MEDIEVAL
SPANISH
EPIC

PENN STATE STUDIES
in ROMANCE LITERATURES

Editors
Frederick A. de Armas
Alan E. Knight

Refiguring the Hero:
From Peasant to Noble in Lope de Vega and Calderón
by Dian Fox

Don Juan and the Point of Honor:
Seduction, Patriarchal Society, and Literary Tradition
by James Mandrell

Narratives of Desire:
Nineteenth-Century Spanish Fiction by Women
by Lou Charnon-Deutsch

Garcilaso de la Vega and the Italian Renaissance
by Daniel L. Heiple

Allegories of Kingship:
Calderón and the Anti-Machiavellian Tradition
by Stephen Rupp

Acts of Fiction:
Resistance and Resolution from Sade to Baudelaire
by Scott Carpenter

Grotesque Purgatory:
A Study of Cervantes's *Don Quixote,* Part II
by Henry W. Sullivan

Spanish Comedies and Historical Contexts in the 1620s
by William R. Blue

The Cultural Politics of *Tel Quel:*
Literature and the Left in the Wake of Engagement
by Danielle Marx-Scouras

Madrid 1900:
The Capital as Cradle of Literature and Culture
by Michael Ugarte

Ideologies of History in the Spanish Golden Age
by Anthony J. Cascardi

THOMAS MONTGOMERY

MEDIEVAL SPANISH EPIC

Mythic Roots
and
Ritual Language

The Pennsylvania State University Press
University Park, Pennsylvania

For Shaula
In memoriam

Al andar se hace camino.

Publication of this book has been aided by a grant from the Program for Cultural Cooperation between Spain's Ministry of Culture and United States' Universities.

Library of Congress Cataloging-in-Publication Data

Montgomery, Thomas, 1925–
    Medieval Spanish epic : mythic roots and ritual language / Thomas Montgomery.

        p.   cm. — (Penn State studies in Romance literatures)
    Includes bibliographical references (p.   ) and index.
    ISBN 0-271-01738-4 (alk. paper)
    1. Epic poetry, Spanish—History and criticism. 2. Spanish poetry—To 1500—History and criticism. 3. Cantar de Mío Cid. 4. Epic poetry, European—History and criticism. 5. Folklore —Europe. I. Title. II. Series.
⌐PQ6058.M66   1998
    816' .03209—dc21   97-13077
                                                                              CIP

It is the policy of The Pennsylvania State University Press to use acid-free paper for the first printing of all clothbound books. Publications on uncoated stock satisfy the minimum requirements of American National Standard for Information Sciences— Permanence of Paper for Printed Library Materials, ANSI Z39.48-1992.

CONTENTS

PREFACE

This study was originally conceived as a synthesis and amplification of work I had done on the traditional content of the various Spanish epics, as well as philological and linguistic analyses of the texts, aimed at interpretation of the mentality each one seemed to represent. I find a coherence in these early works that would probably never be evident to anyone else unless I made the effort to demonstrate it in a unified published form. As it turned out, that effort led further than anticipated: while there are occasional pages summarizing aspects of earlier articles, new slants given to that material and large additions to it have yielded a product I regard as essentially new. Because the topics are wide-ranging, many have been treated rather briefly so as not to lose the overall thread. I hope in the future to deal more fully with some of them.

This book does not espouse or adhere to any of the "isms" that have loomed large in the scholarship of recent decades on Spanish epic. It does not directly address polemic issues. It does make some reference to oral theory, particularly as utilized by Homeric scholars, whose work on myth it also takes into account. For key linguistic concepts it depends on Roman Jakobson and Émile Benveniste as durable guides, and as tacit models in approaching the modes of memory and perception that have shaped the peculiar idiom of medieval Spanish epic.

I will define my use of the terms "myth" and "ritual" in due course. By way of initial clarification, it may be noted that the myth under consideration is that of the initiation of the warrior, known through folk and other literature to have been widespread among the Indo-European cultures.[1] The other great myths, those of creation and of cyclical renewal, have inter-

---

1. Several critics have written on mythological aspects of the *Poema del Cid*. Though by no means unanimous in their interpretation of the term "myth," they tend to identify it with the marvelous, particularly in connection with the lion (Castro 1956; Bandera Gómez 1969). Cesáreo Bandera Gómez sees the hero's mythical stature in moral terms: "El carácter mítico del Cid es inseparable de su ejemplaridad" (115). Peter N. Dunn also emphasizes the Cid's "moral profile" (1962, 349) but develops a more rigorous conception of what constitutes myth, basing himself partly on Eliade and Malinowsky and emphasizing the mythical character of narrative structures in the *Cid*: "The political, social-religious level is where the mythic structure . . . is most readily apparent" (1970, 116–17). The good king is released from evil

connections with the initiation tradition, but those relationships are largely obscured in the sources to be examined here; only the cyclical theme will come in for brief consideration. By "ritual," no religious implications are intended. The minstrel's role before his audience, the language he uses, and the behavior of his fictional characters are all stylized and formalized in ways that find parallels in the performance of religious rites and would have produced an analogous sense of admiration and respect in the audience, but the explicitly religious content of some parts of the poems does not receive special attention in these pages. Part I is devoted to the network of initiation narratives discoverable in Spanish and related foreign sources. Part II deals with various linguistic and poetic traits of the *Poema del Cid* and other texts as concrete manifestations of a deep belief and absorption in an age-old tradition that continued to underpin the sense of identity and propriety of members of Castilian society at the turn of the thirteenth century, as well as modes of perception and thought that supported the mythic vision.

In Part I of the book, translations into English have been provided for all quotations in Old Spanish. Part II concentrates on the mechanics of the epic language more than on content. Hence, translations are usually omitted in this part as potentially intrusive; a knowledge of modern Spanish on the part of the reader will make the analyses clear. For the *Chanson de Roland*, Bédier's (1960) modern rendition of the Old French is included.

Portions of this book were written during a sabbatical leave granted by Tulane University for the fall of 1994, which I gratefully acknowledge. I also thank Mary Montgomery for a helpful critical reading, James Montgomery for technical assistance and advice, and particularly Matthew Bailey for a thorough commentary that led to substantial and necessary improvements to the study. Andrew Lewis, editorial reader for Penn State Press, provided invaluable contributions and advice. Finally, I express deep appreciation for many critical and editorial suggestions offered by Samuel Armistead. Remaining defects are all attributable to me.

---

counselors, for instance, and the Infantes' return to Castile is the reverse of the Cid's triumphant journey to the east. The elaborate study done by Alberto Montaner (1987) shows parallels between the Cid and classical heroes, particularly Herakles, treating them as archetypes. This book, which concentrates on the initiation myth, largely supports the views of Dunn and Montaner, though its perspectives are quite different.

PART I

MYTH

Preliminaries

"Mythological research normally gropes in the dark for a realm of oral tradition that is not directly accessible" (Burkert 1987, 25). It is Walter Burkert, an irreproachable classical scholar, who, among many deeper probings, has made a bold surmise plausible: an affinity, in tradition, of the Trojan horse and the sheep under whose belly Odysseus was carried to freedom from the Cyclops—two highly unlikely means of passing a gateway in an action presumably devised to resemble a rebirth. The analogy, at first surprising, has great instinctive appeal once it is pointed out, like the children's verses (not, of course, composed by children) that, as remarked by Juan Ramón Jiménez, sound familiar the first time one hears them.[1] Medieval narrative also can have that quality. Some narrative traditions appear to have survived for centuries during which the few isolated communities where literacy was maintained took little interest in them. They traveled to various parts of western Europe, where they are now recognizable as peculiar sequences of recounted events. They have mythical resonances. Their survival is surely attributable to oral tradition.

Of the three great classic myths, of origins, of cyclical renewal, and of initiation, the last survived best in the medieval world, perhaps because as an interpretation more of society than of the cosmos, and hence readily secularized, it conflicted least with Christianity. My purpose here is to examine several medieval Spanish versions of a tale that evidently recalls the initiation of a young hero. This tale forms part of nearly every account that has been characterized by critics as epic in Spain, and its several versions are identifiable as variants of an initiation myth that must have been well known in Spain as it was in France, Ireland, and elsewhere, so well known that different oral versions might often encounter and influence each other, and so fundamental that as cultural conditions changed, the myth was

1. "Las canciones de los niños, aun cuando no las hayamos nunca oído, siempre nos parecen familiares, como si su letra y su ritmo nos vinieran de una niñez eterna, inconciente, y sin sentido." (Sánchez Romeralo 1992, 260).

adapted to accommodate them, while always retaining a recognizable core of events that lent ancient authority to its new versions with their new messages.

Lines of influence from one version of the tale to another are not usually traceable, and even if they were, probably the most interesting results of comparisons would still have to do with how various cultures and periods adapted the ancient lore. Some of the successive initiands were derived from historical figures, and each had a distinctive personality that needed to be adjusted to approximate the image of the paradigmatic hero. Without such an adjustment the admired figure would soon fall into oblivion: "The historical character of the persons celebrated in epic poetry is not in question. But . . . the historical event in itself, however important, does not remain in popular memory, nor does its recollection kindle the poetic imagination save insofar as the particular historic event closely approaches a mythical model" (Eliade 1974, 42). The narrative patterns were so firmly embedded in popular memory that they molded not only the figures of Rodrigo de Vivar and Gonzalo, the youngest of the seven infantes de Lara, but also, to a lesser extent, those of Mainet, the future Charlemagne, and even touched secondary figures such as Count Garci Fernández.

The affinities to be proposed here depend not so much on intuitive leaps of the kind that link the two adventures of Odysseus as on parallels among narrative sequences. Little weight will be given to isolated elements or events such as the "Bellerophontic letter," which requests the bearer's murder, or the binational parentage of the hero. These may simply be clichés easily duplicated in societies where messengers were in fact vulnerable and where heroes, as exceptional beings, could be expected to have extraordinary origins and to belong yet not belong to their community. Here the focus will be on coherent series of events unlikely to be replicated by chance. They appear as permutations of the initiation myth detected first by Georges Dumézil (1942) in widely separated parts of the Indo-European world, with key manifestations in India, involving the god Indra; in Rome applied to the human Horatii and Curiatii; and in Ireland, dealing with the hero Cúchulainn. Other principal heroes of this type are Herakles and the Dane Starcatherus. The ideological basis found by Dumézil for the form taken by these tales, through which they reflect a division of society into three strata, giving particular emphasis to the second or warrior class, appears to be attenuated in Spain. Spanish heroes may indeed be set at odds with rulers (representing the first function) and with women (belonging to the third), but triadic symbolism is hard to separate out from manifestations of the widespread preference for threes that marks narrative structures throughout much of the world. (The continued representation of ideologically significant triads is, however, ably supported in García Montoro 1972 and 1974.)

In Spain the two chief heroic figures who replicate the ancient initiatory pattern are Gonzalo, the young Infante de Lara, and Rodrigo de Vivar, known in later life as the Cid. Their stories have added significance in that they suggest an interpretation of the careers of the most notoriously villainous youths of early Spanish literature, the Infantes de Carrión as portrayed in the *Poema del Cid*.[2]

While it is generally true that direct interrelationships among extant texts are elusive, a particular affinity does exist between *Siete infantes* and *Tristan*, which share a number of quite specific peculiarities. *Siete infantes* in turn appears as an earlier offshoot of a legend underlying *La Chanson de Roland*, with which it presents many striking parallels. Without the light thrown by *Siete infantes* and perhaps other congeners, any traces of the earlier initiatory elements would not be recognizable as such in *Roland*.

A great many similarities, most but not all of them convincing, have been identified between Spanish and other heroic traditions, usually French (see, among others, Krappe 1924; von Richthofen 1954; Herslund 1974; García Montoro 1972, 1974; Smith 1977, 87–160; and Menéndez Pidal 1992). While many affinities between Spanish and French epic have been established, the various proposals, considered either singly or together, fall short of forming a coherent whole. Specific claims for influence by one written source on another are usually unconvincing because supporting evidence is scattered and incomplete, or because of chronological contraindications. If many cross-currents seem to be present, but none points to large-scale direct imitation, it may well be because the repeated motifs were common property, widely familiar even across political and linguistic boundaries. For present purposes, where filiations are found, as between *Tristan* and *Siete infantes*, the differences between versions will be emphasized mainly to bring out what they seem to be saying about the cultures in which they appear, rather than to claim directions of influence among them.

The lack of any palpably direct documentary link between the Irish and Spanish tales may leave some critics unsatisfied. By way of justification for

2. Except where specifying their region of origin, Lara, I refer to the seven brothers of Lara as infantes, without capitalization, to distinguish them from the Infantes de Carrión.

the hypothesis of shared origins, a parallel may be drawn with the almost always obscure etymological connections that lie behind the Celtic component of the Spanish vocabulary. Joan Corominas casts doubt upon a great majority of Ibero-Celtic etymologies that have been proposed over the years. Even the ones he is most inclined to favor require tiny leaps of faith of the sort that I advocate here for the tentative linking of stories. One of the strongest etymologies is that of *camino*, from the spoken Latin *camminus*, first documented in Spain in the seventh century. No earlier examples have been found in France or other lands of Celtic settlement, although modern descendants of the word are commonly known in all that territory. Corominas cites an Irish *céinm* and a Welsh *cam* meaning "step," noting that the earliest French examples mean "stretch of road." After piecing together these fragments and dealing also with the problem of long *i* in *camminus*, a reasonably credible Celtic connection can be affirmed despite the great gaps in the evidence (Corominas-Pascual 1980–91, 1:787; von Wartburg 1947, 2:147). More hypothetical is the case of *colmena*, "beehive," for which a proto-Celtic antecedent can be reconstructed on the basis of a Middle Breton *kolouen gwenan*, "straw" or "basket" plus "bees." The admittedly thin evidence does find scattered and imprecise confirmation through wider Indo-European analogies; "luego, estamos autorizados para postular un hispano-celt. KOLMENA" (Corominas-Pascual 1980–91, 1:853–54)—though other solutions cannot be ruled out entirely. Without suppositions of this kind, all traces of Ibero-Celtic vocabulary in Spanish could probably be rejected, leaving no answers instead of the tentative ones advanced. The result would be an impoverishment of Spanish linguistic history. The interconnections here proposed for traditions in folklore present geographical and cultural analogies with the cited etymologies and seem comparably useful.

The narrative to be considered deals with a central theme of a warring society, the initiation of a youthful hero, a model for other youths of his class, but at the same time highly exceptional if not semidivine. The importance of the underlying myth is confirmed by the appearance of analogies in widely separated parts of the Indo-European world. These have been studied by Dumézil (1942, 1969) as expressions of a caste system, existing in reality or perhaps only in principle. The Spanish descendants (as here proposed) of the tale have developed with particular originality one of its key elements, the sexual confrontation.

It might most readily be assumed that the Spanish tradition would be traceable to the Roman version. In fact, no clear evidence of such continuity can be discerned, as will become clear after the medieval permutations of the tradition have been examined.

Dumézil's work provides a basis for the thesis, which at first sight may appear a bit outrageous, that the stories as they have come down find their closest analogies in Celtic tradition. In medieval Ireland, in contrast with the Romance-speaking countries, a strong vernacular written culture was maintained, which has left to today's reader a version of the initiation tale that is considered particularly archaic (Eliade 1958, 85). The transfer of the account from one personage to another occurs within the Celtic sphere (where it is displaced to *Tristan*), along with another highly characteristic form of modification, the separation of narrative elements in time and space, with radical reinterpretation as a concomitant. It was this device of rearrangement, more than any other mechanism, that allowed the tale to take on new life as it was adjusted to conform to changing conditions and beliefs.

A Celtic presence in the Iberian peninsula is attested from the seventh century B.C. and has left linguistic traces and important archaeological remains that indicate the prevalence of tribal wars comparable to those which could nurture a great warrior hero like Cúchulainn—a semidivine figure, since one of his two fathers (he is born of three pregnancies) is Lug, the principal Celtic god (the apparent subject of an ancient inscription found at Osma: MacCana 1983, 25). His story, with different parts datable from the eighth to the twelfth centuries, probably derives from lost earlier lore (Cross and Slover 1936, 137). It is not impossible, in chronological terms, that those lost forerunners had congeners in pre-Roman Celtic Iberia. Whether the heroic tradition persisted over many centuries in Celtic oral culture, and so left traces to reinforce the acceptance and adaptation of the tale imported in medieval times, or whether the tales were brought by jongleurs to a land where they were a novelty, is a matter for conjecture. In favor of the former supposition, some very archaic traits are to be found in the earliest pertinent Spanish text, the legend of the *Siete infantes de Lara*, and other elements, different though equally primordial, come to light in *Mocedades* and in the *Poema del Cid*.

Myth and ritual must often be viewed as two aspects of a single entity, whether or not the content is religious. The initiation myth had been thoroughly secularized by the time of its extant Spanish manifestations, so that any associated ritual would usually have no religious content. In these pages I use the term "ritual" and "ritualistic" to characterize epic performance as a ceremonial kind of activity, supported by preordained forms, both in the actions narrated and in its style of verbal expression. To comprehend either the action or the style, it is important to see how each complements the other to create a total experience. The ritualistic character of the text is inseparable from its direct, dynamic form of expression. This much-admired effect has sometimes been called "dramatic," but that term may be misleading and inappropriate if it is understood to refer to the manner of drama or the theater. Here the proposed approach entails regarding speech as effective action. It sees formalized speech as an affirmation of traditional authority, perceived during performance as a relic of a supposed older, higher order. It recognizes the political function of epic recitation, that "ritualization . . . does not . . . control individuals or society [yet is] very much concerned with power" (Bell 1992, 170). The exercise of power in the absence of physical control is a very tricky matter. The poet or minstrel succeeds admirably at this task. Examples will show how the poem's action and mode of expression reach deeply into the audience's sense of identity—identity with the group and its linguistic tradition.

Beyond the very imprecise gestural level, however, the poem does not encourage or even permit the presenter to put on a show. It is not dramatic in that sense. Instead of placing imitative actors before the audience (the dramatic mode), the ritualized performance works with the physical remoteness of the poetic personages to stimulate the audience's imagination. If the language is equal to its task, the audience participates in the action, losing itself in the words of the poem, not distracted by the metaphors of a stage. I propose to show, using examples from the *Poema del Cid*, that ritual language is an effective medium for this purpose. The language has dramatic qualities, to be sure, but those traits take effect within the ritual framework. At the level of poetic expression and content—the art of composition—all but the most prosaic passages of the poem are ceremonial and point to a ritual performance. At the level of the narrated story—what the characters do and say, the action of the poem—ceremony again is the predominant mode. This atmosphere is promoted by the sense that the poem has the quality of a tale often retold. Even the most overtly dramatic scenes—those where conflicting purposes are worked out by verbal means, with the moneylenders, with the count of Barcelona, and in the court of law—are marked and dominated by formalized speeches, ceremonial turn-taking, and protocol. The way things are said and done, rather than turns of plot, commands the audience's attention. As in ritual incantation, the words move with the action, and any gestural complementation by the minstrel would be secondary, controlled by the words (see Zumthor 1990, 153–57).

Except for instances where its chief concerns are involved, this study does not take stands on the controversial issues that have largely occupied scholarship on Spanish epic over the years. The controversies have sparked much excellent work and in the long run will have given great impetus to research. The extreme arguments may seem to be aimed at reducing the *Cid* to a collection of clichés, either oral or written, but they have led indirectly to moderate syntheses (Powell 1983, 107–8; Montaner 1993, 13–14; Harney 1994, 407–8), which look toward new directions that largely supersede the polemics. The debates—illiterate or learned? tradition or imitation? custom or law? natural or studied rhetoric? myth or politics?—have been expressed in polar terms that disguise the truly significant core of each topic, namely, the productive encounter of each pair of presumed opposites, as well as well-established gradations between them (Zumthor 1987, 141–42). Probes into the relations with cultural contexts have yielded illuminating results (Duggan 1989 is a distinguished example) and will continue to provide insights and deeper understanding of the epic and its world.

Two recent statements by Homeric scholars are relevant to Spanish epic studies. "Whether or not the *Iliad* was composed by a literate singer is immaterial to my argument: the language of Greek epic evolved over a period of many centuries in an illiterate society" (Slings 1992, 100). "The lack of consensus regarding the [formula] has been the greatest hindrance to formulaic analysis, whether for 'proving' that a text is oral or for interpreting the individual Homeric passage" (Martin 1989, 160). Homeric scholars have faced problems similar to ours and have made more productive use of oralist theory in dealing with them. As students of medieval epic begin to exploit more thoroughly the advances of Homeric and oralist scholarship, new perspectives will surely open up.

Orientation

The chief medieval Spanish epic compositions form two groups, one associated with the two counts of Castile, Fernán González and his son Garci Fernández, and the other centered on Rodrigo de Vivar, the Cid. The first includes a *Poema de Fernán González* of distinctly clerical tone, which probably has traditional roots but has undergone much editorial depopularizing. Also pertaining to this cycle of texts are two legends in which

Garci Fernández is a character, although in roles unrelated except for his identity as count: the *Condesa traidora* and the *Siete infantes de Lara*. Though contemporary—the action of the *Condesa* takes place before and again after that of *Siete infantes*—these two legends share no other personages and proceed as though unaware of each other.

Yet they do constitute a group on thematic grounds. Both deal with devious, witchlike women who set about achieving the destruction of their husbands and younger male family members. Both women are ambitious and dangerous and use their gender as a means of manipulating their husbands; both are themselves destroyed in eventual retribution. As variations on a theme, dealing with the same time, place, and ruler, it is implausible that these two tales arose in ignorance of each other. Their concealment of any interrelation imposes a kind of facelessness or generic character on the personages that parallels the anonymity of authorship of the epic and related compositions. They constitute powerful examples of archetypes that survive and evolve whether or not attached to historical models.

The other epic cluster forms a chronological sequence of its own, with no apparent conscious contact with the cycle of the counts except for brief, historically slanted but inaccurate references in *Mocedades*. The texts—to name them in the order of the events they relate—are the *Mocedades de Rodrigo*, parts of the *Cantar del cerco de Zamora*, a chronistic fragment called the *Partición de los reinos*, and the *Poema del Cid*. It appears appropriate to take these works together as a "cyclical poetic life of Rodrigo" (Deyermond 1969, 15) in spite of chronological reversals by which the extant *Cid*, a century and a half older than the surviving *Mocedades*, contains the most recent events, those of the hero's last years. *Mocedades* shows a variety of influences from, or at least elements in common with, the *Cid*, as well as with *Fernán González* and other texts. The shared traits range in type from format, phraseology, and scenes, to reappearance of characters, including for example Pero Bermúdez—the allusive mode almost entirely lacking within the cycle of the counts—and include also the reapplication of a particular kind of event to a different personage, as when the archangel Gabriel of the *Cid* corresponds to Lazarus in *Mocedades*, or when the count of Barcelona as presented in the *Cid* has a counterpart (also called Remont in the chronicles) in another "franco," the count of Savoy, who appears in *Mocedades*.

Mocedades is so much later than the *Cid* that it would not seem to qualify as a source of illuminating insights into the earlier poem. But if it is seen to contain old material, traditional in character, from a source also known by *Siete infantes*, then its claim to authority is strong. As time went on, the historical components of the epic were rejected by audiences in favor of the more durable mythic material, in the process noted by Mircea Eliade (1974, 42) and found for instance in Iranian epic (Hanaway 1978, 79–80) and in the chronicle version of the Cid story (*PCG* 2:608–36).[3] That they were considered important parts of the national or regional patrimony is attested by their inclusion in chronicles. As to their mutual influence, it is compatible with the long coexistence to be posited here. A comparison may be drawn with a finding of a classical scholar, "It is almost true that every Greek myth is connected in a chain of associations with every other Greek myth" (Bremmer 1987a, 6). The material available for Spain is scanty but can lead toward a similar conclusion. The known poetic texts have well-developed stylistic traits in common, constituting a consecrated linguistic format; they surely represent centuries of development. Singers (and writers) cannot have existed in isolation, nor is it believable that a singer would know only one story. If he knew several, they would easily interact in his mind, in a process of cross-fertilization seen also in the ballads: "los romances se comunican entre sí" (Rico 1990, 43).

Cúchulainn and Tristan

The ultimate identifiable prototype of the *Siete infantes* initiation is that of the chief Irish epic hero Cúchulainn, as found in the great saga *Táin Bó Cúailnge*. This account has a palpable link with the extremely popular story of Tristan and Iseut: a companion of the hero, Drust, briefly mentioned, whose name corresponds etymologically to Tristan (Newstead 1959, 126–27; see also Pastré 1994, 322). *Tristan* is in turn reflected variously in Spanish epic, but the latter also gives evidence of more direct descent from ancient tradition. To support these perhaps unexpected and venturesome claims, a good deal of interrelated evidence from the three

---

3. *PCG* will be used throughout as an abbreviation of *Primera crónica general*. The pages indicated (608–36) begin with the incident at Corpes and continue until the Cid's death and subsequent occurrences. The material becomes progressively less epic and more anecdotal in tone, expanding the aftermath of Corpes, the law court episode and the duels, the second weddings of the Cid's daughters, and various peaceful dealings with Muslims, with details that tend to the conventional if not trivial—more reminiscent of a medieval prose romance than of traditional lore.

Spanish epics, *Siete infantes*, the *Cid*, and *Mocedades*, merits examination along with some other legends.

One of the most memorable parts of the *Táin* is the initiation of Cúchulainn. This episode is adapted, and mingled with another adventure of the same hero, in the story of Tristan, particularly in a version of the prose *Tristan* found in just one of its manuscripts (Bédier 1905, 321–95). The *Siete infantes* incorporates some key changes made by *Tristan*, but retains other earlier features, making it appear that the two variants branched off from a common trunk and then evolved independently into their extant forms. The arrival in Spain of the northern legend is less improbable than at first may be supposed. *Tristan* was carried by Breton minstrels or *conteurs* throughout French-speaking territory, which at the time extended to the Scottish border in the north, and in the south to the Way of St. James (Loomis 1959a, 60–63; Menéndez Pidal 1924, 328). The route through Spain was also frequented by Spanish minstrels (Menéndez Pidal 1957, 256–57).

The pertinent parts of the *Táin* (whose fragments date from the eighth to the twelfth centuries) are the following. The hero is Cúchulainn of Ulster, a superhuman figure who at the age of seven is eager to satisfy his thirst for glory and slaughter.[4] One day he leaves his home community to cross the frontier with the next kingdom (Connacht) and fight against three brothers who have killed most of the men of his own land. Upon arriving at the ford where the encounter will take place, he takes an afternoon nap. He awakens when he hears insulting words spoken by the brothers, which cause him to blush deeply—the sleep and the blush mark his transformation into an invincible fighter. He quickly and single-handedly dispatches all three. As he leaves the scene with their heads, the voice of their mother is heard urging her countrymen to pursue the killer.

During his flight in his chariot,[5] the boy stops to capture a fierce stag. He arrives home demanding more men to slaughter, spreading dread throughout the town. In order to avoid deaths among his subjects, the king, with everyone's general agreement, orders the queen with all the young women

4. For ritual purposes, the onset of adolescence is recognized at ages varying from five to over twenty in cultures around the world.

5. Like the Greeks and the Romans, the early Irish used a vehicle termed a chariot by the translators to transport them to the scene of combat, in which they engaged on foot. The techniques of doing battle on horseback, developed in Asia, were slow to spread in the West. The stirrup, for example, was purportedly introduced by the Magyars during their invasion of the Carpathian Basin at the end of the ninth century.

of the community to appear naked before Cúchulainn. The boy hides his face and turns toward the chariot, whereupon the men seize him and immerse him in three successive vats of cold water. After the third his wrath has cooled, and he emerges radiant and beautiful. The queen dresses him in festive garments (implying nudity on his part as well as the women's), and he occupies a place of honor at the feet of the king.

The state of fury, which Dumézil generalizes to numerous cultures, is brought on by the combat and is not under the young man's control; the community must deal with it. The thirst to kill, the ultimate masculine quality, necessary for the survival of the population, is also dangerous to it and must be counteracted, overpowered, by the ultimate feminine quality, seductiveness, which is also necessary for the community's continuation and survival. The essential and benign role of the women was to be replicated in the *Mocedades de Rodrigo*, but radically altered in *Tristan* and *Siete infantes*.

Tristan displaces the anger to a vengeful foreign queen, making it a force threatening the hero's destruction and therefore dangerous to the community. This and other reversals, with respect to the *Táin*, speak for a profound revision of social values. When an Irish giant appears in Cornwall to demand his yearly tribute of youths and maidens, the only knight in King Mark's court willing to accept the challenge to combat is Tristan. He slays his opponent but not before he is wounded by the other's poisoned sword —recalling, with events that follow it, another adventure of Cúchulainn, part of the "Wooing of Emer" (Cross and Slover 1936, 169), although in this story there is no poison.

After weeks of languishing near death, a voyage brings Tristan to the palace of the king of Ireland, whose daughter Iseut cures him. He conceals his identity under the none-too-opaque pseudonym Tantris, because it is the queen's brother whom he has killed and he rightly fears her passion for vengeance. He slays a dragon, is again poisoned when he keeps its venomous tongue (a trophy comparable to one taken in the "Wooing of Emer"), is again cured by Iseut, and proves himself to be the slayer of the beast by producing the trophy he has kept.

He is honored by the royal couple. One day he is enjoying a bath in the presence of the queen and her retinue of ladies, who serve him "moult debonairement," when the queen happens to see that his sword has a notch in it. She matches the notch with a piece that had been left in her dead brother's head, and, possessed by deadly fury, is about to murder Tristan in his bath with his own sword when restrained by a squire. Tristan dresses and as he blushes becomes radiantly beautiful: "Et Tristan se vest et s'en va au palais. Et quant il fut venu devant les barons si oult ung poy de honte, et commença a rougir, et si en fut moult plus bel" [And Tristan dresses and goes off to the palace. And when he came before the knights he had a bit of shame, and began to blush, and so was the more beautiful] (Bédier 1905, 336).[6] The queen cries out for his execution, but those at the court agree that it would be a shame to lose a knight so courteous and handsome. Tristan submits to the judgment of the king, who spares him, citing rules of hospitality and chivalry.

The bath, in the *Táin* a necessary act of purification with sexual implications, retains traces of its ritual function but now has a recreational tone. In *Tristan* the bath serves to place the man at the mercy of the avenging queen, who in the *Táin* was no more than a disembodied voice lamenting the death of her three sons. The courtly tone of *Tristan* brings with it a radical reorientation: the sense of community is gone, motives are personalized and to a degree trivialized, and in a particularly civilizing touch, the queen's wrath is thwarted by chivalric rules of the male-dominated society. Anger, which was resolved by a rite, is still recognized as a problem, but is now blocked by a set of semi-abstract rules. The confrontation between the youth and the woman is less openly sexual and more conflictive, now imbued with deadly hostility between the genders. The woman almost gets control. The hero's role remains passive, as does that of his future lover Iseut, the benign woman who cures. There is no hint of sexual attraction between them at this point. (The Thomas *Tristan*, rationalized here as in many passages, avoids physical contact between Iseut and Tristan and so reduces the sexual implications of these events, by giving the queen the curing role.)[7]

The number of inversions or antitheses in *Tristan*, when compared to the initiation in the *Táin Bó Cúailnge*, is impressive. Still, the essential sequence

6. The sixteenth-century Spanish *Cuento de Tristan de Leonis*, otherwise of little interest for the study of the early versions of *Tristan*, shows the blush to have been preserved for several centuries, indicating its probable importance in the tradition (Northup 1928, 95). It also confirms the ceremonial nature of the occasion by accompanying it by weeks of feasting and dancing. For the ritual initiatory bath, today perpetuated by the Knights of the Bath, see Keen 1984, 65, 79.

7. The Tristan legend is found in a number of medieval versions, none of which can be taken as definitive. The two main poetic versions in Old French, both fragmentary, are by Thomas and Béroul, of around 1180–1200, both probably by Anglo-Norman writers. The version of greatest interest here is in prose and includes only the beginning episodes; Bédier considered it the earliest known Tristan text. I refer to the Thomas version briefly, since it is the one most likely to be familiar to many readers.

of principal events is maintained in such a way as to make fortuitous independent development of the two, when Cúchulainn was such a well-known figure, quite unlikely: the initiatory combat against the hitherto invincible and abusive foe, followed by a bath in the presence of the queen and her ladies, and the transformation, dressing, and honoring of the extremely young hero, during the launching of his warlike career. As killers, women and men have contrasting roles. Whereas Cúchulainn kills wantonly and almost blithely at times (though under oppressive requirements for the maintenance of his honor), the woman's response to a slaying, when the victims are members of her family, is to incite her male relatives to murderous retribution.

Cúchulainn, Tristan, and the Seven Infantes de Lara

Siete infantes is not presented explicitly as an initiation story; the youthful hero may or may not have already seen combat, so the central confrontation in this epic may be part of a replication pattern. Replications of each initiation are normal occurrences in the texts under consideration, appearing as variations that broaden the original experiences by modifying and rearranging the repeated elements. *Siete infantes* is an excellent example of how the events of the underlying myth can be reordered and reinterpreted. Like *Tristan* it moves the bathing scene to the queen's palace and makes her aggressive toward the defenseless hero who has killed her relative. But in other ways it more closely resembles the *Táin*. The sexual element, minimized in *Tristan*, is distinctly present in *Siete infantes*, now in sinister form, and the hero's fury, passed over in *Tristan*, possesses the youth twice. Anger becomes the motivating force of the queen and of the plot itself. For her part, in her devious destructiveness she makes the Irish queen look bland. She appears capable, if left unchecked, of destroying all the men within her reach. It is a verbal transgression of hers, sexual in nature, that sets in motion a series of crimes and retributions among relatives by blood and by marriage. The action is more complex than in *Tristan*, involving a network of familial relationships (see Capdeboscq 1984).

The version of *Siete infantes* I use for this study is that of the *Crónica de 1344* (Catalán 1980, 199–236), considered the earliest and best by Ramón Menéndez Pidal in his later years (1992, 489–90), although I also take into account the version found in the *PCG* and, occasionally, the one found in the *Interpolación de la Tercera crónica general*. The hero is Gonzalo, the youngest of the seven infantes de Lara, who is also their leader. The lady is Doña Llambra, the new wife of their maternal uncle Ruy Velázquez. During the games celebrating her opulent wedding in Burgos, the lady hears the mighty crash of the lance of her young cousin Alvar Sánchez against a *tablado*, a wooden structure used as a target in competitions, and is so overcome by admiration that she declares before the infantes and their mother that she "would not deny her love" to the youth if they were not so closely related: "que non vedaria su amor a ome tan de pro si non fuese su pariente tan llegado." The text goes on to make plain that this declaration of the lady is the cause of the disaster that is to follow: "et por esto que doña Llambra dixo se siguio despues mucho mal" [and from what Doña Llambra said, great evil (or misfortune) ensued] (Catalán 1980, 199).[8] Six of the brothers laugh off this incestuous and adulterous remark as a joke, but a fury analogous to the rage of Cúchulainn comes over Gonzalo. He silently leaves the others, approaches Alvar Sánchez, outperforms him at the *tablado*, and in response to his ritual boasting, remarks that of all the young men present, he seems to be most praised by the ladies. Alvar Sánchez proclaims that they are right to admire him as the best. Unable to tolerate the provocative response, Gonzalo deals the boastful youth such a blow with his fist that the bones of his face are crushed and he falls dead (a method of killing also known in the *Táin*; see O'Rahilly 1976, 138, 209).[9] Llambra raises a great outcry, the uncle appears, and more blows ensue. A

---

8. The churchman Jacques de Vitry, writing in the early thirteenth century, claimed that tournaments were attended by all seven of the deadly sins. Regarding the sin of lust, he maintained that knights would show off their fighting ability in order to obtain the favors of immodest women, and that some would go so far as to display a lady's token as a sort of insignia. "Non carent 7 mortali peccato quod dicitur luxuria, cum placere volunt mulieribus impudicis, si probi habeantur in armis, et etiam quedam earum insignia quasi pro vexillo portare consueverunt" (de Vitry 1971, 63).

9. The ritual boasting and rejoinder have an archaic quality that is most apparent in the original. Everyone knows trouble is brewing after Gonzalo's lance-thrust: "ca Alvar Sanchez começo de dezir sus alavanças tan grandes, porque lo ovo a responder Gonçalo Gonçalez, et dixo: 'Tan bien alançades et tanto se pagan de vos las duennas, que bien me semeja que non fablan tanto dotro cavallero commo de vos.' Et dixol Alvar Sanchez: 'Si las dueñas de mi fablan, derecho fazen en ello, ca entiendo que valo mas que todos los otros.' Quando esto oyo Gonçalo Gonçalez, pesol mucho de coraçon et non lo pudo soffrir, et dexosse yr a el muy bravamiente et diol una grant puñada en el rostro, que los dientes et las quixadas las quebranto, de guisa que luego cayo en tierra muerto a pies del cavallo" [for Alvar Sánchez began to make his boasts so great that Gonzalo was moved to answer, and he said, "You throw the

general melee is averted by the ruling count (Garci Fernández, who is also Llambra's uncle), along with the infantes' father. The following action seems incongruous: the father chooses this moment to place the young men in the service of their uncle. The infantes will now owe their first allegiance to Ruy Velázquez, to the neglect of immediate family ties. Though they are portrayed as mature youths, their transfer to a new master probably reflects the custom called *criazón*, that of sending boys to live and be trained in the house of a powerful relative or friend, which was followed over many centuries in various cultures, and would later apply to the Cid as it had to Cúchulainn (see Cross and Slover 1936, 137, and Ross 1986, 29–30).

The bathing scene occurs some days later at the palace of the alien queen (Llambra is twice anachronistically, as though by a *lapsus calami*, called "queen" in the text). The infantes, as vassals of the lady's husband (who is absent), and as her guests, go hawking "to give her pleasure and service," naively supposing that all rancor between them has been put aside. Upon their return, while waiting for the game they have taken to be prepared for dinner, they go to cool off in a shady place nearby, and here the bathing scene, held in a courtly atmosphere in *Tristan*, is bowdlerized, although the aggression of the lady, the presence of her companions, and the (semi-) nudity of the hero are retained. Mistakenly thinking he cannot be observed from the palace, Gonzalo removes his outer garments and proceeds to bathe his hawk (a common practice). Llambra and her ladies, including the infantes' mother, do in fact watch, and Llambra takes great offense at what she perceives as an attempt by Gonzalo to seduce them by appearing partly undressed.[10] Vowing to obtain revenge, she sends a servant to deliver a rit-

---

lance so well and the ladies are so pleased with you, that it does seem to me that they speak of no other knight as much as of you." And Alvar Sánchez said to him, "If the ladies talk about me, they do right, because they realize that I am better than all the others." When Gonzalo González heard this, it weighed heavily in his heart and he could not bear it, and he rode very fiercely toward him and gave him such a blow in the face with his fist that he broke his teeth and jawbones, so that then and there he fell dead to the ground at his horse's feet] (*PCG*; Catalán 1980, 182).

10. "Quando doña Lambla le vio assi estar, pesol mucho de coraçon, et dixo contra sus dueñas: 'Amigas, ¿non veedes commo anda Gonçalo Gonçalez en paños de lino?; bien cuedo que non lo faze por al sinon que nos enamoremos del; çertas, mucho me pesa si el asi escapar de mi que yo non haya derecho del' " [When Doña Lambla saw him like that, it weighed heavily in her heart, and she said to her ladies: "Friends, do you not see how Gonzalo González is in his linen clothes? I do think he is doing it just to make us feel love for him; indeed, it will grieve me greatly if he gets away from me and I do not get justice against him] (*PCG*; Catalán 1980, 184).

ual insult in the form of a blow with a cucumber hollowed out (as they sometimes were for drinking) and filled with the blood of a bull or a ram.[11] She identifies Gonzalo as "that one with the hawk," recalling the identification of Tristan in the bath—and a similar occurrence in the ancient (eighth-century) story "The Wooing of Emer," in which Cúchulainn is identified in his bath by a token, a piece of a damsel's garment he is wearing as a bandage (Cross and Slover 1936, 169). She instructs the servant to run back to her for protection. The blow with the cucumber evokes uneasy laughter from Gonzalo's brothers, but he becomes violently angry (Cúchulainn's first anger was also brought on by an insult), and they watch the servant for a clearer sign of the meaning of the act. When the man flees as instructed, they recognize that the message came from Llambra. They pursue him, and he takes refuge under her mantle. After an altercation with the lady, they seize and brutally murder him, thoroughly bloodying her clothes as they do so. They depart hastily for home, a few hours' journey away, taking their mother with them.

Llambra has been gravely dishonored; with her ladies, she stages an extraordinary mourning ceremony of several days' duration, placing a bench in her patio and covering it in black, tearing her clothes and "calling herself a widow who had no husband."[12] When her husband arrives after a few days, she cries out for vengeance, which he promises. An honorable man up to this point, now appointed judge of the case, he becomes deceitful and treacherous, plotting the infantes' death, and that of their father as well, at the hands of the Moors.[13] Llambra has used a feminine weapon, grief, to

11. Several *fueros* or medieval Spanish law codes prescribe explicit penalties for striking a man with a cucumber. Clearly the act carries sexual connotations. Several critics have noted that phallic shape of the offensive object. María Eugenia Lacarra goes a step further to suggest that the attack was meant to impugn Gonzalo's virility. She finds in several medieval medical treatises that the cucumber was recommended as an anti-aphrodisiac and accordingly as a remedy for certain conditions that produce male sterility (Lacarra 1993). Whatever the precise implications, this was an extraordinarily uncouth thing for a lady to do.

12. A comparable ritualized provocation to violence, also in the form of a lamentation, occurs in the chronicle account of the siege of Zamora, derived from a lost epic. Arias Gonzalo, having been insulted by Vellido Dolfos, speaks these words: "En mal dia yo naci! quando en mi vegez me dizen tales palabras como estas e non e quien me uengue de quien me las dize" [On a fateful day was I born, when in my old age they say such words and I have no one to avenge me against the one who says them to me] (*PCG* 2:510a22–25). His sons immediately arm themselves and pursue Vellido Dolfos. (In the *Táin*, any remark by woman or man hinting that a knight is less than avid for combat is sufficient to make him go into battle, even if it is to certain death.)

13. Capdelbosc (1984, 205) points out that Ruy Velázquez has been placed in a legally untenable situation, forced to betray his own relatives, either Llambra or the infantes.

dominate, emasculate, and subvert him. She orchestrated the whole event, bringing on the servant's death by provoking the brothers, then claiming to be aggrieved by their predictable, if excessive, reaction. While their response is justified, its extreme violence is rightfully seen as offensive to her. They have been trapped into a criminal act.

At this juncture her active role in the story ends. A distinctive mark of her dealings with Gonzalo in both their violent confrontations, besides their unwholesome sexual overtones, has been the ambiguity of her messages. Gonzalo's brothers reacted to these unexpected and unconventional communications with laughter; only he responded with rage that promptly turned deadly. In the second case, she openly states her intention to make serious trouble by her action. In the first, her remark can be dismissed lightly by most of those present, but it can also be taken as a verbal violation of two cardinal taboos, against incest and adultery. To adduce a possible reasonable explanation for Gonzalo's extreme rage, it may be noted that he is called a legal expert in the father's subsequent lament over the severed heads of the seven brothers. A more important cause, though, given the narrative patterning of the text, is surely found in the tradition of the fury, called *ferg* in Ireland, *wut* and (going) berserk in Germanic. In the Irish saga a few veiled taunts by a friend are enough to bring on the fury, and the hero may even request the taunts (Colum 1967, 68). Llambra's aggressive acts give her power to precipitate the fury. As a woman, she is at risk of disgrace rather than death in this ritualized act of violence, and safe from physical harm until years later, when vengeance is taken for her destructiveness.

Her ambiguities and her ability to threaten the accepted rules give her power over men and eventually over fortresses. When Gonzalo kills her cousin, her anger, like his, seems exaggerated and arbitrary, as though the furor could now affect both sexes. If so, it has lost its useful function in the transformation of the child into the heroic protector of the community and become a grave danger to all. Both Llambra's anger and her grief, after the second killing, are manipulative, aimed at control and destruction, outweighing the gravity of the offenses. The legend seems to condemn aggressive, underhanded women and irrationally enraged men equally—though extreme bravery in combat is still admired.

The initiation tale now leads into its analogue, the tale of death and rebirth—analogical because these passages or crossings also involve travel to another reality, an encounter with strange powers, and permanent change of personality or identity. The tone becomes more mythic than before, the deeds more prodigious and ritualized.

Ignoring supernatural portents much more explicit than mere omens, Gonzalo and his brothers allow themselves to be led off by their uncle into Moorish lands, where, as he had planned, they are ambushed by a huge army. After killing over three thousand, and losing one of their number, they are finally overcome, lined up, and beheaded in the order of their birth under the supervision of Ruy Velázquez.

At the autumnal equinox, "the day of San Cebrián," September 13 on the Julian calendar, the twentieth or twenty-first (with a discrepancy increasing over the years) on the Gregorian, the heads arrive in Córdoba, where the ruler Almanzor has them lined up for identification, although for him there can be no reasonable doubt about whose heads they are. The infantes' father, who through the perfidy of the uncle has been made prisoner in Córdoba, is called upon to provide the names of the eight noble heads from Castile (of the seven and their tutor). The father, overpowered by anguish, takes the heads in the order of their birth and reviews the finest qualities of each son in terms that add up to a portrayal of the ideal knight, but which also have the ring of a medieval (or modern) horoscope. For example, Gonzalo, the youngest, was the one most loved by his mother, distinguished for his courtesy, a good friend and loyal vassal, knowledgeable in the law and fond of judging, a strong warrior and liberal in sharing spoils, champion at the *tablado*, an accomplished talker with ladies and damsels, beloved for his generosity, and formidable in debate.[14]

To console Gonzalo Gustioz in his terrible grief, Almanzor provides the captive with the company of his sister, who conceives a child as a result of their meeting.[15] Gonzalo Gustioz is allowed to go home, and she gives birth a few days later—an oddity that should not be overlooked. The birth leads eventually to another initiation, with another change of tone, dominated by relatively modern elements repeated also in several *chansons de geste*. Gonzalo's double or new incarnation, Mudarra, grows up in Córdoba. He is the very image of his dead half-brother. Still at a tender age, he plays a game of *tablas* or backgammon with a visiting Moorish king. In a fit of pique when he loses, the king impugns the paternity of the boy, who thereupon strikes the visitor dead with a blow of the game board, demands exact knowledge of his identity from his mother, and soon leaves, with an army and Almanzor's blessing, to seek out his father in Castile.

---

14. Only the warlike qualities are observable in this tale.

15. On the topos of the "princesse sarrasine," represented by the sister of Almanzor, by Galiana in *Mainet*, and by Zaida, the Moorish "wife" of Alfonso VI, see note 42.

The game, usually ending with the slaying by means of the playing board, is a sign of the initiation in many accounts and is often accompanied by the questioned paternity (Armistead 1990–91). The birth-rebirth theme now reasserts itself. Gonzalo has journeyed, despite warnings, to the other world, the land of no return as he is specifically told by his tutor (see pp. 76–77), where he suffers, dies, and is marvelously reborn—recall Mudarra's inordinately short gestation period. He returns, bringing power and wealth. Mudarra resembles Gonzalo so closely that he is occasionally addressed by that name—both by his father and, in the ballad "A cazar va don Rodrigo," by Ruy Velázquez. He rejoins his family and is accepted as a son by Gonzalo's mother, through another rebirth, in a ceremony in which she passes him through one sleeve of her garment and out the other. To complete the rite, all make a triumphal procession, with knights and squires, ladies and damsels from the whole region, to Burgos, where the mother will be honored by the count, and Mudarra received as the replacement of the seven infantes—acclaimed as a heroic savior before he has performed any feat to prove himself. There Mudarra meets Ruy Velázquez, whom he is soon to kill, leaving Llambra an outcast.

The foregoing summary—aimed at bringing out the evolution of an ancient theme in the first part, and then the archetypal topics of initiation and rebirth—has necessarily passed over much material, as well as larger themes that enrich this remarkably complex text. Before returning to the discussion of initiations in other epic compositions, it will be of interest to outline a few more elements that attest to the lengthy, complex set of traditions represented by this extraordinary *bricolage*, or composite tissue of inventions. Some astronomical connections have been suggested in reviewing the death of the infantes. Like the wheat crop in Spain, the youths are beheaded (or harvested) at the autumnal equinox (see García Montoro 1972, 114, 120). The harvest was accompanied by such symbolic killings in Mediterranean cultures from ancient times, intended to assure the fertility of the earth in the next year (Burkert 1983, 44–45). Another possible connection suggests itself with the Pleiades, which were visible as a group of seven stars in antiquity, and are so considered traditionally, but were seen as only six in the Middle Ages, as today. The fading one entered folklore as a lost sister in parts of the Mediterranean world (Barnard 1966, 128) and was dealt with variously in folklore worldwide. Several different conjunctions of the Pleiades have also been used around the world to define the beginning or end of the year (Barnard 1966, 119–32). As just noted, the date of the death of the seven infantes is specified as the autumnal equinox ("san

Cebrián"). Perhaps not by coincidence, when the brothers retire to a knoll for respite during what will be their last battle, they discover that one of their number has been lost.

The death-rebirth theme takes on a variation in the story of Gonzalo Gustioz, the father of the infantes. Just after engendering Mudarra, forcibly in some versions, he becomes feeble and nearly blind, walking with a stick like an old man. When Mudarra finds him in Salas, he brings his half of a ring which the father had "parted" on leaving Córdoba for use as an identifying token. The ring's parts fuse together indissolubly when they are joined. When the father brings it to his eyes his sight returns and he is sufficiently rejuvenated to want to do battle with the redoubtable uncle.

A further possible archetype is seen in the pursuit of the uncle, Ruy Velázquez, by the avenging half-brother. The uncle flees from one fortress to another across the northwestern frontier of Castile, then through the lowlands of the Duero until he almost reaches his home, not far from his starting point. Mudarra is always a day behind him, never catching up, as they pass through a jagged semicircle, stopping twelve times. It is possible to interpret this strange trajectory as the successive abandonment by Ruy Velázquez of each of his ill-gotten fortresses, but another sense is also likely. From his home in Vilviestre or from Canicosa, a nearby eminence where the seven infantes had first crossed into Moorish lands, the first stop is almost due northwest; the sixth, nearly due west; and the twelfth and last, to the southwest: the location of the setting sun at, respectively, the summer solstice, the equinoxes, and the winter solstice as seen from those base locations (map in Menéndez Pidal 1934, vi). At the end of the pursuit, Ruy Velázquez loses his hawk—a sign of impending disaster (Débax 1982, 192)—and while looking for it is suddenly confronted by Mudarra, who gravely wounds him and takes him home to be executed. Ruy Velázquez's flight was surely not delineated at random, but it corresponds to no discernible historical reality. It may represent an imaginary topographic calendar, like many prehistoric astronomical calendars that have been identified around Europe, but imaginary in that the successive stopping-points are too far away to be visible from Vilviestre. Ruy Velázquez's years as overlord in Castile have been a period of blight, which ends with Mudarra's arrival. Everything points to a myth of cyclic renewal, with replacement of the old king by a new one who brings fertility to the land.[16] The story is

16. On this topic I have benefited from discussion with my colleague Linda Carroll.

alty to the chieftain, the bathing of the hawk (mainly because of the human baths that are its precursors), the ritual insults, the mourning and "widow's" lament, the border crossing, the diversionary magic prescribed by Nuño Salido when the infantes scorn his warning, the beheadings committed in order, the mourning over the heads with its ritualized language, the game of backgammon or chess (see Menéndez Pidal 1934, 32), the re-birth of Mudarra through Sancha's sleeves, and the triumphant procession and reception of Sancha and her kin in Burgos—to offer a sampling. The scenes of grisly violence that occupy most of the remaining text also take on the inevitability associated with reenactments. They are the games of Lévi-Strauss (see p. 91) turned deadly, and all of them, particularly the slaughter of the infantes and the execution of Ruy Velázquez, have the quality of "acts performed in set sequence and often at a set place and time," which Gregory Nagy (1990, 10) characterizes as the essence of ritual.

In the welter of fateful action, the resemblance of this legend to *Tristan* and the *Táin* may begin to fade from the reader's mind. By way of review, they include the fury (in *Táin* and *Siete infantes*), the killing, the bathing in view of women, the identifying token, the hostile queen, the violence against her (or her daughter) and her shaming, her demand for vengeance, and the lord's order sending the hero abroad.

At the Margins: *Nibelungenlied* and Horatius

Two texts require mention at this point as members of the family of initiation accounts, although they are not clearly presented as such and throw little direct light on the Spanish tradition as here conceived.

The three stories considered thus far form a group within the corpus of initiatory narratives. *Siete infantes*, while intensely Spanish, retains something of the imaginative quality associated with Celtic tradition. It is therefore remarkable that it also has distinctively Germanic traits that come out when it is compared with the *Nibelungenlied*. These have been studied carefully and more or less persuasively by various scholars (including von Richthofen 1954, 151–208; Acutis 1978, 33–62, in schematic form; and Menéndez Pidal 1992, 449–85). To this reader the really impressive correspondence is in the presentation of the powerful, destructive woman. She is not absent from *Táin*; the endless warring that surrounds Cúchulainn's existence is triggered by the jealousy of Queen Medb of Connacht, who urges her husband to acquire at any cost a bull belonging to the Ulstermen. But Llambra is decidedly more reminiscent of Kriemhild and Brunhild, ambitious, scheming, domineering women whose machinations bring ultimate ruin to their menfolk and to themselves. The rivalry and jealousy of these two lead first to the death of Siegfried and finally culminate—typically, on an occasion of great feasting—in the slaughter of nearly everyone in the poem. While Llambra does not go so far as to take part in a physical contest with a man (*Nibelungenlied*, seventh adventure)—hardly thinkable in a Mediterranean culture—she does, like Brunhild, turn her own wedding celebration, with its contests, to fateful purposes, as few if any other Spanish women characters have ever done.

The most exhaustive array of resemblances between *Siete infantes* and a northern text is the one advanced by Erich von Richthofen (1954, 151–208) in his comparison with *Thidrekssaga*, an Old Norse compilation of the thirteenth century based on a precursor of the *Nibelungenlied* but with additions from a number of other sources, some of them unknown. Though von Richthofen gathered together a great number of materials of Germanic, classical, and Romance origin, the affinities he proposes are often nebulous. Regarding one of them, Menéndez Pidal remarked, "Debo advertir que Richthofen señala muchas otras analogías en *Thidrekssaga* que yo no recojo por creerlas lejanas e insignificantes. . . . Sin embargo, estas coincidencias prueban una comunidad de estilo y de fórmulas" (Menéndez Pidal 1992, 484 n. 68). Martin de Riquer, writing on *Siete infantes* and *Roncesvalles*, has shown the weakness of arguments for direct influence based on predictable clichés such as the lament for knights killed in battle. To take an example of the analogies claimed by von Richthofen, he makes a parallel between the death of Ruy Velázquez and two episodes from earlier sources: first, the murder of Odoacer by Theodoric in Ravenna (fifth century), recorded by the seventh-century Byzantine historian John of Antioch, of whose work fragments are preserved in the Escorial library; and second, the grisly slaughter of Jörmunrek as recounted in the Norse *Radnarssdrápa*, probably of the ninth century. The motives and manner of the two deaths are unlike those found in the Spanish story. What the three scenes have in common is extremes of brutality, which in the Germanic sources is visited upon the vassals and families of the victims (von Richthofen 1954, 185–89). In von Richthofen's view, fragments of the recently composed *Thidrekssaga*, recalling these incidents, would have reached Spain in 1256–57 on the occasion of the marriage of princess

Christina of Norway to Felipe, brother of Alfonso X. The legend of the seven infantes would then have originated no earlier than the 1250s.

To von Richthofen's credit, he confessed that he was unable to interpret the welter of sources that he had identified (1954, 185). He also made clear that the closest parallels he found between *Siete infantes* and *Thidrekssaga* represented material of unknown origin.[20]

The only workable explanation for the "comunidad de ambiente" (Menéndez Pidal 1992, 484 n. 69) marking these diverse texts would apparently have to be based on a rich and active tradition of well-known stories, predominantly oral and poetic, and accordingly not traceable, except in the rare instances when a member of the tiny literate minority was moved to write one of them down. A primarily oral mode of transmission is also evidenced by the character of the revisions as seen in the differences among the texts. The references to famous names from the past and faraway places, the touches of erudition, and the appeal to authority typically favored by medieval writers are absent. The revisions are imaginative, including displacements of actions from one person to another, inversions or reversals of events and their meaning, and repetitions that, far from betraying poverty of imagination, round out and complete the sense of the stories without losing sight of their theme, in the present case the initiation. The process of revision would be similar to what happens to ballads as they are handed down and their variants diverge from one another. Revisions performed on written texts have a literal and literate quality that is fundamentally different from the changes by association that take place in the oral sphere. More considerations in this vein will be offered in Part II.

Before leaving the *Nibelungenlied*, one more notable resemblance claims attention. Like Ganelon in *Roland*, Hagen in the German poem is a respected, clever knight, no longer young, influential in the court, who nominates the brash, overconfident young hero, Roland or Siegfried, to head a dangerous military operation in an alien land and continues to manipulate him until he brings about his death (see Wailes 1978, 126–27). The parallels between *Roland* and *Siete infantes* will be examined later; the summary

---

20. Cesare Acutis (1974) has studied some similarities between *Siete infantes* and the *Nibelungenlied*. His particular interest is in abstract forms and relationships that he derives from the narrative. He emphasizes, for instance, that like Etzel (Attila), Ruy Velázquez marries into a sea of family conflicts. His view of the antagonism between Llambra and the seven brothers is innovative and quite different from that expressed here, in that he takes Llambra to be a largely innocent victim, and the infantes as inexcusable transgressors.

just offered fits Ruy Velázquez and Gonzalo almost perfectly, and in both the German and Spanish texts, though not (at least not overtly) in *Roland*, the scheming woman provides the motivation and the background. The initiatory undercurrents of the *Nibelungenlied* and its somewhat baffling character delineations may lend themselves to elucidation in the light of the Irish and Spanish accounts, with their more archaic, paradigmatic quality.

As the medieval initiation tale begins to take shape through its various versions, it may be opportune to look again at the Roman adaptation of the legend, briefly mentioned earlier. A key element, which enabled Dumézil to identify it with the myth of Indra in the East and Cúchulainn in the West, is constituted by the triads it contains. The Horatii and their adversaries are triplets, as the victims of Cúchulainn's initiatory killings are three brothers. In other respects the Roman legend, as best preserved in Livy (bk. 1, chaps. 25–26), is not close to the version found in the *Táin*, which is regarded as particularly authentic. Livy, in making his rationalized text, showed more concern with politics than with archetypes. The Spanish material takes its place in relation to the Celtic (and Germanic) tradition, confirming the probable existence of an initiation account widespread in western Europe. Because of its scant resemblance to the Roman version, it provides no direct evidence to strengthen Dumézil's thesis of an Indo-European tale whose memory persisted in Rome as well as in Ireland, though certainly it broadens the base for that thesis.

Livy's version opens as the Romans and the Albans have been carrying on an inconclusive war. To settle it, they appoint a set of triplets to represent each side in battle, the Roman Horatii and the Alban Curiatii. (*Mocedades* also has this device, with a hundred representing each side—and in another instance, a replication with single champions.) On the field of combat the Albans kill the two older Romans but are wounded while doing so; then the third Horatius separates them by feigning flight and so is able to kill them all. On his return to the city, he finds his sister overcome with grief at the death of one of the Curiatii, to whom she was betrothed. Outraged by her lack of patriotism, he murders her. He is found guilty of a criminal act, but his sentence is commuted on condition that he perform the yearly expiatory ceremony of passing through a symbolic doorway, the *sororum tigillum*. In a supplementary story, years later a member of his gens or clan called Horatius Cocles keeps an Etruscan army from crossing a bridge into Rome by the force of his terrible gaze.

Dumézil's discovery of a complex network of parallels between the

Indo-Iranian and the Roman mythologies gave the primary impetus to his theory of a three-tiered class structure among Indo-European peoples (Littleton 1966, 7–19, 78–82). After the *Táin* the triads were perhaps forgotten in the West (but cf. García Montoro 1972, 1974). Traits shared between the Roman and Irish tales and also found in *Siete infantes* include the combat, the fury, the purifying bath modified to an expiatory rite in Rome and to the bathing of the hawk in *Siete infantes*, and the violence against the woman (Llambra, Finnabair, and Horatius's sister). The violence also appears in Spanish epic texts yet to be discussed. In a number of important respects, however, the Roman story departs from the main current. The initiatory element is absent, the tactic of Horatius is unheroic (as also in *Mainet* as told in the *Gran conquista de Ultramar*; see p. 55), the woman is murdered, which is not the case in the medieval versions, the confrontation with her lacks the sexual dimension, and her role is neither benign nor really threatening. Thus the Spanish tale has received most of the distinctive traits of the initiation from a source other than the Roman version, if this is adequately represented by Livy. That the Roman material is of limited relevance may be unremarkable, since it was not the Romanized population of Spain but barbarians from the north who needed and preserved the image of the ferocious lone hero. To conclude: at the present stage, though the existence of Germanic and Roman records must be recognized and weighed, they do not appear to illuminate the topic at hand.

Las Mocedades de Rodrigo

The next initiation account to be considered, from the *Mocedades de Rodrigo*, also has some notably archaic features, although the work it appears in is a late and decadent example of the epic genre, dating probably to the early 1360s according to Alan Deyermond (1969, 24). No Spanish written source for it is known, and none is likely to exist, given its fabulous character. Though it omits the bath, it retains, from a distant past, essential elements that resemble events encountered in the tale of Cúchulainn. No reminiscence of *Tristan* is observable in this episode, but another segment of the *Mocedades*, to be discussed later, does present distinct parallels with the Breton story.

For comparison with the *Mocedades* and other Spanish stories that are largely independent of *Tristan*, a fuller reprise of pertinent aspects of the initiation of Cúchulainn is required. This segment of the *Táin* is the primary key to all the rites of passage to be examined in this study. The superhuman hero, at age seven, after having mauled and killed many boys, is ready to take on adult warriors to win fame and glory. At first his foster father the king prohibits him from taking arms, but he overcomes the patriarchal resistance. One auspicious day he sets out for the border of his native Ulster to fight against three brothers who have killed off most of the Ulstermen. On arriving at the ford that they protect (most of the encounters of his career will take place in fords), he makes known his presence and then lies down for an afternoon nap. He awakes to hear threatening insults from one of the brothers, which cause him to blush deeply—as noted earlier, the nap and blush are apparently signs of the uncontrollable *furor belli* necessary for his transformation into a prodigious warrior. Although his adversaries have uncanny abilities in battle, he quickly dispatches them one after the other. He takes their heads as trophies and hurries off in his chariot when he hears the mother of the three calling upon her countrymen to avenge their deaths.

On his way he stops in a bog to capture a fierce stag (or two in some versions; see Dunn 1914, 74; Cross and Slover 1936, 150; and O'Rahilly 1976, 147), of which his charioteer is terrified. Cúchulainn reassures the man: "I shall so nod at him and so glare at him that he will not move his head towards you and will not dare to stir" (O'Rahilly 1976, 147), or in an alternative translation, "At the look I shall give at the deer they will bend their heads in fear and awe of me; they will not dare move" (Dunn 1914, 74). True to his word, he subdues the beast with only the power of his look. As he reaches his home community the alarm is spread: he is in the state of *furor belli*, called simply *ferg*, "fury," in Irish, demanding more victims to slaughter. The king, as advised by his people, commands the queen and all the young women of the town to appear "naked" before the boy. The "nakedness" in most versions seems to be limited to the baring of breasts—although the Irish words used, (*a*) *mbruinni*, is ambiguous and may include the torso (Pokorny 1959–69, 1:70). The king presents this exhibition as a test of maturity or masculinity: "And if he be a true warrior he will not resist being bound, and he shall be placed in a vat of cold water until his anger go from him" (Dunn 1914, 77). The queen makes the ritual into an affirmation of feminine power: "These are the warriors that will meet thee to-day" (Dunn 1914, 77; O'Rahilly 1976, 148). At the sight, the boy hides his face in shame and turns toward his chariot; the savage brute seems once again a child. He is seized and immersed as directed; the first vat bursts from the heat, but after a second and a third he is finally cooled. He emerges radiant and beautiful. The queen dresses him in festive garments and he takes his permanent place of honor at the feet of the king, as his childlike quality continues to be combined with intimations of maturity. In the words of one translator, "He made a crimson wheel-ball of himself from his crown to the ground. A shout was raised at the bluish purple about him" (Dunn 1914, 78). A detailed description of his remarkable beauty follows: seven pupils in each eye, seven fingers on each hand, four spots of different colors on each cheek, and several other unconventional traits.

The ceremony represents a reintegration into society of the ferocious lone warrior, who is to become a supporter of the realm and a potential father and family man. The action of the women (150 or 130 of them, depending on the version) is essential. They collaborate with the king, but at the same time the queen's words oppose feminine to masculine power in an apparent act of feminine self-affirmation. The ceremony has further implications: it is a test, or as the king puts it, "If he be a true warrior . . ."; a ritual purification, hence the hero's beauty on emerging from the bath; and given the nudity of the hero and the women as well as the immersion, a symbolic sex act associating the hero's future sexual maturity with his first warlike exploit. With all this impressive symbolism, the rite is only partially effective. Cúchulainn remains wild, though devoted to the protection of the kingdom, and in most versions of the saga, never marries.

In the light of this tale, the initiatory character of Rodrigo's first battle, with the events that follow, appears inescapable. It proceeds as follows: The father of the young Rodrigo—later to be known as the Cid—has been attacked by the neighboring count Gómez de Gormaz in a cattle raid and in turn has conducted a destructive incursion against the count, burning property and taking men, cattle, and "por dessonrra, / las lauanderas que al agua estan lauando" [as a dishonor, the washerwomen who are at the river washing] (303).[21] The count is enraged, particularly by the abduction of the women, and demands an equal battle, with a hundred knights on each side. Some of the captive women and men are returned.

---

21. The association of mass rape with the cattle raid has been seen as particularly archaic, as an example of how ritual acts may sometimes stem from acts that once satisfied biological urges (Burkert 1979, 61–62). Compare Eliade (1958, 83): "Rapine, and especially cattle stealing, assimilate the members of the warrior band to carnivores." Presumably, women were particularly vulnerable to attack and abduction while away from their town and their men, washing clothes in a stream.

Rodrigo, age twelve, is avid for his first fight: "Nunca se viera en lit, ya quebrauale el corazon" [he had never seen battle and his heart was bursting (with eagerness)] (318). He disobeys his father to join his fighting force. With no explanation given—but as a textual signal that this is an initiation —he exercises the honor of launching the battle by dealing the first blows. He quickly dispatches the count and also captures his two sons, taking them as prisoners to his home at Vivar. No report is given of the group battle.

The dead count's three daughters present themselves at Vivar to plead for the freedom of their brothers, dressed in mourning clothes which have turned festive in an enigmatic transformation that appears to echo some half-forgotten tradition: "estonce la avian por duelo, agora por gozo la traen" [then they wore it in mourning, now they wear it in joy] (333). Rodrigo's father refers their request to his son, who reprimands the father (for not assuming responsibility for the death?) but recommends granting the request. The two brothers immediately begin planning a return raid, but the youngest sister, Jimena, seeks to appease them by proposing that they depend on her to make an appeal for justice to the king in Zamora.[22]

Jimena arrives weeping at the royal court and beseeches redress for the wrong done. The king (of León, of which Castile was a dependency) confesses to a quandary: a just decision, one against Rodrigo, may bring an insurrection by the unruly Castilians. Jimena proposes a happy solution: "Give me Rodrigo as a husband, that one who killed my father" (376). The king's adviser seizes upon the idea and urges him to issue a summons to Rodrigo and his father. The messenger, on his arrival in Vivar, gives assurances that Rodrigo is to be honored by the king, but the two remain deeply suspicious. They expect a treacherous act as punishment for the count's slaying, which for their part they regard as a justifiable act of war. Like the *Siete infantes* legend, this text shows serious ambivalence about the initiatory killing.

Rodrigo's mistrust of the king brings on an enraged state that will soon be recognized as the *furia guerrera*, the *furor belli*. He declares to his troops that if the king kills his father, then regicide will not be an act of treachery. As he enters the royal court, all fall back in terror before his gaze: "Quando Rodrigo bolujo los ojos, todos ivan derramando. / Avien muy grand pauor del & muy grande espanto" [When Rodrigo cast his eyes around, all fell

---

22. The geography of the poem is imaginary; Vivar and Gormaz are in fact over a hundred kilometers apart, and Zamora is some two hundred kilometers from Vivar.

back. They were very fearful of him, and in a great panic] (420–21). The father kisses the king's hand; Rodrigo refuses and instead makes a threatening move with his sword that brings a cry for help from the king: "Get that devil away from me!" [A grandes vozes dixo: "¡Tirat me alla esse pecado!"] (425).[23] In the face of Rodrigo's denunciations, the king commands, "Bring me that damsel; we'll betroth this spirited (or proud) fellow" (*este lozano*, 432). Jimena appears, looks Rodrigo over, "Ella tendio los ojos & a Rodrigo comenzo de catarlo," and states, "Many thanks, for this is the count I request" (attributing to him a rank equal to hers, which in fact he does not have).

With that the troth is pledged. The *doncella* (damsel, 433) is now "donna Ximena Gomez" (436). Rodrigo is still furious at the king and expresses displeasure: "Sennor, vos me despossastes mas a mj pessar que de grado" [Lord, you have betrothed me more to my sorrow than to my liking] (438; *pesar* was both "sorrow" and "anger"), but he now calls the king "sennor" and makes no move to avoid the betrothal. He swears never to kiss the king's hand or be intimate with Jimena until he has won five battles. Though he postpones it, his integration into society has begun. The king is amazed: "This is no man; he has the look of a devil!" (343).

Rodrigo will immediately be put to work in the most hazardous defense assignments against the Moors. Subsequently, the first call to arms will reach him during his siesta: a possible reflex of the nap of Cúchulainn.

The tale is thoroughly adapted to Spanish conditions and custom, yet the correspondences with the Irish account are notable. The occasion of the slaughter is a cattle raid in Spain; the *Táin* takes its name from a cattle raid that occurs long after the initiation. In both accounts the child hero, against the wishes of his (foster-) father, takes up arms and single-handedly downs dangerous aggressors—killing three, or killing one and capturing two. (Rodrigo is not alone in the battle, but no account is given of the other combat-

---

23. The late epic ballad "Cabalga Diego Laínez," which relates this incident, recalls the details that appear to be most significant. As Rodrigo and his father arrive to pay their respects to the king, the youth confronts the king's followers, "en hito los ha mirado" [he looked at them fixedly], and issues a challenge that none are willing to take up. Then, when expected to kiss the king's hand, "al hincar de la rodilla——el estoque se ha arrancado. / Espantóse d'esto el rey——y dijo como turbado: / 'Quítate, Rodrigo, allá;——quítate allá, diablo, / que tienes el gesto de hombre——y los hechos de león bravo' " [as he knelt, he drew his sword. The king was frightened at this, and said as though confused: "Get away, Rodrigo, get away, devil, for you have the look of a man and the actions of a fierce lion"] (Díaz Mas 1994, 98–99). The mention of a lion is worth noting. Jimena does not appear in this version; Rodrigo angrily departs with his men, whose court attire mysteriously turns to military garb.

ants.) After removals in time and space in *Mocedades* (as in *Tristan* and *Siete infantes*), the hero arrives at the king's court in the furious state, striking dread into all those present. The hero's look has transfixed a stag in the *Táin*; in Zamora it affects the men at the court. The women (or woman) overcome the power of his look with an even more potent visual stimulus. The ritual sets the young man on the path to socialization as vassal to the king, and also, in Spain, as husband. (Marriage is represented in the *Táin*, as in other Irish sagas, as a less stable commitment than is familiar in the later Middle Ages and in Spain.) Rodrigo's tacit acceptance of the betrothal to an enemy's daughter implies his entry into the larger political world. As in the case of Cúchulainn, the ritual does not complete the transformation that it symbolizes. Rodrigo's anger against the king is not wholly tamed, as manifested in another reference to his devilish look (*Mocedades*, 443). The look again recalls Cúchulainn, who at times underwent grotesque transformations while seized by the *ferg*; one eye became huge and the other tiny, his mouth took on a wolf-like shape allowing a view of his inner organs, his hair became long vertical spikes, and so on.

As a major discrepancy between the two tales, the bath, very essential in the saga, is of course missing in *Mocedades*, along with any suggestion of nudity. These would be hard to retain in a scene situated in a Spanish royal court—although it will be maintained in pages to follow that the bath is ingeniously represented, not only in *Siete infantes*, but also in other Spanish tales, among which only the *Cid* reflects the ancient tradition as accurately in other respects as does *Mocedades*. In general, swimming and bathing are more often mentioned in northern narrative than in Spain, where a negative view of those activities may be evidenced by an edict issued by Alfonso VI, ordering the destruction of all baths in his kingdom, as corrupting and debilitating to members of the armed forces charged with combating the Moors (*PCG* 2:555b27ff.).

The integrating function of the initiation, through which the hero will assume his two essential adult roles in the community, is admirably fulfilled in *Mocedades*. Rodrigo's self-imposed conditions facilitate adaptation to the narrative pattern habitual in these accounts, in which the first battle is replicated with variations. By setting the conditions, he keeps some initiative while submitting to the rules of society. The poem's treatment of Jimena is also notably successful. She takes initiative without loss of dignity in her request to the king, is sexually venturesome without being indecent, and breaks the rules of mourning for a good purpose, bringing both Rodrigo and herself through a crisis with desirable results for each, and turning aside the hero's fury in a manner honorable for all.

Though the bath, crucial in *Tristan* and *Siete infantes*, is absent from *Mocedades*, two episodes involving Rodrigo, one from this poem and one from related epic ballads, can be connected with it. They represent the theme of violence toward women, which also appears in the *Táin* and in other initiation tales. In the absence of bathing, *Mocedades* refers to the related activity of washing clothes while recounting the humiliating abduction of the washerwomen. In the Irish saga, the amazonian queen Medb of Connacht leads a cattle raid against King Conchobar of Ulster, during which she carries off fifty women—whom in one version she has hanged and crucified (Dunn 1914, 135). In reprisal, Cúchulainn stations himself at the frontier between the warring nations and keeps up a constant slaughter of her best warriors. Reaching the point of desperation, she requests a truce but refuses as disgraceful his demand for the return of the women. At this point the fury comes over Cúchulainn. In a replay of his initiatory bath, he undresses and sits in snow reaching up to his waist, which melts around him "a man's length, so great was the fierce ardour of the warrior" (O'Rahilly 1976, 109). To make peace, Medb and her husband offer him their daughter Finnabair as his wife, but Cúchulainn refuses to speak to the messenger they send with word of their offer. As a second messenger, they send an exiled compatriot of his, to whom he responds, "Friend Lugaid, it is a trick." Reassured that the royal pledge is dependable, he agrees to an interview with the king. But the king is evidently (all motives have to be supplied by the reader) afraid to meet with him and sends in his place a jester wearing a crown, accompanied by the girl, to make the betrothal. Apparently further infuriated by the attempt at deceit, Cúchulainn hurls a rock through the jester's head (one of his favorite methods of killing). He impales the jester's body on a pillar-stone, cuts off Finnabair's two plaits, and thrusts a pillar-stone through her mantle and tunic, abandoning her there with the body.

Recalling now *Mocedades*, the parallels again seem too numerous to be coincidental: the cattle raid with the abduction of women, the proposed truce and the demand for the women's return, the *furor belli*, the offer of a wife (relative of the king) as a means of obtaining peace, the mistrust of the king's message, the agreement nevertheless to a meeting. In these shared elements, the only substantial differences are displacements. In Spain it is Rodrigo's fellow tribesmen who carry out the abduction, and King Fernando combines the roles of Conchobar, Cúchulainn's ruler, as seen in the original initiation, with that of Ailill, the enemy king (of Connacht, husband of Medb), in this adventure in which Jimena successfully reverses the role of the unfortunate Finnabair. The rejection and outrageous shaming of the damsel are of course not found in this part of *Mocedades*.

Perhaps they were, however. Perhaps they were to be found in another version of the epic, known now only through the three ballads on the grievances of Jimena (discussed by Montaner 1992), which contain lines also present in the protests of Doña Llambra in the ballad "Yo me estaba en Barvadillo." Yet another parallel appears in a later episode of *Mocedades*, involving the count of Savoy and his daughter, which in turn has a close analogue in *Tristan*. The ingenuity with which the mythic elements are manipulated to develop new meanings, changing their order or their attribution to one or another personage, is truly remarkable. Claude Lévi-Strauss accounts for the technique of rearranging and reattributing preexisting motifs as follows, adapting the everyday term *bricolage* to mythic narrative: "Le propre de la pensée mythique est de s'exprimer à l'aide d'un répertoire dont la composition est hétéroclite et qui, bien qu'étendu, reste tout de même limité; pourtant, il faut qu'elle s'en serve, quelle que soit la tâche qu'elle s'assigne, car elle n'a rien d'autre sous la main. Elle apparaît ainsi comme une sorte de *bricolage* intellectuel" (1962, 30).[24]

The occurrence of the same lines in two distinct ballads, spoken by Doña Llambra after the outrage committed by the seven infantes following the affront of the cucumber in "Yo me estaba en Barvadillo," and by Jimena in "Día era de los Reyes," has been considered by some to be an arbitrary or "impertinent" contamination. But it merits reconsideration in view of the hypothesis here advanced, identifying both *Siete infantes* and *Mocedades* as variations on the initiation tale. The first of these, Doña Llambra's protest, is a close approximation to the epic text, except that the lady amplifies and exaggerates the outrages with which she has been threatened by the seven brothers:

"Yo me estaba en Barvadillo — en essa mi heredad;
mal me quieren en Castilla — los que me havían de aguardar.
Los hijos de doña Sancha — mal amenazado me han,

---

24. To paraphrase this elegant formulation: mythic thinking operates by piecing together whatever odds and ends are available to it, as one might do in a workshop, in a sort of intellectual jerry-rigging.

que me cortarían las faldas — por vergonçoso lugar,
y cevarían sus halcones — dentro de mi palomar,
y me forçarían mis damas, — casadas y por casar;
matáronme un cozinero — so faldas del mi brial.
Si desto no me vengáis — yo mora me iré a tornar."[25]

(Débax 189)

As is well known, Jimena's accusations in the romance "Día era de los
Reyes" at some points take the same form, here indicated by asterisks:

"Con manzilla bivo, rey, — con ella bive mi madre:
cada día que amanece — veo quien mató a mi padre,
cavallero en un cavallo, — y en su mano un gavilán,
otra vez con un halcón, — que trae para caçar.
Por me hazer más enojo — *cébalo en mi palomar.
Con sangre de mis palomas — *ensangrentó mi brial:
enviéselo a dezir, — *envióme a amenazar
*que cortara mis haldas — *por vergonçoso lugar,
*que forçara mis donzellas — *casadas y por casar.
*Matárame un pagezico — *so haldas de mi brial:
rey que no haze justicia — no devía de reinar
ni cavalgar en cavallo — ni espuela de oro calzar."[26]

(Débax 195)

The cited lines of this memorable, confused passage are spoken by each
woman in her own ballad, and some of the accusations are justly applicable
to each of the men. The outcomes of the speeches are the same as in their

25. [Spoken to Ruy Velázquez:] "I was in Barbadillo, on that property of mine; I am hated
in Castile by the ones who ought to serve and protect me. The sons of Doña Sancha [the seven
infantes] have grievously threatened me, that they would cut off my skirts in a shameful place
and feed their falcons in my dovecote, and violate my ladies, married and unmarried; they
killed a kitchen-hand under the skirt of my tunic. If you fail to take revenge, I will become a
Mooress."
26. "I live in shame, king, as does my mother: every day that dawns I see the one who killed
my father, mounted on a horse with a hawk in his hand, other times a falcon that he carries
for the hunt. To grieve me more, he feeds it in my dovecote. With blood of my doves he bloodied my tunic. I sent word to him about it, he sent threats that he will (or would) cut off my
skirts in a shameful place, and violate my damsels, married and unmarried. He killed (or will
kill) a page-boy under the skirts of my tunic. A king who does not do justice should not reign,
nor wear a golden spur." (The doubtful verb tenses depend on what accentuation the forms
receive.)

respective epic sources: Rodrigo's marriage to the good woman, and the death of the seven infantes at the hands of the evil one. Each woman clamors for justice after the killing of a relative followed by a real or imagined sexual outrage (which is not narrated in the extant epic *Mocedades*, but is instigated and then exaggerated by Doña Llambra in both ballad and epic). The boldness of the women who utter these lines is perhaps without equal in the epic ballads.

These alleged humiliations of women lead to consideration of another episode from the *Mocedades*, one which reproduces with considerable accuracy a sequence of events in *Tristan* and which is degrading to an innocent woman. It is again Tristan's first battle, but a later one for Rodrigo. The stories are so similar that they can be told as one.

The hero's lord, King Mark in Cornwall and King Fernando in Spain, receives from a tyrannical foreign power a yearly demand for tribute. The Irish king requires maidens, youths, and horses of Mark. The levy on Fernando is placed by an alliance consisting of the king of France, the pope, and the Holy Roman Emperor, who stipulate maidens and horses. No one at the court is willing to do battle against the requirement. King Mark is at first furious and then, like Fernando, distraught. The hero, who was absent when the demand was delivered, appears and offers to free the kingdom from the oppressor, but cannot do so until he has been made a knight. Each is knighted summarily. Tristan crosses to an island in the Irish Sea, whereas Rodrigo has already crossed the Rhone, each to meet his adversary. The opponent sends messages that the hero answers defiantly. Tristan now reveals his identity to the enemy; Rodrigo will do so after the encounter. The proud representative of the tyrant, the queen's brother in *Tristan* and a count of Savoy in *Mocedades*, is defeated; the brother is mortally wounded but the count is only unhorsed and made prisoner.[27] After a number of adventures in *Tristan*, immediately in *Mocedades*, the beautiful blonde niece (Iseut) of the downed adversary in *Tristan*, his daughter in *Mocedades*, is offered by her father as a wife for the hero. Instead of accepting her, the hero delivers the damsel to his king, as wife in *Tristan* but as concubine in *Mocedades*. The king at first is not interested in marriage or a liaison, but soon changes his mind. The hero is honored in the court, but later the king, Mark or Fernando's successor Alfonso (in the *Poema del Cid*), persecutes

27. A parallel between the count of Savoy in *Mocedades* and Count Remont Verenguel (the historical Berenguer Ramón II) of Barcelona in the *Poema del Cid*—both arrogant *francos* whom the Cid defeats and humiliates—is pointed up by the name Ramón, given to the Savoyard in the chronicle (von Richthofen 1989, 47).

him under the influence of jealous courtiers. A chief difference is that Tristan becomes Iseut's lover, both having succumbed to a love potion intended for use by the married couple, in what may be an addition to the initial "parties anciennes" (Bédier's term) of *Tristan* that connects them to the rest of the story, the part that would come to constitute its main body.

Such close correspondences in two sequels to the initiation serve to confirm the coherence and pervasiveness of all this legendary material. Even though the sequels appear to be a more recent invention, their similarity as they echo the rite of passage is not likely to be accidental. The Savoy episode shows the remarkable flexibility that irony can lend to a tradition. The account is turned to the detriment of French womanhood for the stated purpose of dishonoring France: "embarraganad a Françia" [make France your concubine], Rodrigo tells the king (987). The legend, which must have been widely recognized as French in origin, is manipulated craftily, partly by locating the action in France. The contest between the sexes continues, but the woman has lost all initiative. Rodrigo first feigns interest in marrying the noble Savoyarde himself, then misleads her into thinking King Fernando will marry her, and finally hands her over to him as a spoil of war. Her role is completely passive. The same text that exalts the enterprising woman in the person of Jimena now shows how to degrade the feminine sex, going to extremes that, even when taken as theoretical, speak harshly of the society's system of values.

In another instance of interweaving of legends, the aftermath of these events in *Mocedades* presents a curious parallel with the story of Mudarra. After a pregnancy scarcely longer than that of Mudarra's mother, the count's daughter delivers a son who is seized upon by Spain's desperate enemies, when King Fernando and the young Rodrigo are at the gates of Paris, as a kind of deus ex machina, a pretext to end the war. Both children, born speedily and illegitimately to Spanish fathers and foreign mothers in foreign lands, bring peace, though they do so in completely different ways. Fernando's son eventually becomes a distinguished and respected cardinal.

An apparent reference to the *furor belli*, again in *Mocedades* and in pertinent chronicles, has been studied by Samuel Armistead (1987, with an excellent bibliography on the fury). It appears in an incident that qualifies as a replication of the initiation, although it lacks the distinctive elements except for (perhaps, at a remove) the sleep, the mysterious fury (accompanied by a hot sensation in this instance), invincibility, and of course the killing. While on a pilgrimage Rodrigo befriends a helpless leper and sleeps in the same bed with him—or under the same cape, in a variant. During the night he is

awakened by a remarkable sensation; his companion has blown on his
back, and the breath of air has penetrated through his chest. "Sant" Lázaro
informs him that henceforth when he feels the breath of air he will be invincible. As it happens, Rodrigo has agreed to represent Castile in combat
against a formidable Aragonese champion. Arriving at the scene of the
duel, he requests refreshment in the form of a sop in wine. As he reaches for
it he feels the promised hot breath, and his hand moves instead to his
horse's rein. He quickly fells his adversary. Armistead notes further that the
fury is also recalled, referred to as "corajes," in the Carolingian ballad, "Ya
comiençan los franceses con los moros pelear" (Débax 1982, 217). The
scene is the battle of Roncesvalles, and the hero in question is Reinaldos, or
Renaud de Montauban:

> Ya le toman los corajes — que le suelen tomar
> assí se entra por los moros — como segador por pan,
> assí derriba cabeças — como peras d'un peral;
> por Roncesvalles arriba — los moros huyendo van.[28]

Given the association of the fury with heat, was the cooling effect of the
bath thought by Alfonso VI (p. 34) to dampen the warlike ardor of his soldiers? Probably not; baths presented more palpable risks, but the tradition
may have been well known and could have reinforced the suspicions of the
king and his advisers.

In bringing out the venerable origins of parts of *Mocedades*, the intent is
not to gloss over its generally low literary quality or its irresponsible distor-
tions of basic historical and geographical fact, some of which have been evident in the foregoing summary. The incursion into France, for example, is
altogether fabricated, its motivation expressing a burst of xenophobia that
appears as the ultimate perversion of the healthy if primitive tribal sense
that pervades the *Poema del Cid*. Much of the writing is incoherent, prosaic, and monotonous. As a result of its defects, it has not usually been
taken seriously by critics, but its phraseology is that of traditional epic, it
contains occasional admirable passages taken from different traditions, and
here it has been seen to include authentic and important inherited themes,
giving evidence of a long and honorable textual history. Menéndez Pidal

---

28. "His customary fury comes over him; he moves through the Moors like a reaper
through a wheatfield, he cuts down heads like pears in a pear orchard; upward through Roncesvalles the Moors go fleeing."

and others spoke of it scornfully as a *centón* or patchwork composition, long before a synonym of that word, *bricolage*, became current in a favorable sense among critics fascinated by the intensely intertextual character of mythic narrative (Bremmer 1988b, 53). *Mocedades* is valuable precisely because its juxtaposition of diverse contents such as chronistic materials, uninspired new inventions, popular ballads, and long-standing traditional lore is so transparent. The first documentation of a fragment of the story dates to the late thirteenth century (Armistead 1974), but its beginnings plausibly go back to the lifetime of the Cid (Rico 1990, 20). The part resembling *Tristan*, whose poetic versions probably date from before 1170, with prose redactions beginning around 1230, must have an eleventh-century antecedent, since it preserves matter found in *Táin* but lost in *Tristan*.

By way of summary, *Mocedades* brings together lore that corresponds strikingly with the *Táin*, notably the successful heroic initiation in which the woman or women collaborate, with instances of sexual abuse that cannot be dissociated from each other in *Táin*, *Tristan*, and through the ballads, *Siete infantes*. Some of the correspondences are episodic though compelling; others are found in lengthy and complex sequences. The benign, powerful feminine presence is essential to the successful initiation; but the abuses are disturbingly frequent and degrading, and appear also as an integral aspect of the heroic personality—as also in other myths studied by Dumézil, notably that of Herakles. Though each account—among those already observed and those yet to be considered—fits and amplifies the pattern, *Mocedades*, which relates the initiation of Spain's paradigmatic hero, occupies a central position in this bundle of texts. It does not integrate the tradition—its patchwork quality is irreducible—but it does facilitate integration by the modern observer.

El Poema del Cid

In the *Poema del Cid*, with its biographical component, the interrelation between the story and the actual conditions under which the hero lived is of course much more highly developed than in the other texts that have been considered. The primitive features are better concealed, better blended into a plot based on the realities of the Cid's life and world. One might not expect to find archaic elements at all, especially since the Cid is no longer young in this work, and his initiation is a thing of the past. But there are in fact two young men who take principal roles, and a review of the chief incidents comprising the initiation may now bring them to mind. As seen in the preceding texts, these incidents are the first battle, the nap, the subduing of the fierce animal by the power of the hero's eyes, the bath or immersion, with some reference to nudity, and the subsequent confrontation with and abuse of women and their garments. One or another of these elements is missing from *Tristan*, *Siete infantes*, and *Mocedades*, sometimes more than one; for instance, there is nothing more naked than the main characters' eyes in *Mocedades*, and the animal has disappeared from that poem and perhaps from *Siete infantes*, in which the nap, if not forgotten, becomes a time of relaxation after the hunt. Remarkably, however, all the principle traits are to be found in the *Poema del Cid*. The great difference is that the initiation is a failure and its functions are reversed in order and effect. Some actions are displaced to the nonheroic figures. Reversals and displacements, which have been identified in the foregoing discussion as classic mechanisms employed in each text for the purpose of manipulating the traditional material, here reach a peak of creativity.

For Rodrigo, as for Cúchulainn and Tristan, the much-anticipated first killing, linked to a dramatic encounter with the feminine, leads to an exemplary military career. Rodrigo's victories eventually bring him wealth, which in the *Poema del Cid* he shares judiciously to earn prestige and admiration. For the infante Gonzalo the conflict with the woman is not resolved and leads to disaster. In the *Cid*, the Infantes de Carrión also get off on the wrong foot, with an inversion of values which the poem represents through the inappropriate order of their actions. Their first move was directly contrary to the heroic pattern: the scheming designed to acquire wealth through marriage, with no intention or desire to fight for any purpose, whether glory, wealth, or ennobling marriages. From the perspective of the established heroic trajectory, with its proper sequence of events, they were doomed to failure from the start. If the initiatory sequence still had the force of a belief, as will be maintained in what follows—a belief in a series of actions rather than a more abstract credo or ideology—then the Infantes are put forward as a model of what not to do.

The Infantes' failure in the confrontation with the beast is a key to their total failure. It receives a suitably portentous introduction: the sudden appearance of a lion in the palace hall at siesta time is an extraordinary event. The abrupt and seemingly offhand introduction of "el león" (2222) into the scene suggests, not a routine occurrence, but one acceptable to the audience, needing no explanation or justification, probably an independent, preexisting narrative motif recognized as appropriate for the mythologizing of heroes. Here the hero is of course not one or both of the presumptive initiands, but the Cid, reaffirmed as the established warrior when he dominates the lion by his presence. It is a wondrous deed: "A maravilla lo han—quantos que í son" [All those present take it for a marvel] (2302). The Cid undergoes a transformation comparable to those seen in Cúchulainn and Rodrigo during their initiations when they subdued, respectively, a stag or a king's court with a preternatural look. Américo Castro brought out the transcendence of the moment: "Ritual, sacralmente, el héroe, sin necesidad de otro detalle, se encamina hacia [el terrible animal]. El Campeador histórico se despega del suelo y hace vuelo a la maravilla, al mito" (1956, 7–8). The poem does not specifically attribute the Cid's power over the beast to his eyes. But when animals, like people, look at each other, it is usually eye to eye. Leo Spitzer noted the hypnotic effect of the Cid's presence, referring to "cette sorte d'hypnotisme qu'il exerce sur la bête qui de furieuse devient honteuse" (1938, 529). The Cid's power is surely concentrated in his eyes: "El león, quando lo vio,—assí envergonçó, / ante Mio Çid la cabeça premió—e el rostro fincó" [The lion, when he saw him, was so shamefaced, before the Cid he bowed his head and lowered his muzzle] (2298–99). Compare again the words of Cúchulainn to his charioteer: "At the look I shall give at the deer they will bend their heads in fear and awe of me; they will not dare move and it will be safe for thee" (Dunn 1914, 75–76).

The special quality of the Cid's look, though apparently taken tacitly as general knowledge in this episode, does reappear, and receives considerable attention, in the part of the *PCG* that continues the Cid's literary biography after the point where the *Poema del Cid* ends (see note 3). Moors visiting from other lands are prone to comment on the stunning effect of his look: "Vi yo muchas uezes, quando vinien a el mandaderos de moros, se parauan antel, fincan commo desbaharecidos catandol, tan grant miedo an de la su catadura" (*PCG* 2:629b24–28, also 42–45).[29] "Et quando el pariente del soltan fue çerca del Çid yl touo oio, començol a tremer toda la carne. Et el fue marauillado de quel tremie assy su carne, et touol oio otra uez al Çid; et

---

29. "I often saw, when Moorish messengers came and stood before him, they get addled looking at him, so fearful are they of his look."

el Çid fue por abraçallo; et aquel moro pariente del soltan non lo pudo fablar, fasta vna grant pieça passada" (678a49–b6, also b34–40).[30]

Another circumstance recalling the initiation of Cúchulainn (and perhaps also of Rodrigo, see p. 33) is the hero's siesta. A nap, ordinarily a routine habit, would not command the attention of minstrel and audience if it
did not have some importance in tradition. Both here and in the later
retelling of the event by Pero Vermúdez, it is only the Cid who is said to
sleep; no account is given of what the others may be doing in the meantime,
and only he is awakened:

> En Valençia seí Mio Çid — con todos sus vassallos,
> con él amos sus yernos — los ifantes de Carrión.
> Yaziés' en un escaño, — durmié el Campeador;
> mala sobrevienta, — sabed, que les cuntió:
> saliós' de la red — e desatós' el león.
> En grant miedo se vieron — por medio de la cort.[31]
>
> (2278–83)

The Cid's siesta apparently has its roots in the ancient myth and prepares
him for his impressive action.

If the nap seems a little strange as part of a heroic narrative, the *lagar* or
wine press must seem even stranger. We noted earlier that it would be difficult to locate a bath at or near a royal court in Spain in order to perpetuate
the tradition of the initiatory immersion. Here we have suggested that the
Infantes de Carrión go through an inverted, foiled initiation. No critic
seems to have wondered very seriously why Diego would have chosen a

---

30. "And when the sultan's kinsman came near the Cid and looked at him, all his flesh
began to tremble. And he was amazed that his flesh trembled so, and he looked again at the
Cid, and the Cid moved to embrace him, and that kinsman of the sultan could not speak to
him for a long space of time." Perhaps by coincidence, the sultan's envoy brings a huge collection of "animalias estrannas" as gifts for the Cid. A power similar to that of the Cid is exer-
cised by Horatius Cocles, who holds a whole army at bay, prohibiting them from crossing a
bridge into Rome by the fierceness of his look (Dumézil 1978, 100–101). Other instances
occur in the *Volsunga Saga*: "so bright and eager were the eyes of Sigurd that few durst look
upon him" (111), and his daughter Swanhild has the same quality. Her treatment recalls that
of the Medusa. Her husband has a bag put over her head so she can be murdered—a shame-
lessly sexist touch, since no man would be so treated. (Cited by García Montoro 1972, 55,
from the Morris translation.)

31. "In Valencia was the Cid with all his men, with him both his sons-in-law, the Infantes
de Carrión. Lying on a bench, the Cid was sleeping; know that they had an unpleasant sur-
prise: the lion got out of his cage and broke loose. Great fear reigned throughout the hall."

wine press as refuge from the lion when presumably an audience might expect him to find a room with a door to close or some other protection in or around the Cid's palace. The variant poem followed by the *PCG*, if not the chroniclers themselves, evidently found the wine press implausible and made a revision that demonstrates the fragility of the traditional narrative forms. They speak only of a place that "non era tan linpio commo auie mester" [was not as clean as it should have been] (2:603a38–39), presumably a repository for refuse. Into it the Infante takes such a leap that he loses his balance and falls, soiling his knees.[32]

Not only is Diego's choice of a place of refuge odd; the mere presence of the wine press raises a question, and some modest critical reservations have been expressed about whether such a thing would be found in or around a palace (Such and Hodgkinson 1987, 176n). Whether it would be in use and contain fresh residue is another doubtful matter. The poem seems careless regarding the time of year. In trying to pin down a date, the reader must take recourse to a time reference given at an earlier point: "El ivierno es exido,—que el março quiere entrar" [Winter is over and March is about to come in] (1619), after which events leading to the weddings move rapidly. This would place the weddings around May, after which a second time reference is pertinent: "Í moran los ifantes—bien cerca de dos años," [The Infantes dwell there (in Valencia) for very nearly two years] (2271). The lion episode would then fall in the early part of the year, and not near the time of the grape harvest.

If taken in isolation, the foregoing strictures may be less than compelling. The poem does not have to be exact regarding lapses of time. Other doubts, less than decisive in themselves, nevertheless gather weight as they accumulate. For example, Valencia is not known for wine production in its immediate vicinity. The poet may not have been informed on this point, and it is impossible to deny that he might have imagined a vineyard in or near the city. If he had in mind a typical Spanish town, however, he would have assumed that vines and grains were cultivated at some distance from the center, the nearby areas being reserved for garden crops.[33] How he imagined Valencia is an open question; he had at least heard of the watery *huerta* (1615). In any case the customary location of vineyards raises doubts, because it would be impractical to place a wine press at a distance

---

32. The *Crónica de veinte reyes* sticks to the wine press (Powell 1983, 145). Quevedo received, or else rather predictably chose, the coarser alternative in his re-creation of the incident (Alonso 1973b, 128).

33. On the cultivated areas surrounding the typical city, see Montaner 1993, 561.

from them. Even granting the possibility of nearby vineyards, the military leader's palace would seem a particularly unsuitable place for the untidy operation of wine making.

A perhaps more considerable objection is left unresolved by Alberto Montaner, whose expertise in things Oriental might have allowed him to address it. Though the claim has been contested (e.g., Vicens Vives 1969, 108) and though in their epic, the infantes de Lara receive bread and wine from their Moorish adversaries during a respite in their battle against them, Montaner implies that the Islamic prohibition against wine would have been rigorously observed: "La presencia de un lagar indica la completa cristianización del alcázar moro de Valencia, que, de acuerdo con la prohibición coránica de beber vino, no habría contado con una instalación semejante" (1993, 599). The poet supposes the conquest of Valencia to have been completed some two years before the lion episode. If the Christians were not depending on Moorish plantings, and only started to grow grapes after settling into the city, they would have had no use for a wine press at the time of the lion's escape, since vines do not begin bearing a usable crop until five or six years after they are planted.

Epic "allows myth to take precedence over reality as we know it" (Nagy 1990, 8). The introduction of the wine press involves enough implausible presuppositions to give the impression that it was recognized as a frank fabrication, and that neither the minstrel nor his audience were concerned about strict verisimilitude regarding it. As the story of the Infantes is pursued in the discussion to follow, and as further evidence strengthens the idea that they go through a version of the traditional initiation, it will become increasingly believable that the poem has found a way to bring the bath to the palace, as *Mocedades* had failed or neglected to do. We may note in passing that this is not the only detail in the poem that the hearer was allowed to take with a grain of salt. For instance, the *juglar* could not expect his audience to accept literally the conversation in Castilian, complete with wordplay, with Búcar, newly arrived from Morocco, or the superhuman blow that ends that dialogue—or the easy duping of moneylenders, or the ready unmaking and remaking of marriages, or, in fact, the whole fable of the third *cantar*. The *Poema del Cid* is more self-consciously literary, in the sense that it creates its own artificial reality, than either *Siete infantes* or *Mocedades*.

The nap, the lion, the look, and the wine press all fit better into the mythic pattern than into a portrayal of daily realities, and surely their spontaneous reinvention by a poet unacquainted with the preexisting pattern is implausible. The four elements correspond, allowing for thoroughgoing reversals and displacements, to the nap, stag, look, and tubs of water in the tale of Cúchulainn. In the *Cid* the first three actions are attributed no longer to the initiand, but to the established hero. The Infantes fail the lion test,[34] and the purification accomplished by the immersion turns to contamination. Diego takes an unclean bath. His garments, like those of Finnabair, Llambra, and Jimena (in her imagination) are sullied, as recalled in the court of justice by Martín Antolínez: "¡Más non vestist—el manto nin el brial!" [You never again wore your cloak or tunic!] (3366), in a possible oblique reference to the traditional nudity of the initiand. Another implication, at least remotely possible, would put the Infantes in the same class with the three women just named, who are said to be treated as prostitutes —implying the degradation that surfaces again at Corpes.

The subverted initiation will now proceed to a second phase, the battle itself. Whereas the heroes of other tales have been avid for their first opportunity to kill an enemy, the Infantes, already shamed for having fled before the lion, are panic-stricken by the arrival of an army from Morocco. They speak as though aware that they have reversed the prescribed initiation procedure: "Catamos la ganançia—e la pérdida no" [We considered the gain and not the loss] (2320). According to the rules, winning should come before winnings; *ganar* and *ganançias* have the same double sense. The ritual makes no allowance for a "pérdida." Loss in battle, in the ritual context, would mean loss of life. The Infantes missed their chance to lead heroic lives by reversing the order, putting marriage before the first test. They have not taken the necessary step into adulthood and will continue in

---

34. Much has been written about the significance of the lion (see, e.g., Smith 1977, 137–40). Without denying the many symbolic values of the beast, it seems like the inevitable choice as a threatening animal, since the alternatives would be a boar, a bear, a stag, or some other, more exotic animal. In Ireland the stag was also an obvious choice; though the lion was known as a heraldic creature, none would be imagined roaming the bogs. In the far North the normal fearsome beast of literature is the bear, or of course the dragon. Bowra (1952, 154) has noted a deliberate vagueness in epic descriptions of monsters. The lion's status as literary cliché was so well established as to permit deft parody by Chrétien de Troyes in *Yvain*, where the hero encounters a lion who by some chance has been wandering in a French forest and has been attacked by an (equally foreign?) serpent. In the course of destroying the reptile, Yvain is obliged to cut off the lion's tail. The lion expresses its infinite gratitude in gestures part doglike, part courtly (3392ff.). Yvain is now forever to be followed by a tailless lion, and the grotesquerie will be politely ignored by everyone. (On Celtic prototypes for Chrétien's lion, which include the stag, see Chotzen 1933.) Armistead (1987, n. 29) acutely brings out parallels between the Cid's lion and Grendel in *Beowulf*. Both enter the hall where someone is sleeping and are subdued in a one-to-one encounter by the hero, though others are present.

limbo: "Esto es aguisado—por non ver Carrión" [(freely) The way this looks, we'll never see Carrión] (2322): as untried, immature youths, they were never ready to leave home. "Bibdas remandrán—fijas del Campeador" [The Cid's daughters will be left widows] (2323): their lives, their very identity, bizarrely expressed in terms of the Cid's family, are in jeopardy. All this is presented, of course, with heavy irony, which is possible because there are two Infantes and their thoughts are spoken and audible. As often happens, they are overheard, and their desperation is made known to the Cid. Acting more in accord with historical reality than with heroic myth, he offers to excuse them from the battle, extending a right that was given to young men in the first year of their marriage (Michael 1980, 2335n). But his manner of doing so shows that neither he nor the poem's ethic approve of this custom. He makes the connection between their married state and their cowardice paratactically:

> "¡Dios vos salve, — yernos, ifantes de Carrión!;
> en braços tenedes mis fijas — tan blancas commo el sol.
> Yo desseo lides — e vós a Carrión,
> en Valençia folgad — a todo vuestro sabor."[35]
>
> (2332–35)

The reference to the women is openly sexual; "tan blancas commo el sol," in the context given, surely refers to the unclothed body. The order of the Cid's observations is significant: sexual intimacy of the Infantes, warlike ardor of the hero, homesickness of the youths who have not formally left their family environment through a successful first combat.

The offer, given the conditions surrounding it, is gravely insulting and must be refused. As confirmation that this will be an initiatory combat, the older of the two brothers, Fernando, requests and is granted the honor of launching the battle by striking the first blows (as reported later by Pero Vermúdez; the page where the incident was first narrated has been lost [expurgated?] from the manuscript). He approaches a Moor but then turns to flee: "vist un moro,—fústel' ensayar, / antes fuxiste—que a él te allegasses" [You saw a Moor, you went to test him, you fled before you got to him]

---

35. "God save you, sons-in-law, Infantes de Carrión! You hold in your arms my daughters, white as the sun. I want battles and you want Carrión. Take your ease in Valencia, and your pleasure." *Folgar*, here rendered as "to take one's ease," was also customarily used to designate the sex act. That meaning need not be taken here, but it could never be absent from an audience's mind.

(3318–18b). The verb *ensayar*, "to test, to prove (oneself)," as will be noted again, is used tellingly in the initiatory context. Pero, who had been appointed to watch over Fernando, kills the Moor and gives the youth his horse to conceal the disaster, since (to offer a modern gloss) it reflects seriously on the reputation (*ondra*) of the Cid's family, to which Pero also belongs. An indication that this aborted initiation episode had once had an existence apart is seen in its awkward integration into the narrative, which requires the audience to believe that the failed exploit could somehow have been conducted in secret, when in fact the "first blows" were an opening to the general battle, a signal indicating the time and place of its first joining, so that it was important that it be visible to all. The poem simply does not confront the problem of having the action both public and secret, and thereby allows the Cid to praise the Infantes, when the battle is over, for their presumed participation in it, while also allowing Pero Vermúdez the opportunity for his resounding denunciation of Fernando later on at the court of justice.

The bishop takes over the delivering of the first blows (again with *ensayar*): "por esso salí de mi tierra—e vin vos buscar / por sabor que avía—de algún moro matar. . . . Pendón trayo a corças—e armas de señal, / si ploguiesse a Dios—querríalas ensayar" (2371–76).[36] This time the *ensayo* is distinctly public. Says the Cid, "Afé los moros a oio,—idlos ensayar. / Nós d'aquent veremos cómmo lidia el abbat" [the Moors are in view, go test them. We from here will see how the abbot fights] (2381–82). Don Jerónimo's first killings are watched carefully: "Ensayávas el obispo,—¡Dios, qué bien lidiava!" [He proved himself, the bishop. God, how well he fought!] (2388), and he is kept "a oio": "El que en buen ora nasco—los oios le fincava" [He who was born in a propitious hour kept his eyes on him] (2392). The contrast is clear with the rout of Fernando, which seems to happen invisibly.

A great victory ensues. The Infantes are still concerned about wealth, and alone among the Cid's forces are impressed by their new riches. They even seem inclined to believe that they deserve them (see Duggan 1989, 38–39),[37] but the others, the most active in the fray, noticed their absence, and rumors of their cowardice fly, prompting their decision to go home,

36. "For that purpose I left my homeland, and came to seek you out, because of the urge I had to kill a Moor or two. . . . I have a banner emblazoned with hinds, and arms with my insignia [knightly rather than clerkly emblems]; if it please God I would like to test them."

37. After the battle, amid the general euphoria, the Infantes seem for a while to be highly regarded by the Cid: "Grandes son los gozos de sus yernos a dos, / daquesta arrancada que lidiaron de corazón" [Great is the joy of his two sons-in-law / over this victory in which they

and on the way, to do injury to their wives: "después en la carrera—feremos nuestro sabor" [later on the road we will do our pleasure] (2547). Following the logic of the initiation tradition, they see the women as the cause of their trouble.

The poem makes it clear that the Infantes failed to complete the passage from self-centered infantilism to an adult devotion to family and nation, since they married before being initiated as warriors, and for the wrong reason, to enrich themselves rather than to protect and serve their wives. They are not lacking in warlike skill (2245–46), but that has become irrelevant. Being untried, they are untrue. Joseph Campbell says of tribal initiation in general: "If an initiation should fail, the individual's personal system of reference, and consequently of sentiments, would remain essentially infantile and therefore aberrant, isolating, painful, and frightening" (1956, 90). These remarks fit the poem perfectly. As misfits, the Infantes de Carrión threaten the harmony of the Cid's *mesnada*. A wrong step in the still partly mythical scheme allows for no later correction. "When the primary urges of the adolescent remain unsocialized, they become inevitably a threat to the harmony of the group. The primary function of all myth and ritual, therefore, is to engage the individual both emotionally and intellectually in the local organization" (Campbell 1959, 467). The unanimity of the *mesnada*, in which no opposing opinions have arisen up to this point, is disrupted as a result of the Infantes' failure. The Cid finds himself obliged to prohibit his men from ridiculing their cowardice and false pretensions. Their duplicity thus introduces a false note, driving a wedge between the leader and his vassals. The audience, too, sees the hero as deluded. Opinions diverge. A single failure touching the leader affects the health of the social group.

The remaining basic element related to the initiation, the shameful or dishonorable treatment of women, is made the last of the sequence in the *Cid*. In the *Táin* it is separated from the rite of passage but is still accompanied by the *furor belli*. The hero either marks the woman as a prostitute (Finnabair), bloodies her clothing and threatens the same accusation (Llambra and Jimena in the ballad), or makes her a royal concubine (the Savoyarde). The physical abuse is most extreme in the *Cid*, in the crime of Corpes, where references to concubinage are also present.

---

fought so wholeheartedly] (2507–8). For various critical attempts to deal with the last hemistich, see Montaner 1993, 602. The two lines should probably be considered together; "sus yernos" directs the focus to the Cid's viewpoint, and the second line could be an instance of unmarked indirect discourse, rather frequent in the poem, as in many medieval texts.

The repeated use of the verb *ensayar* gives further indication that the initiation rite lurks in the background of the Corpes incident. The verb has taken on the tone of a technical term referring to the testing and proving undergone by the hero. Of its nine occurrences in the *Poema*, three refer to the glorious initial combat of the bishop Don Jerónimo, two to the Infante Fernando's failure in the same battle—which serves as a prelude to the bishop's success—and two to Corpes. Two other instances are not relevant, referring to the use of swords in other circumstances—by the Cid against Búcar, and by the Infante Diego during the judicial duels.

The strange locale of the Corpes episode, its imaginary geography and legendary history (Griza, Álamos, Elpha [2694–95]), its counterpoint of sinister and bucolic aspects, and the evening's sexual acceptance followed by the morning's brutal rejection, all point to a story that was once more complete in its details and its motivations.

The *Siete infantes*, with its ritual boasts and challenges issued when Llambra's young cousin Alvar Sánchez and the infante Gonzalo conduct their deadly dispute as to who is most praised by the women, provides background for this misadventure. To be a hero, the man needs the praise and support of women and works to achieve them by admirable warlike deeds. Rather than praise, the Infantes de Carrión expect scorn from their wives, and twice they declare their intention to silence them before they voice the scorn publicly: "después en la carrera—feremos nuestro sabor / ante que nos rretrayan—lo que cuntió del león" [Later on the road we will do our pleasure, before they confront and condemn us for what happened with the lion] (2547–48); "Assí las escarniremos—a las fijas del Campeador, / antes que nos rretrayan—lo que fue del león" [So we will disgrace the daughters of the Campeador, before they confront us with the incident of the lion] (2555–56). The verb *retraer* seems to be used as the antonym of *alabar*, in the senses "reprobar, reprender públicamente," and more strongly, "censurar, condenar públicamente," when Doña Sol chooses the same verb in her prediction that the censure will be even broader after this further indignity: "rretraer vos lo an—en vistas o en cortes" [You will be censured before an assembly or a court of law] (2733).

The Infantes have had to submit to the mockery of the Cid's men, but the contempt of the women looms as something even more intolerable. Like Gonzalo (see p. 151), they adopt the solution of physically silencing their critics. Though unwilling to hear any reference to the lion, the Infantes bring it up themselves as they begin their attack on the women. The last words they ever speak to them are, "nós vengaremos—por aquésta la desondra del león" [by this deed we will avenge the disgrace with the lion] (2719). They will have no answer for the noble words of Doña Sol, "Dos espadas tenedes—fuertes e taiadores" [You have two swords, sturdy and sharp] (2726). With cinches and spurs, both designed for use on horses, they debase the women and by extension their parents. The abuse proceeds wordlessly until they achieve their purpose of silencing the reprehension that they know is the women's minds: "Ya non pueden fablar—don Elvira e doña Sol" (2747). Here the key verb *ensayar* reminds the audience, with a masterly touch of irony, that this is a debasement of the consecrated initiation: "ensayándos' amos—quál dará meiores colpes" [testing themselves (to see) who will give better blows] (2746). Félez Muñoz uses the same verb when he comes upon the unconscious women in the wood: "¡Ya primas, las mis primas,—don Elvira e doña Sol, / mal se ensayaron—los ifantes de Carrión!" [Oh cousins, my cousins, Doña Elvira and Doña Sol, they have tested themselves in an evil manner (or wrongly), the Infantes de Carrión!] (2780–81). The Infantes steal the clothes they have not bloodied, consistent in their degraded behavior.

As they leave, they debase yet another phase of the knightly test, the ritual boasting: "Por los montes do ivan, ellos ívanse alabando . . . 'non las deviemos tomar por varraganas—si non fuéssemos rrogados.' . . , La desondra del león—assís' irá vengando. / Alabándos' ivan" (2757–63, again 2824).[38] The misappropriation of the boasting (called *gab* in French epic, where it is common), in which the Infantes also engaged after Fernando's secret failure against the Moor in the battle against Búcar (2340, 3324), reaches the height of indignity when applied to the shaming (*escarnio*) of women, reflecting on the Infantes' masculinity, as does their choice of weapons for the punishment of their wives. The extreme irrationality of the Infantes' act, which has puzzled critics and has seemed a weakness in the poem, gains in authenticity when seen within the pattern of violence against women and the broader scheme of the initiation. These patterns are surely not the only forces that shape the episode, but they are perhaps the most primitive and the basic guide determining the course of action.[39]

To sum up, in the *Poema del Cid* the initiation rite reaches a new level of

38. "Through the forest as they went, they continued boasting . . . 'We should never have taken them as concubines, if we had not been begged to do so . . . so the dishonor of the lion will be avenged!' They boasted as they went."

39. Gifford (1977) has suggested a connection between the Corpes episode and medieval fertility rites related to the Roman Lupercalia. The proposal offered here seems to provide a

manipulation of order of events, of personages to whom they refer, and of their effect. In the tales of Cúchulainn and Rodrigo, an established order is followed, beginning with the killing of enemies, the fury (and the taming of the beast, omitted or transformed in Rodrigo's case), and the confrontation with the feminine and with nudity (again omitted in *Mocedades*), with the egregious violence against the woman occurring sometime later. Each of the components, except for this last, contributes to the formation of the heroic characters. Within that pattern, the confrontation with the feminine counterbalances the murderous act with its accompanying fury. In the *Cid*, where the order is marriage-beast-battle, each element has negative results. Two are displaced: the taming shifts to the Cid and the victory in battle to Pero Vermúdez. The effects are all likewise negative in *Siete infantes*, begun with a marriage, though not that of the hero, followed by the confrontation with the woman, fury, and killing in Burgos, all replicated in the scene with the hawk and cucumber in Barbadillo.

Recalling the status of Finnabair, who is put forward as a peace offering or reward by her parents, it is noteworthy that like Jimena, the Savoyarde and even Llambra fulfill that role (although Jimena and Llambra are relatives, not daughters, of the ruler). Llambra's marriage is a reward offered to Ruy Velázquez, who during a Castilian siege of Zamora led a counterattack against Leonese raiders, "et porque fizo mucho bien en aquel dia ouol después a dar el conde Garçi Ferrandez por muger a doña Llanbra, que era su prima cormana" [and because he performed great deeds on that day, Count Garci Fernández would later give him Doña Llambra, his first cousin, in marriage] (Catalán 1980, 199). The *Siete infantes* legend may have been thought of as beginning after the initiation had taken place, since there is no hint that Gonzalo's killing is his first, and the infantes have been knighted previously by the ruling count. The other elements are present, however, including the fury, the partial nudity, and the confrontation with the woman—which is marked by an element of vengeance in all the stories. The power of the eyes is perhaps replaced by the hawk, an attribute both of Gonzalo and of his double Mudarra. The hawk, with its fabled eyesight, its spectacular speed and apparent sovereignty in the air, its ferocity, and other qualities, can be a potent symbol for a number of things, but a better repre-

---

stronger basis for the episode, but is compatible with some of the details he cites, particularly the physical surroundings: caves, spring, and sinister woods. There was of course nothing to prevent combination of elements of diverse origin, or perhaps the reversal of what seems to have been a joyful public celebration in Rome to a vicious secret abasement.

sentation of the eye would be hard to find if a substitute were for some reason desired. Instead of a powerful look, Gonzalo has his hawk. He even
takes it into combat, and his inexplicable use of it to strike Ruy Velázquez
in the face could perhaps be taken as a substitute for the eye-to-eye contact
of other legends.[40] Later he bathes his hawk instead of himself, after the
bird has undoubtedly killed and has bloodied its talons. (This substitution
has a rough parallel, though surely not its origin, in the reduction of bap-
tismal immersion to a dab on the baby's forehead.) Gonzalo is then identified by Llambra to her servant as "aquel que vees que tiene el açor en la
mano" [that one you see with the hawk on his hand] (PCG; Catalán 1980,
184), recalling the identification by tokens of Cúchulainn and Tristan in
their baths.

For the seven infantes, as for the Infantes de Carrión, and in direct contrast with Cúchulainn and Rodrigo, every phase of the narrative sequence
has negative results, making disaster progressively more inevitable, domi-
nating and guiding the plot of each tale. The Mocedades and the Cid, taken
together, confirm that to be a complete man, the hero needs the support of
a woman of noble spirit, and that the purpose of his heroic career is to protect and sustain her and her children. The Cid states his great hope in life in
these terms: "¡que aún con mis manos—case estas mis fijas . . . e vós,
mugier ondrada,—de mí seades servida!" [that yet with my hands I may
marry these my daughters . . . and you, honored wife, may be served by
me!] (282b–84). Jimena's wish, likewise expressed in prayer, is "¡Tú que a
todos guías—val a Mío Çid el Canpeador!" [Thou who guidest every one,
aid the Cid Campeador!] (241), with of course no reference to herself. The
infantes in both epics, in contrast, have no productive relationships with
women, and therein seems to lie their infantilism. They accordingly have no
productive future.[41] In this and in other ways—their direct reaction to each
new circumstance, for instance—epic lives are presented as predetermined
by inscrutable forces. It is worth repeating that with the partial exception
of the Poema del Cid, the works show forces acting and figures responding,
rather than concepts governing personal motives. Stories have their own
kind of meaning independent of ideology; the fixity of abstractions cap-

40. The initiations of Indra and Cúchulainn are accompanied by the release or capture of
birds. Further investigation of this detail in Indo-European tales may be desirable.

41. The term "infante," in the fictional narratives, may be applied to a royal prince, as with
Mainet, but more often it seems to imply that the youths either will not survive or will slip into
literary limbo (compare "Billy the Kid," "the Sundance Kid," in the lore of the Old West, who
by definition could not live into middle age).

tures, at best, only part of the story and cannot replace it as a reflection of human experience. The epic texts make exemplary use of narrative as a tool for the interpretation of existence.

Mainet

Once the basic pattern has been established and reconfirmed by its complete, if inverted, recapitulation in the *Poema del Cid*, other tales of epic cast can be seen to belong to the tradition or to draw upon it for important motifs. The best example of this phenomenon is the *Mainet*, an *enfances* or *mocedades* of Charlemagne, set in Toledo—one among many varied texts on this hero's purported youthful deeds, which appear in many parts of Europe (Jacques Horrent 1987, 61–63; Sharrer 1992). The Spanish *Mainet* is found in two versions, in the *PCG* (2:340–43) and in the *Gran conquista de Ultramar* (Cooper 1979, 1:561–92).[42] The former is a brief, sober account, similar in tone to other texts of epic origin as reproduced in the *PCG*, although its probable French provenance is supported by the form it gives to personal names. The second version has traits of French romance, being more detailed, with some explanation of personal motives and rationalization of events. Its geography is imaginary, but curiously, it Arabizes most names, so that for instance the heroine, Galiana in *PCG*, is Halia, her father Galafre is Haxem, her pretender Bramant is Abrahin. It forgets some components of the primitive pattern as identified in this study, to be noted below, but clarifies some motivations, for instance when it makes explicit that the hero comes to Toledo as a mercenary because he has been rendered destitute at home. It places his age at fourteen or perhaps fifteen at the time of this adventure, on which he is accompanied by his foster father and his tutor, whereas in the *PCG* his behavior makes him seem a bit older. The *Conquista* also rationalizes his victory over his gigantic adversary as a less than fully heroic act; he cuts off the opponent's hand when it is raised to strike another Christian knight. Further, it specifies that the name Mainet

---

42. A fragmentary French *Mainet* begins much as the Spanish versions do, takes place in Toledo, and has the same principal names: Mainet, Galienne, Galafre, Braimant. It lacks, however, the initiatory implications, and soon turns into a story of palace intrigue. In French literature Galienne is one of many personifications of the "païenne amoureuse et compatissante" identified by Bédier and by Knudson (1968–69, 449), who chooses to call her the "princesse sarrasine" and provides bibliography.

([Carles] Maines with a diminutive ending) is intended to conceal his identity as future emperor of the Franks, and at the same time to prefigure his greatness. The legend of his *enfances* in Spain is also recalled in the Spanish epic *Roncesvalles* fragment, lines 54–66 (Menéndez Pidal 1965, 110).

The chronicle version, which invites particular comparison with the *Mocedades de Rodrigo*, is as follows: At odds with his father King Pepin, Mainet crosses into Moorish Spain to offer his services as warrior to the lord of Toledo. Another motive for his arrival is the attraction by reputation of the lord's daughter Galiana. As he and his knights approach the city, she and her ladies come out to meet them. "E luego que Galiana llego a ellos, omillaronsele todos menos Mainet. Ella quando aquello uio, nol connociendo, touosse por desdennada" [And as soon as Galiana arrived where they were, all knelt before her except Mainet. And when she saw that, not knowing who he was, she considered herself scorned]. In response to her inquiry, his tutor responds that the youth is of high lineage and bows to no woman except the Holy Virgin. He does not reveal his name.

After some weeks the city is attacked by Bramant, a powerful Moor and unwanted suitor of Galiana. The Moors of Toledo and their Frankish allies go to meet the attackers, but Mainet remains in his quarters sleeping (in the *Gran conquista*, his guardians have locked him in to keep him from plunging into battle and risking his life in his youthful ardor). The battle seesaws for most of the day. Mainet wakes to find himself alone. Thinking he has been betrayed and abandoned, he begins a loud lament in the course of which he declares his identity. From a nearby parapet, Galiana hears him. "Con grand sabor que ouo de fazerle algun plazer por quel amansasse et se pagasse della . . . fuesse poral palacio o ell estaua. Maynet quando la uio, non se quiso leuantar contra ella nin recebirla."[43] (The choice of the word *amansasse*, "to tame, as a horse," suggests an initiatory ferocity that is not otherwise clearly present.) Very displeased, she rebukes him with Oriental indirection: "Don Maynet, si yo sopiesse aquella tierra o dan soldada por dormir, pero que mugier so, yrme ya alla morar; ca semeiame que uos non auedes a coraçon de acorrer uuestra companna que esta maltrecha en el ual Somorian o lidian con Bramant. E digouos que si mio padre sopier que non fuestes y, que uos non dara buena soldada."[44] He begins, "If I had a horse

43. "With the eager desire that she had to give him some pleasure so that she might tame him and he might be pleased with her, she went to the palace where he was. Mainet, when he saw her, would not rise to meet her, or give her a greeting."
44. "Sir Mainet, if I knew that land where they pay soldiers to sleep, although I am a woman, I would go there to live; for it seems to me that you are not eager to help your com-

and arms . . . ." She offers them, including the sword Joyosa (a gift to
her from Bramant), on condition that he take her to France, see to her conversion, and marry her. He agrees readily though unwillingly: "Galiana,
bien ueo que e de fazer lo que queredes, pero sabelo Dios que a fuerça de
mi, e prometouos por ende . . . " [Galiana, I see clearly that I must do what
you wish, but God knows that it is against my will, and I promise you
therefore . . .]. Compare the words of Rodrigo: "Sennor, vos me despossastes mas a mj pessar que de grado. / Mas prometolo a Christus que
vos non besse la mano . . ." [Sir, you have betrothed me more to my sorrow
than to my desire, but I promise to Christ that I will not kiss your hand . . .]
(438–39). She brings weapons and personally helps him to arm himself,
"ayudol ella misma a armar."

On the way to the battle, he comes upon a fallen cousin and, weeping,
vows vengeance. This is the closest approximation in this story to the offense that triggers the *furia guerrera*. He thereupon cuts down "doze de los
meiores de Bramant, et muchos de los otros" [twelve of Bramant's best and
many of the others]. On hearing of this, Bramant emerges from his tent
(where he has been playing chess to show his disdain of the Toledans, according to the *Gran conquista*), and a mighty duel ensues. Bramant asks
the name of his opponent, who reveals it, "et dixol que nunqua iamas
tornarie a su tierra. E respondiol el inffant: 'Esso que tu dizes en las manos
de Dios yaze' " [And he told him he would never again return to his homeland. And the prince answered, "What you say rests in the hands of
God"].[45] Mainet receives a terrible blow, but then severs the arm of the
Moor, now called a giant, retrieves his fallen sword Durendart, and pursues him, wielding two swords and killing many as he goes, until he finally
overtakes and dispatches his quarry. He takes the Moor's head and ties it
to his horse's breastband, "ca la querie dar en donas a Galiana" [for he
wanted to present it as a gift to Galiana]. The battle is won, and Mainet has
two swords formerly belonging to Bramant, both known from the *Chanson
de Roland*, Durendart as Roland's weapon and Joyosa as his own.

Word arrives that Pepin is dead, and Mainet wishes to return and as-

---

pany, which is near defeat in the vale of Somorián where they are battling Bramant. And I tell
you that if my father learns that you were not there, he will not pay you well."

45. Compare the response of Rodrigo to threats of the champion from Navarra in the
Crónica de Castilla (see p. 40): "Don Martin Gonçales, sodes buen cauallero. Et non son estas
palabras para aqui, que este pleito por las manos la auemos de librar, que non por las palabras
vanas. Et todo el poder es en Dios, & de ende la onrra a quien el quisiere & touiere por bien,
& a quien entendiere que sera mas a su seruiçio" (Armistead 1955, 135).

sume the throne (in the *Gran conquista* he needs to save Burgundy and its duke from the abuses of his own two ill-born half-brothers). The king of Toledo intends to prevent the departure of the Christians. Mainet and his companions feign a hunting expedition to escape, and his foster father returns for Galiana, who bravely faces great dangers and hardships, surviving seven weeks in the wilderness, before reaching France, where she becomes Christian and queen.

As in the case of Rodrigo, the combined sexual and warlike confrontations are wholly successful, and the woman's singular initiative is indispensable to the launching of the youth's heroic trajectory. The power of the eyes is reduced to a haughty reception to her two advances—not recognizable in itself as the same detail, but similar in the way it is overcome by her effrontery—her effort to tame him, and her proposal of marriage, which is met by displeasure and at the same time by acceptance. Acceptance in turn immediately becomes total commitment—soon yielding a love-token in the form of Bramant's head. As *femme impudique*, in the Moorish context Galiana ranks high merely by being alone with a male outsider, and higher yet for her bold proposal of marriage, and the physical contact and possible seminudity involved in arming the knight—usually a task reserved for servants. The bath in which the hero is identified is plausibly replaced by an enclosure or private room. (All these compromising features are avoided in the *Gran conquista*, as is the face-to-face confrontation, replaced by a dialogue through a locked door.) The abusive treatment of the woman, reduced to rude disdain, is amalgamated with the confrontation. Mainet's arrogance is subdued not by a contest of eye-power, which might believably have been won by a veiled Mooress, but by words chosen to shame him (comparable in tone to those addressed by the Moorish princess Zenla to Gonzalo Gustioz, father of the seven infantes de Lara, who also compares herself to a man [both chronicles; Catalán 1980, 196, and 212–13]). Though the Oriental irony is a fine literary touch, the verbal rather than visual encounter may be a remnant of an earlier version situated on French soil, since there was no language in which the newly arrived foreigner and the Toledan princess could possibly have conversed. This problem is often ignored, of course, in medieval literature, but rarely is it so extreme.[46] The remaining key elements of the initiation are well represented in *Mainet*: the sleep before battle, the subsequent *furor belli*, and the prodigious killing. Also, as in each other case, the lone hero is indispensable for the achieve-

---

46. In the rationalized *Tristan* of Thomas, the author carefully informs the reader that Tristan studied languages and learned Irish.

ment of victory.

Mainet is in all probability of French origin (see Horrent 1987, 62), although its hints of Oriental mystique are worthy of a Spanish text and suggest fruitful contacts among minstrels from north and south. The two French accounts, *Tristan* and *Mainet*, when taken together, give evidence of an artistic imagination contrasting with that of the Spanish epic tradition. They develop an atmosphere of palace life, with conflicts among diverse individuals, in which the warlike tribal mentality moves to a secondary plane. Archetypal elements fade, as when the confrontation with the feminine is less clearly set against the *furor belli*. Given the ambiance of *Mainet*, the reader imagines a professional French minstrel exercising his inventive talents and repertoire, which would include stories offering magic boats, dragons, giants, and genteel courtesy to an audience expecting a diversion, whereas the earthier Spanish tales reflect folk concerns, and the quaint details—the hawk, the washerwomen, the sop in wine—seem to carry submerged symbolism.

A narrative trait that would seem to be basic to the initiation theme is obscured in both *Siete infantes* and in *Mainet*. In neither is it clear that the first killing recounted is the initiatory act, the first one ever committed by the youthful hero in an adult setting. (In the *Gran conquista* version of *Mainet*, earlier killings are in fact narrated, though one may doubt whether the victims are represented as adults, and Cúchulainn kills many boys before his formal initiation takes place.) This omission or suppression demands some attention, even though its importance cannot be evaluated. Since all the basic texts contain replications of the principal initiatory rite, the episodes in *Siete infantes* and *Mainet* might qualify as replications without losing their significance. Another interpretation would see the confrontation with the feminine, which is absent from many replications, as the distinctive mark of the chief rite. As another possibility, the chronicles may offer rationalized versions. Being sober historians, the compilers may have chosen to suppress the claim that a child could quickly cut down the best warriors available to the enemy (though Mudarra escaped their censorship). All these factors probably came into play to some degree.

Other Manifestations

Several quasi-epic tales that are told of historic personages, though they are not heroic, show influence from the initiatory pattern that becomes evident once *Mainet* is recognized as a member of the tradition. The most complete of these is the story known as the *Condesa traidora*, concerning Garci Fernández, the second count of Castile, and his two murderous French wives, particularly the second one.[47] In this case, before summarizing the story, it may be opportune to present an outline that fits both it and *Mainet*.

The chief male character, traveling because his status as ruler is threatened at home—in Castile or in France—crosses the Pyrenees, concealing his identity, and reaches a domain where a young woman awaits his arrival with the hope or expectation of being delivered from an intolerable situation involving her family or an unwanted suitor. After some evasive delay, he reveals his high rank and identity to her in a private meeting. His purpose is a vengeance killing, which he accomplishes with her assistance. In recompense, he either offers or agrees to marry her. Subsequent to the killing, he and his lady must quickly and secretly escape to the his own land, where they can now be acclaimed as rulers.

Later in the *Condesa traidora*, in an apparent reversal of the theme represented by Galiana's presentation of a horse and arms to Mainet, the second wife, entrusted with the care of the count's warhorse, feeds it bran instead of barley, so that it looks healthy but is weakened. The result is correspondingly reversed: instead of carrying the rider to victory, the horse falls during the battle, and the count is fatally wounded.

The *Condesa traidora* is not really a version of the initiation. The most important components of that tradition are absent. What remain are several motifs that are familiar from the tradition and group themselves in comparable fashion: the border crossing, the killing associated with sleep, and the marriage—consummated, no doubt improperly, before the killing—as compensation for a favor, with eventual dire results.

The count takes a French wife whom he meets as she passes through Burgos on her way to Santiago. Later, after six years of marriage, at a time when he is incapacitated by illness, she escapes to France with a noble

---

47. In tracing later modifications to this story found in fifteenth-century versions, Vaquero (1990, 45, 108–15) shows apparent influence of orally transmitted versions, probably lost ballads.

Frenchman who has sought her out while also on a pilgrimage. When the count recovers, he travels to their land disguised as a poor pilgrim, intent on the revenge necessary to the restoration of his honor. He arrives at the French gentleman's palace to find that the latter's beautiful daughter by a previous marriage, Doña Sancha, has been mistreated by her stepmother and has conceived an intense hatred of the older couple. She has been waiting (for a time that seems much longer than the illness of Garci Fernández) for deliverance from their abuse by just such a noble visitor as the count. She manages to speak to him and learn his identity. She offers him an opportunity to avenge his dishonor and to name his reward to her; he offers marriage, which they consummate that same evening. She keeps his presence secret and, on the third night, installs him under the bed where her elders are to sleep, with a rope tied to his foot, remaining present by the bedside herself on the pretext of fondness for her father. When the father and stepmother are asleep, she pulls the rope as a signal, and the count emerges to decapitate the sleepers and gather up their heads. With these trophies he and Doña Sancha flee to Castile. The detail of the rope has the appearance of a remnant from an older story in which such a device would have had a useful function. Here it serves as a metanarrative signal reminding the hearer that the young woman is in charge of the whole proceeding.

The double murder and the taking of heads seem particularly archaic, especially since Garci Fernández is an otherwise bland figure. The pride taken by the pair in their exploit also has the quality of an ancient fiction. They publicize the complete story in Burgos, as the count proclaims: "agora so yo pora seer uuestro sennor que so uengado, ca non mientra estaua desonrrado" [I am suitable to be your lord now that I am avenged, for I was not while I was dishonored] (*PCG* 2:428b33–35). The Castilians receive Doña Sancha as their ruling lady, "et plogoles mucho con la uenida del conde et de quan bien se sopiera uengar" [and were very pleased with the count's coming and how well he had managed to avenge himself]. The reader must wonder if irony is intended, since the count has acted under the domination of a woman. Virtuous during the first years, Doña Sancha then begins to reveal an evil nature, although "quanto en maldat de so cuerpo" [as for wickedness relating to her body], she maintains secrecy.

The historical Garci Fernández ruled Castile at a time of cruel Moorish incursions. Though the *PCG* gives him much credit for developing his region and keeping peace with his Leonese king, he lost important territories to the Moors and led some poorly conceived military operations. His son Sancho, later represented as a wise and successful ruler, rose up in opposition to him. The Moors took advantage of the division, and Garci Fernández led a diminished force into battle against them, at which time he was fatally wounded. Contributing to his failure and death, according to the legend, was Doña Sancha's quasi-poisoning of his horse. Later, according to the legend, she made a more forthright attempt at poisoning that was less successful. Finding her son's presence an obstacle to her desire to marry a Moor, she poisons his wine, but he is forewarned and vows to behead her unless she drinks the lethal draught. So she joins Llambra, a cousin of the same count and presumably her contemporary at the court of Burgos— though the two are never mentioned together—as another vicious destroyer of men who eventually comes to a cruel end through the agency of a youth of the succeeding generation.

The tale of Garci Fernández leads us to consider the legend of his father Fernán González, one of the best known Spanish narrative traditions, preserved in a clerical poem (*Poema de Fernán González* = *PFG*; Catalán 1980, 34–180) and several chronicle versions (including *PCG*, chaps. 684–720), an introductory segment of *Mocedades* (to line 61), and several ballads. The *PFG* includes a number of primitive elements found in the *Condesa traidora*, but they have been scattered through the tale, with their order changed and their sense diminished if not lost. They appear as narrative clichés used to enliven a text devoted mainly to political conflicts, battles, and sermon-like passages. The way these non-Christian details are used shows an awareness of their continuing interest to an audience, along with authorial indifference to the symbolic or traditional meaning they once had.

In the *PFG*, the protagonist is kidnaped as a baby and raised in the wilderness. While still quite young, he realizes he has a mission to rescue the Castilians from threats of Moorish conquest and resolves to lead them. Instead of any hint of an initiation, he offers up prayers. Upon reaching the Castilian community, he is received as a conquering hero (Catalán 1980, 58, stanzas 183–85). Like Tristan and the infante Gonzalo, he is hated by a queen. She sends a letter to the king of Navarra (as Ruy Velázquez sent one to Almanzor) proposing his ambush (recalling the infante Gonzalo and his brothers) and imprisonment (like the elder Gonzalo). In an act that brings to mind Zenla, the sister of Almanzor, the ruler's sister, Doña Sancha, helps to end his imprisonment, in this case by carrying him, still in chains, on an all-night trek to freedom. Like Galiana in *Mainet*, she offers her aid in exchange for a promise of marriage (as noted by Horrent 1987, 63). After the escaping pair take refuge in a wood, the episode most reminiscent of the older legends takes place. They are discovered by an evil archpriest who threatens to divulge their whereabouts unless the princess yields to his sexual demands. She pretends to accede, invites the archpriest to remove his breeches, and then holds him while the count, still in chains, kills him with his own sword. Motifs familiar from the other tales include the (attempted) violence toward the woman, the undressing, and the killing. Though close resemblances to the traditional forms are absent, the inclusion of an evil cleric may indicate the persistence of a tradition, since the author is usually careful to keep his version orthodox, proper, and favorable to the clergy.

Like Garci Fernández, the count now crosses the border into Castile, where he is acclaimed as ruler, and the wedding to the enterprising lady is joyfully celebrated. At a later point the tradition of narrative replications is honored when the count is again imprisoned by a hostile ruler, this time in León. Doña Sancha travels to the royal court disguised as a pilgrim (recalling Garci Fernández). In an audience with the king, she appeals to his concern for the continuation of royal and noble lines and requests the removal of the prisoner's chains, "diziendol que el cavallo travado nunqua bien podie fazer fijos" [telling him that a hobbled horse could never properly make children] (*PCG*; Catalán 1980, 155). She spends the night with her husband—recalling the role of Zenla—and next morning trades clothes with him, making possible his escape. The king, piqued but attentive to her eloquence and mindful of her royal birth, allows her to depart in peace.

Obviously, given the great range and variety of events to be found in the vast body of folk literature, these similarities to the heroic tradition need to be recognized as more than coincidental. But it is equally clear that the traditional details of *PFG*, which are some of its most colorful touches, have lost any direct or deliberate connection with an initiation legend. The passivity of Fernán González is surprising in a figure second only to the Cid as a great Castilian hero, and very similar to that of his son Garci Fernández. Each is dominated by his wife or wife-to-be, particularly at the moment when he commits murder. So a killing is linked to the feminine, as is the case in the traditional initiation—but in a very different way, since these women plan the act, severely compromising its heroic quality. As in the tradition, they are indispensable participants; but there the resemblance ends.

Both of these women's roles are strongly marked for gender; little or nothing they do could plausibly be done by a man. Since the parts they take have points of similarity, but one of them turns out to be highly virtuous and supportive of her husband, and the other perverse and destructive, they add complexity to the already multidimensional image of woman. Though she is absolutely essential to the man's functioning, her place remains irrevocably subordinate. In several of the tales her status is reduced to that of an article of exchange, offered in marriage as a reward to a man. Her proper role is to support the man in his worthy causes. For doing so she is honored. If, however, she imposes her will on the man, there is danger that the causes are unworthy.

These lessons are reinforced in yet another legend related to the initiation tradition, a chroniclers' adaptation of the supposed epic *Cantar de la mora Zaida*. Whether or not its source was really an epic poem, as Menéndez Pidal and Jacques Horrent have maintained (Horrent 1987, 128–30), it is largely fictional, with only a partial historic base, and in view of the material assembled in this study, its author appears to have woven a number of heroic motifs into its fabric. As told in the *PCG* (2:553–55), the legend affords a clue to why the courtship and purported marriage (historically a concubinage) of the Moorish princess Zaida to Alfonso VI produces unhappy consequences.[48]

The segment begins with high praise of Abenabeth, the Moorish king of Seville, and his daughter Zaida, as well as an encomium of King Alfonso. So impressive was the king's fame that "non de uista, ca numqual uiera . . . se enamoro del donna Çayda, [and here is the clue] tanto que fue ademas" [not by sight, for she had never seen him, . . . Doña Zaida fell in love with him, so much that it was excessive]. Excess continues to characterize her initiative, as well as willfulness, "commo las mugeres son sotiles et sabidoras pora lo que mucho an a talent" [as women are subtle and cunning as to what they have a great desire for], recalling the persistence of Galiana. Zaida sends messages to Alfonso offering him cities and castles in New Castile if he will marry her and agree to a meeting between them. The king is happy to make the marriage and becomes a friend and ally of Abenabeth. Together (in this fiction) they decide to invite the Almorávides from Morocco to act as protectors of their mutual interests. The Almorávides soon get out of control, overrun much of Spain, and kill Abenabeth.

Years later, when Alfonso's son by Zaida has reached adolescence, the king sends the youth, to whom he is strongly attached, to take part in a battle against the Almorávides at Uclés, one of the towns Zaida has given to him. The son is killed along with his protector in a distressing scene, and

---

48. Like Almanzor's sister in *Siete infantes* and Galiana in *Mainet*, Zaida represents the topos of the "princesse sarrasine"; see note 42.

the king grieves deeply, soon afterward beginning a mighty campaign of retribution against Córdoba. The chronicle records no further words of judgment, but clearly seems to associate Zaida's fateful impulses with the tragic events. It has consistently distorted the facts in such a way as to imply that association, following its chief Latin sources, the chronicles of Toledano and Tudense. The Alphonsine chroniclers were evidently aware that this was a popular legend, and they followed it by another, more accurate version of the historical events of those years, taken largely from the Arabic source Ben Alcama (*PCG* 2:557b42–558a30).

Though caution is in order, it is possible to read in all these tales the message that women who are too skilled at getting "lo que mucho an a talent," too self-centered rather than supportive of male interests (which are understood to include family interests), bring misfortune even if they do not will it. Women as well as men must understand that women's actions cannot be inconsequential. This sense is a constant from the Irish tale forward. The account originally reflected an initiation rite in which women took a necessary part. Now it has lost its initiatory character but has maintained the confrontation with the feminine. From the beginning, the nature of this confrontation, benign or hostile, has determined whether the hero's future endeavors will succeed or fail. A hostile encounter always implies overstepping the bounds of feminine propriety. In this instance the overstepping alone seems to be sufficient to produce misfortune. King Alfonso is not blamed for taking a Moorish wife; the story, by its selection of adverse events, turns the focus to Zaida.

La Chanson de Roland

Of the narratives to be considered in this study, *Roland* is the furthest removed from the earlier patterns, particularly in that it eliminates the woman. Nevertheless, its correspondences with *Siete infantes* form a remarkably complete tale. A number of the similarities have been pointed out over the years, beginning in very fragmentary fashion by German scholars early in this century; later by Alexander Krappe (1924); and most comprehensively by Angelo Monteverdi (1945, 360–62). For him the parallels were evidence that a Spanish author had adapted the *Roland*, working strictly from one written text to create another, *Siete infantes*. A good many more significant resemblances will be pointed out here than were shown by

Monteverdi, perhaps twice as many. When brought together to make a story, they yield a coherent and complete tragic narrative.

In successive studies, Menéndez Pidal makes an increasingly strong case for a historical starting-point for the Spanish epic—namely the attack by Count Garci Fernández against the Moors at Deza in 974—and in addition for an "aire de familia" (1992, 485), relating it to the story of the Harlungen, two brothers executed by their uncle King Jörmunrek, according to the late Norse epic compilation, the *Thidrekssaga*. In a late statement on the matter, he passes over a French derivative of the Harlungen narrative, *Les quatre fils Aimon*, part of the epic cycle of Renaud de Montauban, whose resemblances to *Siete infantes* are indeed vague and whose story is unheroic, but which he had previously admitted as the only French poem with a connection to this Spanish text. As for the parallels drawn by Monteverdi with *Roland*, he dismisses them as "imprecisas y vagas semejanzas" (1992, 450) in a discussion of the relative chronology of the two epics. Possibly in a less sensitive context, in which his historicist theory were not threatened, he would again have admitted an "aire de familia."

While *Roland* and *Siete infantes* follow similar patterns, their differences are also profound. These begin with the structuring of language and of motivations, two aspects whose interrelation will become evident. In *Siete infantes* the characters are moved by unseen, impersonal forces, reacting directly, without reflection, to each new circumstance that arises. As E. G. Quin says of Irish saga, "every step is made to seem fore-ordained" (1968, 57). Of the European epic texts and romances that this reader can bring to mind, only the *Táin* has this mythic quality to such a marked degree. In *Roland*, by contrast, actions are the products of individual wills. Accordingly they are justified in debate and built on stated reasons, though the reasoning is primitive and often faulty. The motives of each individual, when at variance with one another, frequently provoke conflicts. Their expression takes the form of succinct explanations or arguments as to the best course of action, leading either to group decisions, as when Charles agrees to deal with Marsile, or else to individual determinations, as in the reiterated discussion between Oliver and Roland about whether to sound the Olifant. In this contrast between modes of expression, *Siete infantes* is more primitive and *Roland* prefigures the development of later prose forms.

In content, too, the French poem is further evolved, having dispensed with the initial killing and other trappings of the initiation, including any confrontation with the feminine—though it has perhaps retained the *furor belli*. Before considering the differences more fully, it will be useful to sketch the resemblances. A single story outline is applicable to both texts. First, the characters: The hero, the youngest infante Gonzalo or Roland, is irascible and impetuous, which is to say that he represents a primitive idea of bravery, of the unsocialized hero who fights alone and who may be a danger to his community as well as its protector. His behavior is ruled by an unbending military code, which he may apply too strictly, too unthinkingly, for his own good or that of his allies. A deep rancor or rivalry exists between the hero and his maternal uncle or stepfather. This bitterness seems to antedate the beginning of the story, although in *Siete infantes* it is amply motivated by Llambra's aggressive excesses. While no woman appears in the pertinent part of *Roland*, the feminine link between hero and villain—Gisle, Charles's sister and Roland's mother, now married to Ganelon—would afford potentially powerful motivation for friction. In both stories the older man is admired as brave and forceful. He is politically powerful and close to the ruler (Garci Fernández or Charlemagne; the resemblance of Hagen in the *Nibelungenlied* to the two villains, Ruy Velázquez and Ganelon, has been noted).

The reason for the hatred between Roland and Ganelon, the basic force propelling the poem's action, merits some further consideration. Gisle appears with some frequency in the later French epics, but as a passive figure providing no clues. In medieval society, the bond between a youth and his maternal uncle was particularly strong, often outweighing the father-son relationship; Charles's favoritism toward his nephew might be seen as normal, and just as normally resented by the stepfather. A largely covert traditional belief that Roland was Charlemagne's own son by his sister is forcefully advanced as the motive for favoritism by Rita Lejeune (1961), who sees novelistic psychological interaction in the scene. In both *Roland* and *Siete infantes* the main characters form a close-knit family group with a passive mother at its hub, within which the destructive impulses develop. An additional probable source of hostility, to be taken up shortly, is related to the gift economy still dominant at the time of these texts, very evident too in the *Poema del Cid*, and contrasting with the exchange economy which was soon to gain prominence: the young man is extremely generous, a quality essential to the hero, whereas the older one is avaricious.

The story in general: The older relative works to control the destiny of the younger one. He betrays the hero, at the same time betraying his ruler, with dire consequences for the nation. His actions bring about the death of the hero and eventually lead to his own judgment and horrible execution.

The story in its particulars:

The offense: Gonzalo strikes his uncle, who wounds him in return; Roland proposes Ganelon for a dangerous mission, provoking a fit of fury and threats of lifelong hatred and retribution. In both cases the ruler puts a temporary end to their dispute, but as events unfold he appears weak, unable to guide events or to stop their deadly course. At this very moment, when the malevolence of the older man is most evident, the most complete trust is placed in him.

The traitor crosses into the territory of a Moorish potentate of fabulous wealth, who has an immense army. He declares to the Moor that the youth, Gonzalo with his six brothers or Roland with the twelve peers, presents a grave danger to him and the only obstacle to his conquest of all Castile (in *Siete infantes*), or all Spain (in *Roland*). He promises to expose the youth with his companions and a small force to attack by a Moorish army, in Moorish territory near the border of their homeland.

As the battle approaches, the youth receives dire warnings from his tutor Nuño Salido or from his companion Oliver, but ignores them. During the conflict Roland refuses to call for help; the seven infantes request help from their uncle but it is refused. Both Roland and Gonzalo recognize the betrayal too late. The Christians slaughter huge numbers of Moors but are reduced to the immediate band of brothers or comrades, then killed off one by one. Nuño Salido and Oliver, whose warnings might have averted the debacle if heeded, die heroically. The hero is the last to die.

The consequences of the battle in Castile and in France are devastating. Castile is held in the grip of Ruy Velázquez, who seizes the count's fortresses, and a blight falls over the land. The French lose huge numbers, including their best heroes. The traitor is finally brought to judgment, and his body dismembered, spread-eagled before an armed mob, or drawn and quartered.

In *Siete infantes* as in *Roland*, the historical ingredient is limited to a few names of people whose existence is verifiable; events recounted are products of fancy, although scholarly attempts have been made to find historical parallels with the climactic battle. The geography of *Roland* is basically imaginary. The essentials of the familiar story may be reviewed as follows:

As it opens, the emperor Charlemagne has conquered all of Spain except for Zaragoza, which is held by King Marsile. To end the Christian threat, the Moorish ruler sends a messenger to Charles offering him great wealth, and pledges to travel to his capital at Aix-la-Chapelle and convert to Christianity with all his forces, if the French will retire across the Pyrenees. He of course has no intention of keeping his promise.

On receipt of this message, Charles holds a council of war. Opinion is divided within his group; among those opposed to trusting the Saracens is Roland, while those in favor include Ganelon. The latter opinion prevails despite Charles's misgivings. The next task is to appoint an emissary to deal with the Moors. Roland and several others offer to go but are brusquely rejected by Charles. Roland nominates Ganelon, his "parrastre," with the general approval of those assembled. Ganelon erupts in a furious attack in which he pledges enmity to the death against his stepson and all his comrades. It is not clear why his wrath is directed only at them and not at the emperor, who makes the appointment. In the face of his threats Roland bursts into laughter, upon which Ganelon nearly loses his mind with rage. The fateful atmosphere is accentuated when, on receiving the glove symbolizing his appointment, he drops it. He departs in the company of the Moorish messenger Blancandrin.

On the way to Zaragoza, Ganelon inflames Blancandrin against Roland, blaming him for the war and claiming that he is the chief danger to the Moors and the main obstacle to their conquest of all Spain. In Zaragoza he continues to lie regarding both Roland and Charlemagne and to misrepresent his designated mission. After a series of dramatic and courageous confrontations, he promises to bring about the departure of the French from Spain, and to arrange for Roland with a small force to act as rearguard, exposed to attack and annihilation at the hands of a great Moorish army.

Ganelon receives costly presents and returns to the French camp to report falsely that Marsile has agreed to Charles's terms. He nominates Roland as captain of the rearguard, sending him with 20,000 others (against 400,000 Saracens), including the flower of France's knighthood, to what will be certain death. Charles weeps, but as usual cannot go against the recommendation. By this time he is convinced of Ganelon's treachery.

As the rearguard, widely separated from the main body of the army, moves toward France, Oliver sights the approach of a huge Moorish host. He urges Roland to sound his horn, the Olifant, to summon help. A debate ensues in which Oliver speaks sensibly but Roland, supremely proud and confident, refuses to open himself to criticism and shame by acknowledging any need for support. The battle is recounted at painful length. When it is obviously too late, Roland sounds his horn. Charles returns to find only corpses. He pursues and wipes out the Moorish army. A replication follows in which an even greater Saracen host arrives from Cairo and is destroyed.

Considering again the two epics, we find extreme differences in the causes and motivations for the clashes between the hero and his elder relative. Gonzalo is infuriated by remarks made by both Doña Llambra and Alvar Sánchez, whom he murders—remarks regarding the acceptability, based on their warlike prowess, of men to women. Both the murder and the sexual contention contribute to the conflict between nephew and uncle. No words are spoken except for ritual challenges. In the *Chanson*, words are the substance of the conflict; actions are limited and symbolic. The terrible fury seizes the treacherous elder relative, leading not to a killing in the initiatory vein but to a devious manipulative plan of destruction—though motives are primitive and of epic dimensions. (It is possible to see a partial transfer of the fury to Ruy Velázquez, making a clearer parallel between the confrontations found in the two versions.)

The events in the Spanish tale spring straightforwardly from the display of female perversity. While there is no effort to account for the origins of the lady's impulses, the resulting violence requires no further explanation. In the *Chanson*, motives are set forth with some care by the author. But it must be said the decisions made—here as later—are extraordinarily bad, that the whole plot hinges on foolish choices, first, to trust the obviously false Saracens, then to send the worst possible emissary to them alone, with no one to check on what he does (an omission that many in the audience would not fail to note), and later to leave Roland in command of the rearguard, isolated from the other force, and charged with making responsible decisions when Oliver has earlier pointed out his dangerous impetuousness (255–57). While the grandiose tone of the poem may bring this off artistically, the fact remains that to accept the story, the hearer or reader must accept Charles's impotence in the face of the opinion prevailing among his vassals, which in turn is naive and unrealistic. The epic power lies in the events, not in their contrived underpinnings.

A possible explanation for the poor match between the action and its causes would be that the poet's audience was quite familiar with the outlines of a primitive inherited story, satisfied to hear it retold in an exclusively masculine setting, and pleased to hear an author or presenter elaborate on the quarrels that might have led to the tragic unfolding of events. Motivations are thus seen to be divorced from real military experience, just as are the geography, the French names and Occidental mentality attributed to Moors, the numbers, the alternation of horrendous blows and prodigious horn blasts with fainting and weeping during the battle, and so on. On this view the *Roland* is a frankly artificial literary creation, an adaptation of a traditional story line that employs a preexisting paratactic and formulaic style and plays with these inherited elements to please and move an audience no longer imbued with the primitive heroic spirit. It is escape literature that cleverly conserves fundamental lore while doing a vast variation on it. Like the initiation narratives seen earlier, it creates its message by modifying earlier tales. However, it steps out of the world of real values more radically and more deliberately than they, to inaugurate a new genre whose authors will increasingly cultivate variations for their own sake.

Roland's derisive laughter prompts a comment on the only two incidences of laughter in the *Siete infantes*, which are used metatextually as a form of punctuation, as signals of displays of perversity or treachery that will move the plot into new phases. Doña Llambra's unseemly praise of her cousin provokes laughter in the six brothers, and apparently in their mother as well, but it triggers Gonzalo's fury and leads to the killing of the cousin, together with the violence that follows. The second instance is similar: when Llambra's servant strikes Gonzalo with the blood-filled cucumber, the brothers laugh, perhaps in startled confusion, but he is infuriated by the act and even by their reaction to it. They all watch the servant run to Llambra for protection, to ascertain that she is in fact the author of the insult, then brutally murder the man and sully her clothes. As before, the impropriety has produced both laughter and death-dealing fury. Similarly, in the Chanson, Roland's laughter provokes in Ganelon a deadly reaction identifiable with the *furor belli*, though, as always in the poem, it is superficially rationalized. Ganelon forthwith begins to plot Roland's death. The fury functions differently in the two stories, seizing the hero in one and the traitor in the other, in a type of inversion by now familiar in the texts of the initiation tradition.

As a plausible background for the "haine obscure, ancienne" (Bédier 1926–29, 3:413) that underlies the plot of Roland, I suggest the gift economy prevalent at the time the poem was composed. This economic system was the object of extended study by Marcel Mauss, and was analyzed again with great sweep and subtlety by Benveniste (1971, 274–79). It is fundamental in the *Poema del Cid* (Duggan 1989, 16–42; Montgomery 1994a), where the hero gains good will and prestige through adroitly managed magnanimity, and the villains are covetous. Ganelon's single explicit charge against the hero, when near the poem's end he defends himself before the tribunal, is expressed in a defective and ambiguous line, "Rollant me forfist en or e en aveir" (3758; Bédier: "Roland m'avait fait tort dans mon or, dans mes biens"), defective in that it has eleven syllables instead of the normal ten, and ambiguous because *forfaire* had a broad range of meanings, "to offend," "be guilty," etc. How does one offend (or do wrong to, or be excessive against) another in gold and wealth? Ganelon supplies a convincing answer in his other complaint against Roland, made to the Moorish emissary Blancandrin: all the French will support Roland, says Ganelon, because "Or e argent lur met tant en present, / Muls e destrers e palies e guarnemenz" (398–99; Bédier: "Il leur donne à profusion or et argent, mulets e destriers, draps de soie, armures"). Like the Cid, Roland is successful within the gift economy, a widespread system in tribal societies that, as opposed to the exchange economy that began to dominate in France toward the end of the twelfth century (Duby 1974, 257), involves the judicious bestowing of lavish gifts with the expectation of receiving favors later on. This system of "générosités nécessaires" (Duby 1974, 56) allows for a veneer of gentility, but in fact the acceptance of gifts, which may be difficult to refuse, imposes serious, even life-threatening obligations upon the receiver.

Ganelon complains of Roland's openhandedness and the resulting fidelity to him evinced by the French. With regard to Ganelon himself, the poem implies a grasping nature, capable of betrayal for a price (515–19, 844–47; see also Brault 1978, 1:133–35), and even Roland, after firmly resisting such a thought, finally accepts it: "Que Guenelun nos ad tuz espiez, / Pris en ad or e aveir e deners" (1147–48; Bédier: "Ganelon nous a tous trahis. Il en a pris pour son salaire de l'or, des richesses, des deniers"). Gonzalo's generosity is celebrated in his father's eulogy over his severed head, "Muy granado en partir vuestro aver" [Very great in sharing out your wealth], with particular liberality toward needy "dueñas e donzellas" [ladies and damsels]: "davades las vuestras donas quando veyades que era mester, muy de voluntad" [you gave your gifts when you saw that it was necessary, very gladly] (*Crónica de 1344*; Catalán 1980, 210–11), "a los vuestros franquear . . . a las unas proveiades vos e a las otras davades" [giving freely to your own . . . some (women) you provided for and to others you gave] (ibid.: *Interpolación de la Tercera crónica general*); recalled also in the epic ballad, "Pártese el moro Alicante," which speaks of Gonzalo as "repartidor de su haber" [sharer of his wealth] (Menéndez Pidal 1986, 116). Ruy Velázquez, in contrast, uses a mean-spirited request for money, from his nation's enemy, as a pretext for sending Gonzalo Gustioz, the seven infantes' father, to his death in Córdoba: "Cuñado, vos sabedes bien que me costaron mucho mis bodas, et el conde Garçi Ferrandez non me ayudo y tan bien commo yo cuede e el deviera; et Almançor prometiome que me darie muy buen ayuda por ellas, et vos sabedes que assi es" (*PCG*; Catalán 1980, 186).[49] Gonzalo Gustioz is supposed to carry both a verbal and a written request, but upon his arrival in Córdoba neither he nor Almanzor expresses any awareness of the alleged promise. In this text the contrast between the generous and the ungenerous personage does not motivate their conflict, but it undoubtedly serves to mark the good and the bad character. The *Chanson*, having suppressed the feminine element that is a strong presence in all the other tales, would have the economic motive to fall back on under the conditions of the gift economy.

The difference in the language of motivations in the two texts is well exemplified in the wording of the respective offenses. After Gonzalo has bested Alvar Sánchez in the target exercise, the latter "començo de dezir sus alabanças [*boasting*] tan grandes," moving Gonzalo to observe, "Tan bien alançades, et tanto se pagan de uos las duenas, que bien me semeja que non fablan tanto dotro cauallero commo de uos" [You throw the lance so well, and the ladies are so taken with you, that it really seems to me that they talk about no other knight as much as you], to which the other responds, "Si las dueñas de mi fablan, derecho fazen en ello, ca entienden que ualo mas que todos los otros" [If the ladies talk about me, they are right to do so, because they realize that I am better than all the others] (*PCG*; Catalán 1980, 182); ". . . todos los otros que y sodes" [(variant) "all you others who are here"] (ibid. 196 [first series of pages]: *Crónica de 1344*). At this, Gonzalo rushes forward and crushes the bones of his opponent's face with a death-dealing blow of his fist. In his resulting attack on Gonzalo, Ruy Velázquez says nothing to him. When Gonzalo utters a remonstrance and a threat after being struck, Ruy silently strikes again before the fight is stopped by others.

When Roland proposes Ganelon for the dangerous mission to Marsile in Zaragoza, the stepfather responds with fifteen lines of accusations and threats (286–91, 296–301, 305–7), with an interpolation by Roland that may be taken as typical of the language used, containing abstractions and generalizations, an appeal to others' opinion, and manipulation of his adversary as he offers to take the mission for which the emperor has already rejected him:

49. "Brother-in-law, you know well that my wedding cost me a great deal, and count Garci Fernández did not help me with it as well as I expected and he should have, and Almanzor promised me that he would give me very good help with it, and you know that it is so."

"Orgoill oi e folage.
Ço set hom ben n'ai cure de manace;
Mais saives hom, il deit faire message:
Si le reis voelt, prez sui por vus le face!"
(293–95)[50]

The pithy style is rich in concepts, maintaining a necessary distance from the situation it encapsulates and at the same time preserving the paratactic mode of epic tradition. Direct discourse can govern action, whereas in *Siete infantes* speeches, like other acts, are with rare exceptions determined by circumstances. In both texts the speeches are highly stylized and serve to create scenes of ritual intensity.

The account of Ganelon's behavior and appearance in this episode includes a number of oddly selected details. Recalling the traditional initiation, with the offensive remark (like the one to Cúchulainn) producing the fury, which in turn leads to a killing, along with the nudity, the potent gaze, and the radiant beauty after the purification, one must wonder whether the similarity of the details applied to Ganelon is purely fortuitous. Obviously no initiation takes place, but could the author be making an allusion to it in this passage? Ganelon receives the appointment to the mission,

E li quens Guenes en fut mult angoissables.
De sun col getet ses grandes pels de martre
E est remes en sun blialt de palie.
Vairs out les oilz e mult fier lu visage;
Gent out le cors e les costes out larges;
Tant par fut bels tuit si per l'en esguardent.
(281–85)[51]

---

50. "Ce sont propos d'orgeuil et de folie. On le sait bien, je n'ai cure d'une menace; mais pour un message il faut un homme de sens; si le roi veut, je suis prêt: je le ferai à votre place." The judgmental, generalizing tone of line 294 is also typical of the prose transformations of Spanish epic; e.g., after the victory at Alcocer, the Cid of the poem says, "¡Oíd, Minaya, sodes mio diestro braço!" [Hear, Minaya, you are my right arm!] (810). In the chronicle he intones, "Aluar Hannez, todo algo que uos omne fiziesse merecedes lo uos muy bien a guisa de muy buen cauallero" [Alvar Fáñez, anything that any man might do for you, you deserve it very well in the manner of a very good knight] (*PCG* 530a2–5). Not even brief formulaic praise is found in the *Siete infantes* text. The elaborations are of course earmarks of a literate mentality.

51. Bédier: "Et le comte Ganelon en fut pénétré d'angoisse. De son col il rejette ses grandes peaux de martre; il reste en son bliaut de soie. Il a les yeux vairs, le visage très fier; son corps est noble, sa poitrine large: il est si beau que tous ses pairs le contemplent." A variant of the

Distress turns to deadly fury as he throws off his cloak and displays his body, his eyes flash, his face is fierce, and his beauty is impressive to all. A strange spectacle, but less so if read as a reference to an inherited set of formulas, particularly the blush and the beauty of Cúchulainn and Tristan. Recall that Gonzalo also removes his outer garments, and his physical appearance creates a strong (this time negative) impression in Llambra that motivates the subsequent action of the story.

It is at this point in both narratives, where the elder knight is threatening the life of the younger one, that the youth's fate is placed in his hands—directly in *Siete infantes*, as Gonzalo and his brothers are entrusted to their uncle in a relationship like that of the *comitatus* or roving military band, an institution of northern Europe dating from Roman times.[52] The warriors' duty to their leader overrode family ties, as happens in this story. They handed over to him any spoils, in accordance with the gift economy, and in return received sustenance (as also in *Siete infantes*) and enjoyed a camaraderie based on ritual feasting.[53] The image of the hero as an invincible wild man flourished within this framework, and heroic literature perpetuated it, although more often than not in a negative vein, as in *Siete infantes*, where the dominant theme was the man's destruction, or in *Mocedades* where it was his taming. In the two tales at hand, the stepfather/uncle seems unable to kill the youth within the confines of his own society and so depends on the greater destructive forces of an alien world to achieve his purpose. His dependence on that world necessitates betrayal of his own nation and alienation from it before leading to his execution—though only after he nearly escapes punishment. Ganelon's claim that his vengeance has

---

second hemistich of line 283 suggests the "blush" of Cúchulainn and Tristan more precisely: "si fu ben colorez" (Segre 1989, 2:40); again, the line was rendered in the Bavarian *Ruolandes Liet* (c. 1172) [as cited in French translation]: "son visage était noble, son teint était ardent" (ibid.). The High German translation was made from an early, authentic source manuscript, probably better than the Oxford according to Segre (1989, 1:20). Again at l. 326, this version declares (1418) that Ganelon has the look of a she-wolf (Brault 1978, 1:398 n. 23). Compare the transformation of Cúchulainn when seized by the *furor belli* (p. 34).

52. To form a *comitatus*, or band of *Harii* or berserkers, a leader would bring together a group of young warriors who would pledge their loyalty to him and devote themselves to robbing and pillaging under his direction (Benveniste 1973, 64, with reference to Tacitus, *Germania*, 13–14, and also p. 92). Oman (1953, 13–14) explains that they were too unruly to be trusted as members of Justinian's legions.

53. On a feast not found in medieval *Siete infantes* texts, but recalled in local folklore, in which the seven brothers are visited by a deity called the Virgin, see Menéndez Pidal (1934, 196). The site near Soria of this legend is today known as the Sierra del Almuerzo, where a prehistoric artifact is identified as the table at which they sat.

been a private matter is only overcome by a judicial duel. So public justice and the good of the state prevail against the personal morality of the *comitatus* and the clan—as happens also in the trial and judicial duel of the *Poema del Cid* (Lacarra 1980, 96–101).

After the offense, which in *Siete infantes* is replicated against the malevolent "queen" in his absence, the traitor in each account begins secret dealings with the Moors. These transactions are very different in the two narratives. Ganelon sounds out Blancandrin on his way to Zaragoza and proceeds as noted above to set up the trap for Roland's forces. Ruy Velázquez sends a letter to Almanzor in Córdoba containing two requests. The second one is followed: to lay the trap for the seven infantes. The other, however, is not. Almanzor reveals only the first request to Gonzalo Gustioz, the seven infantes' father, and chooses not to comply with it: instead of putting the father to death he provides the instrument of his eventual revenge, by supplying him with feminine company while in prison. So this instance of nonfulfillment of a request becomes the basis for a new plot and a satisfying final outcome. Only at this point is adverse fate foiled; only Almanzor, in this story, makes an independent decision. No such device appears in *Roland*, where the tide of events appears inexorable (except that at the very end, when the traitor is about to go free, the youthful Thierry steps forward to propose a judicial duel with Ganelon's supporter Pinabel, and his victory is taken as a divine judgment against the accused). Both narratives achieve tragic grandeur as the sweep of events, combined with individual character flaws in Roland, and subjection to an impersonal fate in *Siete infantes*, carries the heroes to their doom.

In both tales the hero refuses to listen to warnings, Roland through pride and adherence to the military code, and Gonzalo through a simplistic sense of duty reminiscent of the *comitatus*, when after seeing signs too explicit to be called mere omens, his tutor Nuño Salido marks a line across the path into Moorish territory, declaring that once it is crossed there can be no return: "si esta rrisca pasades, yo non yre conbusco adelante mas, ca bien llana miente veo vuestra muerte, ca yo tales agueros veo que nos muestran que nos nunca mas aca tornaremos a nuestros lugares" [If you cross this line, I will go no further with you, for I very plainly see your death, because I see such omens that show me that we will never again return to our homes] (*Crónica de 1344*; Catalán 1980, 201).[54] He goes on to recommend

---

54. The apparent site of this incident, a hill behind Canicosa (Menéndez Pidal 1934, 195), is today a wood of singular eerie beauty, thanks in part to a reforestation project carried out in the years of the "democracia orgánica."

that they have their mother perform some diversionary magic if they insist on continuing. Gonzalo answers him harshly, giving no reason, but prohibiting him from speaking further. Here another comparison of the two texts will bring out contrasts in narrative technique. Gonzalo says only this: "Don Nuño Salido, dezides mucho mal en quanto fablades, e muerte buscades si oviese quien vos la dar, e digovos que si non fuesedes mio amo, como lo sodes, yo vos mataria por ello, e de aqui adelante vos digo e vos defiendo que non digades mas en esta razon, ca non nos tornaremos por vos, mas vos que sodes ya de hedat tornadvos para Salas si quisierdes" (ibid., 201).[55] This is one of the longest speeches in the Spanish text, loosely constructed as is normal. The words express no idea, they are strictly directive and designed to allow for no deviation from their message.

As a parallel to the response to Nuño's warning, for the purpose of demonstrating the contrast, a suitable selection is Roland's rejoinder to Oliver's first warning that a Moorish attack against the rearguard is at hand:

> "E! Deus la nus otreit!
> ben devuns ci estre pur nostre rei.
> Pur sun segnor deit hom susfrir destreits
> E endurer e granz chalz e granz freits,
> Sin deit hom perdre e del quir e del peil.
> Or guart chascuns que granz colps i empleit,
> Que malvaise cançun de nus chantet ne seit!
> Paien unt tort e chrestiens unt dreit.
> Malvaise essample n'en serat ja de mei."
>   (1008–16)[56]

The news of impending battle prompts no decision from Roland; like Gonzalo, he is ready for a fight, with no thought to tactics and no regard for the consequences. Instead, he launches into a pre-battle harangue, per-

---

55. "Don Nuño Salido, you speak much ill in all you say, and you invite murder if there were someone to commit it, and I tell you that if you were not my tutor, as you are, I would kill you for it, and from here on I <tell you and> prohibit you from speaking any more on this matter, for we will not return on your account, but you who are advanced in age, go back to Salas if you wish."

56. As rendered by Bédier: "Ah! que Dieu nous l'octroie! Nous devons tenir ici, pour notre roi. Pour son seigneur on doit souffrir toute détresse, et endurer les grands chauds et les grands froids, et perdre du cuir et du poil. Que chacun veille à y employer de grands coups, afin qu'on ne chante pas de nous une mauvaise chanson! Le tort est aux païens, aux chrétiens le droit. Jamais mauvais exemple ne viendra de moi."

haps directed to all within earshot, that borders on the theoretical in some
of its irrelevances, such as the duty to endure heat and cold. These timeless
reflections lead to a call for mighty blows, to considerations of future fame,
characteristically expressed in terms of double negatives, then the rather
abstract generalization on "pagans" and Christians, and the final statement
of personal resolve. The references to self, to duty, and to what people will
say, all reinforce the single baldly directive line (1113), "Or guart chascuns
que granz colps i empleit," but they subordinate action to motive; they sur-
round action with personal decisions. These lines are not what warriors
need to hear before battle. They are the words of an author directed to an
audience aware that it has opinions: a self-conscious author and audience.
Comparison of these two texts suggests a medieval recapitulation of a tran-
sition undergone in ancient Greece with the expansion of literacy:

> The Homeric Greeks experienced or represented speaking, thinking,
> feeling, and acting as originating outside the self, typically in the
> speech of the gods: they "had to" act rather than "decide[d] to" act.
> The Classical Greeks came to see speech and action as originating in
> the mind and progressively more under the control of the self. It is
> this new way of seeing speech and action which allowed for the in-
> creased control and responsibility that we speak of as the rise of self-
> consciousness. The proposed route to this self-consciousness is the
> experience of writing. (Olson 1994, 242)

The exclusively external motivations found by David Olson are in fact
more neatly represented in *Siete infantes* than in Homer, where a character
may distinguish between internal and external motivation. Thus Agamemnon, in excusing himself for dishonoring Achilles by confiscating his concubine Briseis, blames Zeus, Fate, and the furies for temporarily interfering
with his judgment (*Iliad* 19:100ff., cited by Olson 1994, 240), showing an
awareness of individual initiatives that is scarcely reflected in *Siete infantes*
(except in the decision of Almanzor)—or in *Mocedades*—whereas in the
Poema del Cid it does come to the surface, as in—"Conbidar le ien de
grado, mas ninguno non osava" [They would gladly have invited him, but
none dared to] (21, also 20, 74–77, 704 and 710, 2334, 2355–57, 2379,
3118–19).

Don Nuño later rejoins the seven and, like Oliver, wages a mighty battle
before falling in the face of hugely superior numbers. Both Gonzalo and
Roland realize finally, in the thick of the battle in which they know they
must die, that their stubborn, unquestioning faith in the traitor has been

misplaced. These are exemplary instances of the anagnorisis or disclosure recommended by Aristotle for high tragedy, but seldom actually practiced by Greek dramatists, and not often found in subsequent authors.

In *Roland*, direct discourse is used as an instrument or tool of aggression. It controls action as an agent of personal will. In *Siete infantes*, in the case of insults, provocations, requests, refusals or agreements, and laments, direct discourse is action. At other times it is no more than a gloss on what takes place. As in folktales, characters are thought of as types, and their speeches bear little of the stamp of the individual. People respond directly and immediately to circumstances with no visible or audible reflection (except in an interior monologue of Nuño Salido, in which he analyzes his lack of choices other than to rejoin the seven infantes [Catalán 1980, 201: first series of pages]). What is true of the characters applies also to the authors: the poet of *Roland* controls and manipulates the epic form with skill and deliberation; he develops an individual voice. The author of *Siete infantes* appears to stay much more within the framework handed down to him. He lets the story tell itself, injecting few effects. Effects are very much present, but of other kinds: a powerful structure that gives sense to the narrative by its manner of organization; archetypal figures that move in accordance with the underlying meaning of the text; a sense of a brutal existence unmediated by the artificiality of language. The ostensibly artless creation of those effects is in fact a high artistic achievement rooted in the narrative mode. Authorial reflections and devices would be irrelevant in such a structure, and perhaps were not even available to the composer of this text.

On the level of narrative content, the contrast between *Siete infantes* and *Roland* is accentuated in the climactic battle scene. The Spanish text is permeated with archaic folk motifs. After lying transparently to persuade the seven brothers to fight against the huge Moorish host, Ruy Velázquez somehow transports himself to where the Moors are, with Nuño Salido following close behind. Ruy exercises an unaccountable power over the Moors as he directs them to wipe out the Castilians; after hearing his words, Don Nuño rushes back to warn his pupils. They are soon surrounded. The tutor retracts his former warnings, urges the young men to victory, and rides against the enemy and to certain death. After the two hundred horsemen accompanying the seven infantes have been killed along with more than a thousand Moors, the youths retire to a knoll to rest, where they discover that one of their number has perished. They arrange a truce so that they can send to their uncle for help. He refuses their request. Three hundred of the uncle's knights desert him to join the six remaining brothers as the battle resumes. When those reinforcements have all been cut down and the six are too tired to raise their swords, the Moorish chieftains grant them respite, take them to their tent, let them disarm, and offer them bread and wine. Ruy Velázquez arrives and intimidates the chieftains by threatening to have Almanzor execute them if any infante goes free. The Moors seem terror-stricken by the thought that he will convert to Islam, be granted all of Almanzor's power, and persecute them. He appears not as a combatant but as one in authority, immune to danger from either side. The battle again resumes, and the six kill an additional 2060; then, disarmed and exhausted, they are beheaded in the order of their birth as Ruy Velázquez supervises in the manner of a priest making a sacrifice. The similarity of the proceeding to a harvest ritual has been noted (p. 21). Each of the uncle's actions arouses shocked indignation in the reader, who nevertheless feels each one to be inevitable.

The corresponding scene in *Roland* is full of prodigious deeds and pathos. The sense of an individual author concentrating on individual exploits is constant. Since the traitor is absent, the focus of conflict shifts to the disagreement between the two comrades, Oliver and Roland, who express their motives with force and with reasonable clarity, and to the noble individual struggle and generous impulses of each knight who falls. For this reader at least, no clear trace of the cosmic or archetypal forces that underlie the Spanish text is discoverable.[57] The Frankish heroes are magnificently human. In their self-consciousness, their loyalty, and their grandeur they reflect no clear vestiges of the collective, impersonal, rather generic imperative that moves everyone in *Siete infantes*.

Given the way *Roland* and *Siete infantes* both retell the same story of offense, tragedy, and retribution from beginning to end, it would be very difficult to deny their relationship. Given their radically different physical settings and intellectual and artistic grounding, it seems indefensible to claim a relationship based strictly or primarily on written intermediaries. A background in oral tradition is indicated for both. *Siete infantes* is plainly

---

57. A possible exception is the emphasis in both texts on the ordering of severed heads or of corpses after the battle has become a massacre. As noted, the infantes are slaughtered in the order of their birth, and their father follows the same order in his lament over the heads. Roland brings seven bodies, "par uns e uns," and arranges them "en reng" before Archbishop Turpin, who pronounces a brief elegy and benediction (2184–97). Both expressions quoted suggest ordering, though they are a little ambiguous; Bédier renders them "Un par un" and "sur un rang" [in a row], but an alternative meaning "in order of rank" seems plausible. Of a dozen translations of the poem, into English, German, and Spanish, that have been consulted, all choose "in a row" except one, which prefers "in rank" (Butler 1932). The ordering may be a predictable cliché, or it may be a trace of a once-significant detail.

kin to *Tristan* as well as to the initiation tradition; in *Roland* that heritage is effectively obscured until *Siete infantes* is recognized as a key to it. This does not make the Spanish text a missing link, because no linear development can be established. Rather, the two texts appear as members of a widespread, well-known tradition that has left marked mythic traces only in *Siete infantes*.

Listing of Narrative Elements

For quick comparison and reference, the narrative elements that make up the initiation tales and similar accounts are listed here, showing the texts in which each one appears. Except as otherwise noted, the citations of the *Táin* refer to the boyhood initiation of Cúchulainn. The entry *Siete infantes* refers to the account of the seven brothers; the story of Mudarra is cited separately. The count of Savoy episode is likewise distinguished from the rest of *Mocedades*. *Roland* is not included because it is too far removed from the initiation tradition, though it could come under 5, 8a, and 12.

1. Child hero. Explicitly stated: *Táin*, *Tristan*, Mudarra, *Mocedades*, *Mainet* (in the version of the *Gran conquista de Ultramar*). Only implied: *Mainet* in the *PCG*.

2. Travel to or passage over a border or watercourse before the killing: *Táin*, *Tristan*, *Siete infantes*, Mudarra (second killing), *Condesa traidora*, count of Savoy, *Mainet*. In the *Cid*, the Infantes also travel—to their failures in Valencia and in Corpes.

3. Sleep before killing: *Táin*, *Condesa traidora* (the victims sleep), *Mocedades* (before second battle), *Cid* (before encounter with beast), *Mainet*.

4. Killing: *Táin*, *Tristan*, *Siete infantes*, Mudarra, *Condesa traidora*, *Mocedades*, count of Savoy (defeat only), *Cid* (failure), *Mainet*.

5. Fury: *Táin*, *Siete infantes*, Mudarra, *Mocedades*, count of Savoy.
   5a. Eye power: *Táin*, *Siete infantes* (if transferred to hawk), *Mocedades*, *Cid* (displaced to the established hero), *Mainet* (turned to haughty look).

6. Confrontation with the feminine ("femme impudique").
   6a. Breasts: *Táin*.
   6b. Eyes: *Mocedades*.

6c.   Words: *Tristan, Siete infantes, Mainet.*

7.   Bath / immersion: *Táin, Tristan, Siete infantes* (the hawk), *Cid* (in the wine press).

    7a.   With identification by a token: *Táin* ("The Wooing of Emer"), *Tristan, Siete infantes.*

    7b.   Attack by angry queen: *Tristan, Siete infantes.*

8.   Dressing of the hero: *Táin, Tristan, Mainet, Cid* (reversed: clothes sullied and never worn again).

    8a.   Radiance/blush: *Táin, Tristan.*

9.   (possibly not distinctive): The hero's identity is kept secret and then revealed: *Tristan, Mocedades, Condesa traidora,* count of Savoy, *Mainet.*

10.   Promise of marriage or concubinage.

    10a.   Made by the damsel's elders (parents or ruler): *Táin* (Finnabair), *Siete infantes, Cid.*

    10b.   Offer made to keep peace: *Táin* (Finnabair), *Mocedades.*

    10c.   Offer made by damsel: *Condesa traidora, Mocedades, Mainet.*

    10d.   Offer made by hero to ruler: *Tristan,* count of Savoy.

11.   Violence against woman of another clan or tribe: *Táin* (Finnabair), *Siete infantes,* ballads based on *Mocedades,* count of Savoy, *Cid.*

12.   (possibly not distinctive): Excess leading to misfortune.

    12a.   On part of man: *Siete infantes,* count of Savoy.

    12b.   On part of woman: *Siete infantes,* Zaida.

13.   Long-term effects of the initiation or killing.

    13a.   Beneficial and necessary: *Táin,* Mudarra, *Mocedades,* count of Savoy, *Mainet.*

    13b.   Disastrous: *Tristan, Siete infantes, Condesa traidora, Cid.*

Recapitulation: The Road to Corpes

To summarize the thesis put forward in the preceding pages, it has been maintained that the memory of the ancient account of the initiation of the young warrior, as propounded by Dumézil, provided the narrative background for large parts of all the principal medieval Spanish epic texts, as well as several minor tales. The exception is the lost *Cantar del cerco de Zamora,* a major text which, being devoted to the middle part of the Cid's fictional career, contains no initiation. It does, however, include an element of each heroic career studied by Dumézil, namely a shameful action or series of actions: the Cid fails in his duty to protect King Sancho from his treacherous murder by Vellido Dolfos, and fails to kill Vellido in retribution (see Montgomery 1994b). In the accounts that do include the rite of passage, only in *Mocedades* and in *Mainet* is it completed successfully and auspiciously. The youthful Rodrigo of *Mocedades*, while still in the furious state that was necessary for triumph in his first combat, confronts the king and forward woman together, as they act in concert to prepare the wild youth for his eventual entry into society as a mature, ideal vassal and husband. After many and varied replications of the initial killing, the same hero (granting the probability that both poems formed part of the standard juglaresque repertoire) emerges in the *Poema del Cid* as a model of political and knightly virtue, whose expertise as a warrior is at the service of those two social roles. The *Poema* makes those roles the basis for its action. To maintain that focus, it disregards the fact that the historical Cid had a son. The first concern in life of the epic Cid is the well-being of the women of his immediate family: "que aún con mis manos—case estas mis fijas, . . . e vós, mugier ondrada—de mí seades servida" [that yet with my hands I may marry these my daughters, and you, honored wife, be served by me] (282b–83). To these goals of his political and military enterprise, the extended family or *mesnada* is also dedicated. The Cid's conquests are directed toward those ends: "entrad comigo—en Valençia la casa, / en esta heredad—que vos yo he ganada" [enter with me the city of Valencia, this property that I have won for you] (1606–7), as are his gifts to the king. But his two roles, the domestic and the political, come into conflict when the king mistakenly or impotently supports the marriage of the daughters to the Infantes de Carrión. The inadequacy of the Infantes' initiation then becomes a barrier to the realization of the Cid's mission in life.

Mocedades, with its successful initiation, provides the necessary point of contrast which underlies the interpretation here advanced of the failure of the Infantes de Carrión. The initiatory rite of *Mocedades* is less than exemplary, however. At its late date of composition (c. 1360), it absorbed many ambivalences from a culture in crisis and became in part the account of a ritual rebellion or ceremonial role-reversal. Rodrigo terrorizes the king as well as his court and puts his own conditions to the acceptance of Jimena's hand: first he will fight and win five battles in the field. Much of the rest of the poem will be devoted to completing that prolongation of his rite of passage (though omissions in the single manuscript make counting the battles problematical; see Armistead 1963–64). At this point Jimena's active part in his formation as a warrior is completed, and she will not appear again in *Mocedades*. Not only does Rodrigo take charge of his own initiation; he continues to defy and threaten King Fernando I, who is portrayed, in a gross distortion of history, as weak and childish. Later Rodrigo becomes the king's supporter, but scarcely less objectionable than before, overbearing to the point of interrupting the ruler as he speaks, contradicting him, and overriding his will in dealings with other potentates. If the *Mocedades*, the *Cantar del cerco de Zamora*, and the *Poema del Cid* are taken as parts of the same hero's biography, his defiance toward the king of León and Castile persists down to the very prelude to the third poem. As a possible clue to such continuity, five battles are attributed to the Cid in the *Poema*, during an encomiastic summary of his exploits (1333). The number five would have to come from some external source, since it does not correspond to any grouping of battles to be found in the poem itself (as noted by Deyermond 1969, 162–63). Presumably the five battles are the ones pledged by the youthful Rodrigo in a lost earlier version of the *Mocedades* legend.

The continuity among epics, though probable, is not necessary to the proposed interpretation, since in any case the initiation and related traditions rank as cultural givens and as such lend meaning to the contrast between Rodrigo's initiation and the experience of the Infantes de Carrión.

The critical events of the initiation are the same for Rodrigo and Cúchulainn. In both cases, the hero does his first killing in single combat, though others are present as witnesses. Subsequently his terrible fury, which gives special power to his eyes, is turned aside by the *femme impudique* as the ruler presides over a confrontation symbolizing the approach of sexual and political maturity. The youth's character must still be tempered over time by further combat and by postponement of sexual fulfillment. As seen against the background of this pattern, the Infantes de Carrión do everything in the wrong order, with disastrous results. Placing marriage (and material gain) first is the fundamental error, after which all manly challenges are impossible to meet: the beast arouses fear instead of feeling it; the bath is shameful and disconnected from the feminine. The first combat is a secret failure, especially in contrast with the highly public success of a warrior-priest. Having revealed themselves as liars and plotters, the Infantes seek to avoid the confrontation with the feminine by killing their wives "before they bring up what happened with the lion" (2548, 2556). The scene of the crime again may echo the bath, as it does in *Táin*, with seminudity and, in the *Poema*, a secluded spring which will restore the women to life. The *Poema* continues its revision of the tradition as the Infantes stage a perverse test, "ensayándos," with unworthy weapons (cinches and spurs appropriate to the domination of animals), failing as before in their murderous intent. To Doña Sol's noble reinterpretation of what is happening, "Dos espadas tenedes . . . mártires seremos nós . . . atán malos ensienplos non fagades" [you have two swords . . . we will be martyrs . . . do not commit such an infamous deed] (2726–32), they make no verbal response; they are not operating in the same cultural or moral context as the woman who is able to make a clear-headed and eloquent assessment of the unfolding events. The reversal of events of the initiatory text and bath is perhaps further emblematized by the act of the night before, "mugieres en braços" (2703), which ought to occur only long after the initial ceremonial confrontation with the feminine. A particularly violent reversal is the transfer from men to women of the ritual nudity that characterizes some initiation ceremonies. Details aside, the progression (1) marriage, (2) failed tests (beast, Moor, Corpes), (3) degraded sexual confrontation, does make up a distorted mirror image of the heroic sequence, (1) test (killing, beasts), (2) sexual confrontation, (3) marriage leading to mature domestic and political relationships. The Infantes' regression leads nowhere but to continued delusion as they imagine they should have married better. They are doomed never to mature; they will always be infantes.

The unaccountable and incongruous elements of the Infantes' marriage and its three sequels, namely the scene of the lion, the failed "primeros golpes," and the Corpes incident, when viewed within the framework of the initiation, take their place as mythical matter. In that light the irrationality of much that happens in those episodes comes out more clearly, and at the same time acquires coherence. This is not to say that other elements, from the obscurely archaic to hagiographic and political motifs roughly contemporary with the poem's composition, may not also be present.

The interpretation here offered of *Mocedades* intersects at many junctures with the analysis done by García Montoro (1972), in a book rich with insights and significant details which treats many points more completely than is done in these pages. García Montoro's study concentrates on representations of the tripartite scheme of Dumézil, and while some of his arguments are brilliantly persuasive, others seem forced. The proposed ancient "ideology" of three classes, one of rulers and priests, another of warriors, and a third said to be of producers but in effect including everybody not in the first two groups, had largely broken down in many cultures and in their folklore as early as Roman imperial times, when military and governmental functions were taken over by the same individuals. Under these conditions, the symbolic triads could easily be absorbed by the narrative three's so prevalent in the storytelling of many cultures, where they may have no ulterior meaning.

As conditions made the earlier principles obsolete, the heroic initiation, once a powerful expression of the distinctive place of the warring class in society, survived the weakening of the triad, sometimes as a continuing celebration of the hero and sometimes as a condemnation of the single-minded, untamed aggressor. Each version represents a revision stemming from repeated second thoughts on the murderous youth as model adolescent. The most formidable heroes, such as Herakles and Cúchulainn, do reprehensible things and lead tortured lives. The Ulsterman, for instance, when his supremacy is threatened by an only son who promises to become even greater than he, resorts to a secret weapon to kill him (see p. 160, note 38). With the evolution of the tradition, *Tristan* grafts courtly values onto the unfortunate career of its hero, whereas *Roland* attributes the hero's ruin (or apotheosis)[58] to his individual traits of character. The woman, always dangerous, becomes a destructive witch in *Siete infantes*, one who confounds the heroic ideal, but that same legend shows her also as a victim of violence and presents other women in supportive roles as mother or avenger. These varied functions are also seen in *Mocedades*, and (with the abuse attenuated) in *Mainet*. The *Poema del Cid* upholds the heroic ideal partly by portraying its reverse, and also by adapting it magnificently to twelfth-century conditions and wisdom. From that admirable mutual adaptation of hero and culture, there can be only decline; when Rodrigo overshadows and bullies the king a century and a half later in *Mocedades*, the tradition has been subverted, reaching a critical level of decadence. Remarkably, it is still fully recognizable, and the initiation is positive in its results.

---

58. Robert F. Cook interprets Roland's decision not to sound his horn as an affirmation of feudal ideology, an act of "heroism and conformity" (1987, 246), and supplies an excellent bibliographical summary on the varied interpretations of the poem (ix–xvi). The mythic framework proposed here seems equally applicable whether the author intended to present Roland as a model of proper behavior or as the incarnation of folly. The ambiguity may well have been deliberate, in light of the ambivalence that is evident in the treatment of most of the heroes, ancient and medieval, seen throughout this study.

As narrative is inherited from earlier times, evolving with the changes of society and its values, readjustments in its structure will leave some of its parts obscure. But it has been said that Greek myth, through whatever changes it undergoes, always keeps its identity (Parker 1987, 189), and great staying power is also to be found in the medieval initiation tale as it continues to authorize the building of new structures around it. A hero newly appearing among a people may be authenticated, for example, by assimilation to a preexisting pattern. If earlier meanings are blurred, the wonder and excitement carried by the tale may nonetheless remain unabated, especially if the linguistic and stylistic form of the text retains the flavor of past times. Some aspects of poetic form that reflected inherited modes of thought and expression, mainly in the *Poema del Cid*, will be the subject of the second part of this book.

PART II
POETICS

El Poema del Cid: Looking Inward and Outward

The *Poema del Cid* is obviously the best surviving example of medieval Spanish epic style, although it shows signs of writerly editorializing that would bar it from any claim to "purity." One trait that supports its authenticity as a traditional work is its use of two linguistic registers. When the minstrel addresses his audience, he adopts a simplified syntax with little grammatical subordination and a conventionalized system of verb tenses. By contrast, when his characters converse with each other, their language is more complex, expertly conveying the subtleties of human interaction and often carrying forward the narrative thread, in a style closer to everyday speech. The distinction between the two linguistic registers highlights the contrast between the narrator as performer before an audience and the narrator as the director of the interaction among the poem's characters. His control of both groups, the audience and the fictional characters, is a key to the power and immediacy of the work. It is his presence among the two groups that brings them together. And, as I will attempt to demonstrate, the ceremonial behavior of the poem's personages enhances the ritualistic quality of the performance. An ingenious interpretation of ritual offered by Lévi-Strauss helps the reader to appreciate the process under observation: ritual is a game, with its rules and its competitiveness, in which all participants become winners (1962, 47–49). The rules are elaborate: on the internal face, looking at the content of the poem, rules of propriety and etiquette predominate, and in dealing with the audience, the requirements of poetic form are paramount. The poem's successful interplay of internal and external dimensions produces a winning combination in the game being played. Further, just as the figures within the poem are professional combatants, the minstrel engages in competition with other minstrels to attract, hold, and control an audience.

To an extent, the synergy of inward and outward direction is identifiable with the harmony of form and content that has attracted the attention of some linguists, as when Dell Hymes speaks of "form-meaning covariation and patterning based upon it" (1981, 333), and Paul Friedrich describes a mythical idiom: "The underlying nuances of myth are felt to be somehow consonant with the surface of sound" (1986, 39). The identification of form and content comes through to the reader of *Siete infantes*, for example, in spite of its mask of prose, more clearly than to the reader of its relatively advanced congener *Roland*, for in *Roland* ancient motifs are subordinated to the author's design, whereas they are the very stuff of *Siete infantes*.

My aim in what follows is to identify traits of the language and content of the poems, particularly of the *Poema del Cid*, that give evidence of a persisting mythical mentality, traces of an archaic perception of humanity's place in the world. The harmony of language and thought ranges from the smallest to the largest poetic units, from the phoneme to the overall structure. This most easily becomes clear to the observer who accepts the principle that in this genre, stories are knowledge in themselves, rather than a means of arriving at knowledge that is more properly expressed in abstract and general terms. Knowledge exists by being communicated, and in the epic the form of communication is the narrative. The story of the Cid is about a man acting in his society. Neither he nor his poet are men of ideas in a modern sense. The *Cid* departs from tradition, however, in literary developments such as the elaboration of individual wills and motives, the subtleties of interaction among personages, with attendant ironies, or the conversion of the Cid and others into accomplished declaimers, assimilated in this sense to the author or performer himself. Such departures from an inherited model or matrix are artistically successful: the poem is a transitional work.

Eliade brings together the two directions developed by the minstrel in these terms: "Il ne s'agit pas d'une connaissance 'extérieure,' 'abstraite' mais d'une connaissance qu'on 'vit' rituellement, soit en narrant cérémoniellement le mythe, soit en éffectuant le rituel auquel il sert de justification" (1963, 30).[1] We may propose a codicil: the audience experiences the myth ritually, as the critic says, but does so more intensely because the poem's characters live ritually. Their speech is accordingly "ritual in the broad sense of the term: greetings, and fixed politeness formulas, formal behavior" (Bloch 1977, 285). Maurice Bloch implies a contrast between these conventions and the more institutionalized varieties of ritual, which take the form of acts or expressions of power or authority. With slight

1. "It is not a matter of external, abstract knowledge but knowledge that is lived ritually, whether in narrating the myth ceremonially or in carrying out the ritual that it supports."

modification, both of Bloch's categories, greetings and fixed politeness formulas, are applicable to the kinds of formalities found in the poem. They appear respectively as introductions to direct discourse (which involves interaction between the poet's voice and those of his characters) and as hortatory expressions. These forms are essential to the idiom of the poem and to the images it develops of its personages. In the first verbal pattern now to be discussed, the conventional speech that conditions the realization of the characters as literary creations is intermingled with additional conventions to which the narrator's own voice adheres.

Introducing Direct Discourse

The poem's peculiar way of leading into direct speech entails collaboration between the narrating voice and the speaking personage. The analogy with politeness formulas is pertinent, taking etiquette as a necessary factor in the shaping and defining of society (Lincoln 1989, 75). In the poem politeness also serves as the basis of a dynamic through which the presenter reaches out to his audience. The mechanism is comparable to that of a formal introduction of two people who have not met before: here the narrator presents the person who will speak, who then addresses a third party by name. Each of the two speakers uses a line of poetry comprising predetermined though variable patterns of syntax and content. The second of the two lines, in which the speaker addresses his hearer within the poem, is the locus of most of the work's epithetic language. Taken together, the two lines lend gravity to the text, providing an excellent example of a kind of formulism of patterns that is truly epic in tone. Unlike the simple repetitions of word groups that have sometimes been called epic formulas whether or not they are conducive to an elevated style, these patterns contribute notably to the dignified tone of the text.

The first line of the introduction, which is delivered by the narrating voice, is normally structured as follows: identification (usually by name) of the speaking subject, with an optional epithet or grammatical complement, and a verb. As a variation, the speaking subject may be named in a previous line. The second line, which begins his or her speech, names the person addressed (this is an essential component of the pattern) and usually applies an epithet to that person. It might be expected that the verb of the first line would be a verb of speaking, a *verbum dicendi*, but this is so in less than half the cases. The most common substitute is (1) a verb of motion. Progressively less frequent alternatives are (2) verbs of ceremonial action and (3) those of feeling or perception. As examples, "se levantó" (3199, etc.) in the law court fits the first two categories, "alegrós" (2442) the third. Dámaso Alonso noted, in his first published commentary on this pattern, in 1944, that the absence of the *verbum dicendi* in these introductions probably bore a relation to the technique of oral delivery, while for the modern reader it contributes an emotional, dramatic tone to the text (1973b, 116). He studied the trait more systematically in a 1969 article (1973c, 199) as a distinctive mark setting the *Cid* apart from French epic, and stated his intention to reexamine it as a stylistic device, but this last project never reached print. The introductions that are reduced to a simple *dixo*—which, as just noted, are exceptional—propel a dialogue already under way, giving it rapidity, e.g. in 136, 139, 141, 146, as the verbal exchange between Martín Antolínez and the moneylenders gains momentum. The pattern with a verb replacing *dixo* serves to inaugurate a verbal exchange and often creates an effect of stately ceremony. This pattern or template is particularly common in the early part of the poem, where most utterances are brief and isolated. The pattern in skeleton form is: line 1: identification of the subject who is to speak, verb (of motion, etc.), epithet or complement; line 2 (which begins the quotation): the name of the addressee, an epithet. Examples from near the beginning of the poem follow:

(*verbum dicendi*)

        Fabló Mio Cid — bien e tan mesurado,
        "¡Grado a ti, Señor, — Padre que estas en alto!"
        Esto me han buelto — mios enemigos malos."
                               (7–9)

(type 2, verb of ceremonial action)

        Meçió Mio Cid los ombros — e engrameó la tiesta:
        "¡Albricia, Álbar Fáñez, — ca echados somos de tierra!"
                              (13–14)

(type 1, verb of motion)

        Una niña de nuef años — a oio se parava:
        "¡Ya Campeador, — en buen ora cinxiestes espada!"
                              (40–41)

(type 1)

> Llegó Martín Antolínez — a guisa de menbrado:
> "¿O sodes, Rachel e Vidas, — los mios amigos caros?"
> (102–3)

(type 2)

> Rachel a Mio Çid — la manol' va besar:
> "¡Ya Canpeador, — en buen ora cinxiestes espada!"
> (174–75)

(type 2)

> Reçibiólo el Çid — abiertos amos los braços:
> "¡Venides, Martín Antolínez, — el mio fiel vassallo!"
> (203–4)

In the first hundred lines, only the speech of the people of Burgos, which is not addressed to anyone in particular, breaks the mold. The first and fourth examples show adaptation of the conventional epithet to suit personages other than knights and nobles, and the second is abbreviated, since the first line of the speech is also the last. In situations where the epithet is not called for, it is usually replaced with a suitable formulaic phrase (as in the first and fourth examples) rather than simply omitted. Tender, ironic, or intentionally ambiguous substitutes, such as "amos sodes ermanos" (2230), stand out clearly against the conventional background of formulaic praise (for more examples, see Montgomery 1990–91, 62–63). Except for equivocal instances such as 2230, it is true in the *Poema*, as it is in Homer (Block 1986, 157–58) that there are no negative or insulting epithets in the poem.

The author of the *Poema* displays a fine command of technique in sharing this ritualistic verbal pattern with his epic creatures; indeed, it is how he establishes harmonic contact between himself and them. A further point of contact, which I will discuss later in connection with the poem's metonymic manner, is in the clearly established sense of where each action occurs. Ritual activity is by definition linked to a particular place, one having a solemn if not hallowed aura (Nagy 1990, 10). As for the location of an epic performance, it might be humble, but it would be recognized as distinct from ordinary places, at least at the time of the performance. Each of the speeches just cited occurs in a different specific location. The speeches and places define and punctuate each other: the last look at his property (7–9), the entry into Burgos (13–14), the passage through Burgos ("¡Dios, qué buen vassallo, si oviesse buen señor!" [20]), and the pause at the hero's place of lodging (41). Each of these scenes closes with a speech that functions to summarize and interpret it. As the poem then proceeds, it uses the technique less regularly, but the introduction of direct quotations continues to be done with great skill as a means of "narrative evaluation" (Pratt 1977, 48), of organizing and bringing out the sense of the text for a listening audience. Each place is solemnized by the words spoken there, and each speech is enclosed spatially.

Places

Places are also a basic structural element of the *Poema del Cid* in their own right. This is to be expected in the earlier parts, those devoted to travel, where the impression of reality and factual accuracy is enhanced by the frequent naming of towns and topographic features, and each successive event happens in a different locale. After the conquests are finished, however, the manner is maintained, and it is only rarely that some vagueness is felt as to where an action or speech is taking place. A corroborating counterexample is the first mission of Alvar Fáñez to the king. He finds Alfonso in "Castiella" (871); the imprecision is noticeable because it is exceptional. Exemplifying the normal habit, the dealings with Raquel and Vidas are segmented and organized by six crossings of the river Arlanzón. The law court scene is preceded, and prepared artistically, by arrival in Toledo, relocation to San Servando, and return to the city. Then it is formed by comings and goings within the court, by advancing to hand over or receive swords, and as minimal punctuating movement, by rising to speak. On a larger scale, the beginning and the end of the Cid's migration are each marked by the viewing of a scene in its significant details—the ruined buildings in Vivar and the lands and sea around Valencia: the Cid's two chief properties, which define his successive stations in life.

The poem's emphasis on movement to and from specified places will receive further analysis in connection with the metonymic mode of expression adopted by the poet (pp. 146–47). The longest segment without significant movement is the one dealing with the count of Barcelona, in which (as in *Roland*) change of speaker provides a substitute. In each new "paragraph" throughout the poem, the audience is systematically reminded that it is in a new place, one that has specific associations with given speeches and actions.[2] The hallowing effect of the poem's associations is felt even today by the traveler who arrives at one of the sites and reflects on what was purportedly said or done: "That happened here!" Like the site of a ritual, an event retold, even if known to be imaginary, cannot be separated from the location attributed to it.

Hortatory and Other Directive Modes

Ritual activity usually has some kind of narrative content, in which the conductor of the ceremony represents an imagined personage whose identity he partly assumes. In comparable manner, especially in a preliterate environment, the epic minstrel identified himself to some degree with his heroic characters. Like them, he operated in a primarily oral environment, a fact intimately and deeply reflected in his manner of using language (compare Martin 1989, xiv). In the *Poema del Cid* the presenter and his heroes speak with analogous intentions: to capture and keep the attention of the hearers, either the audience or the listeners within the poem, to engage them emotionally and to develop consensus, as well as to give essential information. The assimilation therefore works in both directions: the heroic characters, to be seen as admirable, must be skilled speakers.

Like the authorial voice, the reported discourse within the poem functions bidirectionally: when the Cid speaks to influence the actions or the opinions of other characters, he reaches out to the audience as well. When his speech acts are most overtly intended to modify or elicit behavior, when they are acts of advising, requesting, and particularly of commanding, they move the minstrel's audience powerfully, though the responses of that group are confined to the realm of the imaginary. The hortatory utterances, which constitute the great bulk of those spoken by the poem's characters,

2. With its peculiar structuring of narrated experience, the poem would be a useful source of information for linguistic investigations into the nature and functioning of the mind, for which narrative offers fundamental clues. "Narratives also give evidence that the mind actually requires certain kinds of information in order to operate successfully. There appears to be a need for orientaion in terms of the organism's location in space, in time, in a social context, and with relation to ongoing events. . . . Hence the frequent provision of settings, not only at the beginnings of narratives, but at whatever points the orientation may change" (Chafe 1990, 97).

are among its most potent communicative devices: they produce vivid inter-action, they bring the characters' force of will home to the audience (or reader), and they fuel the forward movement of the particularly dynamic poetic form that is Spanish epic. Their style is of great importance; they need to be good examples of skilled speaking, suitably adapted to the status and the personal traits of each addressee. This last requirement brings mat-ters of courtesy to the fore and creates further parallels between the internal discourse of the poem and the communicative process linking minstrel and audience during performance. The mutual identification of the two sets of hearers, internal and external, people addressed within the poem and the minstrel's audience, is one of the poem's remarkable achievements.

A study of the hortatory modes in the poem should accordingly throw light on the work's peculiar immediacy and dynamism and its ability to ab-sorb the attention and enter the consciousness of the reader—qualities that have not lent themselves to easy analysis. In the verbal artistry needed to achieve these effects, in the skill of speaking well, good form and good con-tent are inseparable. Such ability may be different, for example, from ver-bal expertise in reasoning or in explaining or analyzing, different from the art of arguing a case or delineating a character. Such functions are chiefly properties of prose, and the *Cid* is an eminently poetic text, synthesizing form and content, words and experience. Speeches operate in oral space be-tween people, showing keen sensitivity to feelings and hierarchies; they are courteous and tactful unless combative. In all this the *Cid* distinguishes it-self sharply from *Fernán González*, in which principles of disputation are indeed followed, yielding a prosaic and dehumanized result.

The poem's initial hortatory speech sets a tone of persuasive subtlety and civility that will be maintained throughout. At first it hardly seems like an exhortation. The words of the nine-year-old girl take mainly the form of a recapitulation of information already given by the poet (25–28)—though this time personalized by the use of *nós* forms—on the conditions of the hero's banishment, to which are added formulaic praise and a prayer on his behalf:

> "¡Ya Campeador, — en buen ora çinxiestes espada!
> El rrey lo ha vedado, — anoch d'él entró su carta
> con grant rrecabdo — e fuertemientre sellada.
> Non vos osariemos — abrir nin coger por nada;
> si non, perderiemos — los averes e las casas

e demás — los oios de las caras.
Çid, en el nuestro mal — vós non ganades nada,
mas el Criador vos vala — con todas sus vertudes sanctas."
(41–48)

While the speech has other implications, its immediate burden is hortatory:
a plea to leave Burgos quickly and peacefully, intimated by words of quite
different apparent content (47), together with a simple prayer (48). A ceremonial closure to the scene ensues, as the child turns to reenter her world,
excluding the hero: "Esso la niña dixo—e tornós' pora su casa" (49).

This single example suffices to show the poem's author as master of a
technique of powerful persuasion. As a performer (or perhaps by way of an
intermediary performer) he exercises analogous power over the audience.
Through a stylized linguistic construct blending form and content in its
rhythmic patterns, he develops a sense of a collectivity, of tribal unity
against a hostile force. The child makes no reference to the transaction she
is conducting between the people of Burgos and the hero, nor does she state
explicitly their feelings of solidarity with him and helplessness in the face of
the royal order. When she says, "el rrey lo ha vedado," "lo" needs no expressed antecedent. The absence, on the surface, of these elements in no
way interferes with understanding; rather, it confirms the preexisting mutual comprehension and agreement among the various parties, strong
enough to make explanation and entreaty superfluous. The Cid's silence
(exceptional in the poem, in which requests normally receive answers)
again heightens the effect for the audience. The girl is a poetic device, a
voice that defeats the enforced silence. Since she is eloquent in her stylized
humility, the artificiality of the device is perfectly acceptable.

On another level, her words are an incursion by the poet upon the scene,
in that the language is plainly his, intended to mold audience opinion, and
is not believably the phrasing of a child. He undermines the distinction between the fictional listener (the Cid) and the performer's audience, by
catching up the latter in the action. The young girl's words compel agreement, blurring the lines separating all parties: speaker, hero, presenter, and
audience.

A chief determinant of the language used in this scene is the sense of hierarchy. The child is near the bottom of the social scale, and she speaks for
the people of Burgos collectively, as they face with difficulty an appeal for
aid from a neighbor more powerful than they. Her words, especially the di-

rect, humble appeal for understanding of "Non vos osariemos abrir," would sound apologetic and undignified if spoken by an adult. Awareness of hierarchies is likely to show itself in any hortatory speech.

This leads to consideration of the poem's closest parallel to the unspoken plea of the child, found in Minaya's third mission to the king (1845–54). Here as before, no overt request is made. Minaya reaffirms the Cid's loyalty to Alfonso and tells of the hero's battle with Yuçuf and the resulting booty, to conclude, "e envíavos dozientos cavallos—e bésavos las manos" (1854), a dual declaration of vassalage, echoing "a vós tiene por señor—e tiénes' por vuestro vassallo" (1847). The request is clear though unstated, because it has been made twice before; it is part of the background knowledge that unites the audience and the fictional figures with the minstrel. So a discussion of this mission necessitates consideration of the previous one, the second ambassade before the king. It has been a model of diplomatic language, in which the number and length of polite expressions is an index of the degree of formality. In this second speech before the king, the introductory formulas occupy four lines (1321–24), with a hortatory formula in each: "¡Merçed. . . .!" "besávavos las manos," "los pies e las manos," "quel' ayades merçed." The narrative runs from 1325 to 1333, five lines are occupied with the offering of gifts, and the final one is a declaration of loyalty, "razónas' por vuestro vassallo—e a vós tiene por señor" (1339), to be repeated in 1847 with only an adjustment to the different assonance. In addition to the plea for the lifting of sanctions, "quel' ayades merçed" (1324), Minaya requests the liberation of the Cid's wife and daughters. The verb forms are as self-effacing as possible: "Merçed vos pide el Çid . . . saldrién del monesterio . . . irién pora Valençia" (1351–54). The first of the three ambassades, shorter than the others, uses the same formula because there are fewer exploits to recount and because modest expectations are conducive to discretion in the application of pressure, "quel' ayades merçed" (880), but ends with a request for future action couched as a prediction: "Grado e graçias, rrey, commo a señor natural, / esto feches agora,—ál feredes adelant" (895–96). The boldness of the future tense, which only in this phrase replaces the subjunctives and conditionals of Minaya's petition, is attenuated by the implied promise it carries: the Cid will continue to work to gain royal favor. Further, this remark seems to anticipate the ellipsis of the third mission, whose unstated assumptions, because they are by implication shared, serve as silent reaffirmations of the sense of community. Leaving assumptions tacit also allows for pithiness of expression; a number of the memorable lines of the poem, such as line 896, are in fact hortatory circumlocutions.

The exhortations observed thus far, covering some forty-five lines, contain not one imperative verb form. In the dealings with the moneylenders, the Cid likewise avoids any use of the imperative. He broaches the matter to Martín Antolínez with the customary circumspection, declaring his ambivalence and proposing a collaborative action: "con vuestro consejo—bastir quiero dos arcas, / inchámoslas d' arena" (85–86). In the strenuous and elaborate negotiations conducted by Don Martino, imperatives gradually appear, but their first introduction occurs, as often happens in the poem, in preliminary transactional phrases, those referring to the personal interaction which is part of the dialogue in progress, with subordinate subjunctives expressing the desired action: "amos me dat las manos / que non me descubrades" (106–7). Having established an air of conspiratorial secrecy —fabricating a transitory in-group—and promising wealth, he repeats the lie that the Cid has withheld money from the king, strengthening the illusory in-group while reaffirming his sense of solidarity with the audience, who shares with him the knowledge of the irony being created. Only after laying this groundwork does Don Martino move to imperative verb forms, "prestalde" (118) and "prended las arcas—e metedlas en vuestro salvo" (119), followed by the forceful imperative of the oath, "con grand jura—meted y las fes amos / que non las catedes—en todo aqueste año" (121–22). The moneylenders then proceed to persuade themselves of the profitability of the transaction, and the dealing begins. The use of imperatives ceases except for operational verbs: "dezitnos del Cid" (129) and "amos tred" (142). When the usurers appear before the Cid, hierarchical considerations come to the fore; he asks them for nothing, assuming instead the role of benefactor: "de lo mío avredes algo, / mientra que vivades—non seredes menguados" (157–58). Second-person (plural) imperatives only reappear when Don Martino urges the lenders to take their valueless chests, "levaldas . . . ponedlas" (167), playing further on politeness conventions by ironic reversal. Then imperatives are once again abandoned, and Raquel's request for a tunic as commission reaches a new level of verbal indirection and delicacy: "Cid, beso vuestra mano—en don que la yo aya" (179).

It is of course the Cid's responsibility to command, and he has at his disposal a liberal supply of formulaic patterns for the purpose. The introductory "Oíd" makes a command recognizable without being too direct.

Particularly effective also are expressions designed to forestall any possible disapproval, which the hero's superior position allows him to use graciously: "Oíd, varones,—non vos caya en pesar . . . quiero . . . sed menbrados—cómmo lo devedes far" (313-15), "Lo que yo dixier—non lo tengades a mal, / en Casteión—non podriemos fincar" (530-31), "Si vós quisiéredes, Minaya,—quiero . . ." (1257), and "Si a vós ploguiere, Minaya,—e non vos caya en pesar, / enviarvos quiero . . ." (1270-71). Minaya makes his own ingenious variation on this pattern to propose a plan of action to his lord: "Campeador, fagamos—lo que a vós plaze. / A mí dedes ciento cavalleros . . ." (1128-29). He continues with subjunctives; in the poem this form is favored over the imperative in many hortatory sentences. Even under great stress the subjunctive may be chosen, as when young Félez Muñoz discovers his cousins languishing between life and death: "¡Despertedes, primas,—por amor del Criador!" (2787). And even in such dire straits, Doña Sol's first words, besides being deeply touching, are elaborately courteous: "Sí vos lo meresca, mio primo,—nuestro padre el Canpeador, / ¡dandos del agua,—sí vos vala el Criador!" (2797-98).

The more specific devices for diminishing the directness of commands and related utterances, such as supplications and requests, fall into two main categories, separated by a rather uncertain line: the grammatical and the phraseological. The grammatical devices are numerous and express subtle gradations of forcefulness. Their variety in such an apparently plain-spoken text justifies some detailed consideration. They include the use of several tenses, moods, and persons, other than the second-person plural imperative, which is much less frequent than the sum of its substitutes. The present subjunctive is generally seen through examples of its contexts to be less peremptory than the imperative:

> Aquí vos llas acomiendo — a vós, abbat don Sancho,
> déllas e de mi mugier — fagades todo recabdo.
> (256-57)

> Digades al conde, — non lo tenga a mal . . .
> (977)

> A mí dedes çiento cavalleros, — que non vos pido más,
> vós con los otros — firádeslos delant.
> (1130-31)

(The Cid appoints four emissaries:)
Cavalguedes con çiento — guisados pora huebos de lidiar;
por Sancta María — vós vayades passar,
vayades a Molina . . .

(1461–63)

Pues esso queredes, Çid, — a mí mandedes ál.
(1694)

dédesme vuestra amor.
(2032; the Cid addresses the king)

bien me lo creades — que él vos casa, ca non yo.
(2204)

("Creédmelo bien" would have enjoined belief, rather than acceptance of an assurance; also in 2714.)

These forms can be intermingled with imperatives, as in the first example: "prendetlas . . . fagades . . . bien las abastad" (255–59). As an added factor, certain verbs tend to one mood or the other; for instance *prendet* occurs six times, but *prendades* is not used in main clauses.

The first plural subjunctive can provide a genteel way of coaxing, as when Minaya urges the Cid, "pensemos de ir nuestra vía" (382), and in the same vein, "tornémosnos" (2625). Other examples are "demos salto a él" (584) and the hero's call for collective action in "vayámoslos ferir" (676) and "todos iscamos fuera" (685). When the Cid says, "inchámoslas d' arena" (86), neither he nor his interlocutor Martín Antolínez is expecting to perform the task himself. The third-person subjunctive can have hortatory force: "de noche lo lieven" (93), "í nos cante el gallo" (209), and "dénme mis espadas / mios averes" (3155, 3206). Menéndez Pidal (1954–56, 345) adduces a number of additional second- and third-person subjunctive forms as having "valor de imperativo."

Most of the forms with *vós* as the subject of a hortatory verb are directed to single individuals. This might be expected as a concomitant of the polite implications of the subjunctive, but in fact the pronoun *tú* is seldom used, and I have noted only ten instances of the singular imperative (see also Menéndez Pidal 1954–56, 324–25). The conditions for its use are specific: prayers (365, 3665), commands addressed by the Cid to his nephews Félez Muñoz (3628) and Pero Vermúdez (3302), the challenge issued by

Pero Vermúdez to the elder Infante before the court (3316, 3329), the similar challenge of Muño Gustioz (3383), words directed to Muslims ("Acá
torna, Búcar" [2409]), and dialogue among Muslims ("Acayaz, cúriate
d'éstos" [2669]), where a subordinate addresses a superior, and the choice
of *tú* suggests that the poet was aware that Arabic did not use an honorific
comparable to *vós*. Since *tú* is rare, only three hortatory subjunctives occur
in the second singular: "cúriesme" (twice in 2352), "oyas" (2634), in each
of which the Cid addresses a nephew, and "lieves" (2903), where he speaks
to his *criado* Muño Gustioz.

The imperfect subjunctive is used in third-person desiderative sentences
(1897, 3339) and in one case where the Cid addresses the king with
extreme deference: "Fuéssedes mi huésped, — si vos ploguiesse, señor"
(2046). The response may be gracious enough, but the verb chosen clearly
reflects the hierarchy: "mio huésped seredes, — Çid Campeador, / e cras feremos — lo que ploguiere a vós" (2049–50). The king, as ultimate authority,
has in practice if not in principle his own verb system, reminiscent of the
Iliad, where, properly enough, "in the language of Zeus, commands,
threats, and predictions comprise *one* and the same category" (Martin
1989, 53, emphasis his). The king is also more liberal than other speakers
with direct commands to individuals: "Id e venit" (888), "Levantados en
pie" (2027), and "besad las manos, que los piedes non" (2028). Exceptionally, the king is the recipient of an imperative when the Cid tells him "sed
en vuestro escaño" (3118). Presumably in connection with the dual meaning of *ser*, "to sit" and "to be," the form *seades* is not used in the sense
"sentaos."

Those of lesser rank mingle imperatives with less abrupt forms to maintain a gentlemanly tone, often (as noted earlier) displacing the command
form from the act commanded to a verb pertaining to the dialogic intercourse going forward: "¡Oídme, cavalleros . . . todos armados seades!"
(1685–87), "amos me dat las manos / que non me descubrades" (106–7),
and "catad cómmo las sirvades" (1359). The habit of finding substitutes
for the imperative makes all the more noticeable the insistent repetition of
"comed, conde" (which had been *comde* into the thirteenth century) to the
vanquished count of Barcelona, in a clear reaffirmation of group identity
and rejection of the inept outsider.

Though the king's future tense has a special force as a directive, the Cid
may also use it in addressing subordinates: "por Molina iredes, — í iazredes
una noch" (2635, followed by imperatives) and "vós iredes comigo" (3064,
also 1808, 2621). Some directive force remains when the action is to be de-

layed: "ál feredes adelant" (896, Minaya) and "por tu boca lo dirás" (3370, Martín Antolínez). The first plural attenuates a commanding tone: "Mesuraremos la posada—e quitaremos el rreinado" (211). A future form directed toward the audience has a hortatory effect in "odredes lo que fablava" (188). The conditional "veriedes" (726, 1228, 2158, etc.), spoken to the audience, has a counterpart also in dialogue: "saldrién del monesterio" (1353) and "bien casariemos con sus fijas" (1374). "Sabet" is also useful both in expostulations to the audience and in dialogue, often in litotes or antithetical statements: "Por muertas las dexaron,—sabed, que non por bivas" (2752) and "más nos preçiamos,—sabet, que menos no" (3300).

Besides variations in verb forms, and combined with them, a number of auxiliaries are available to make commands less direct. *Mandar* has singular subjects in both "Mandad coger la tienda" (208) and "mandedes buscar" (1072), and is favored for offering gifts: "mandédesle tomar" (3515). *Pensar* also admits imperative and subjunctive: "pensad de cavalgar" (1688), "pensedes de folgar" (1028b), and first plural "pensemos de cavalgar" (320).

Gradations are particularly numerous with *querer*: "Enviarvos quiero" (813, and 1271, 1274), "fablar querría" (104, also 538), and phrasing where two forms of the verb are paired, aptly emphasizing harmony of wills: "Si vós quisiéredes, Minaya,—quiero saber rrecabdo" (1257) and "Mas lo que él quisiere,—esso queramos nós" (1953); in a message, "no lo quiera olbidar" (1444); and in the king's formal request for the Cid's approval of the marriage, ten lines long (2072–81), with hortatory force escalating from "cometer quiero un ruego" to "¡dándoslas!" *Poder* carries a hortatory tone in "A nuestros amigos—bien les podedes dezir" (830, also 423) and an ironically desiderative sense in "pueden aver sospiros" (3358).

Yet another means of bringing delicacy to the making and granting of requests, a seemingly unidiomatic passive construction, comes up in this exchange between Don Jerónimo and the Cid: " '. . . pídovos un don—e séam' presentado, / las feridas primeras—que las aya yo otorgadas.' / Dixo el Campeador:—'Desaquí vos sean mandadas' " (1708–10); also "d'aquí sea mandada" (180) and "de mí seades servida" (284). All of these participles are in assonance, as they are in most of the twelve passive constructions noted by Menéndez Pidal (1954–56, 343), but the examples here have none of the forced quality that marks the repetition of participles, for instance, in *Fernán González*, and their function as courteous circumlocutions, not only as devices to make rhymes, seems to be confirmed in *Mocedades* (a point that will discussed more closely).

To reinforce this last conclusion we may turn from grammatical devices and cite the phrases adduced to forestall disapproval that accompany some hortatory utterances: "Lo que yo dixier—non lo tengades a mal" (530) is followed by "quiero" (533, 534). Other turns of phrase have already been noted, such as "Oíd, varones,—non vos caya en pesar" (313) and "Si a vós ploguiere, Minaya,—e non vos caya en pesar" (1270), as well as "Si vos cayesse en sabor" (1351) introducing conditionals "saldrién" and "irién." Minaya's "Campeador, fagamos—lo que a vós plaze" (1128) introduces subjunctives. The attenuating formulas are often less explicitly linked to the command: "Temprano dat çevada,—¡sí el Criador vos salve!" (420, also in 879–80), "¡Cavalgad, Minaya,—vós sodes el mio diestro braço!" (753, again 870), and "En buen ora nasquiestes de madre; / pensemos..." (379–80). Some of the poem's epithetic language has the function of mitigating and formalizing hortatory speech—inevitably, since so much of the direct discourse is hortatory, and epithets nearly always help to introduce speeches (as typically in 71, 2350). Finally, in a turn of phrase found in a prayer, the sense of courtesy normally observed toward humans is adapted to suit the otherworldly sphere. A metonymic displacement aptly provides desired indirectness in "válanme tus vertudes,—gloriosa Sancta María!" (217) and "¡Vuestra vertud me vala,—Gloriosa, en mi exida!" (221).

The foregoing accumulation of examples shows an extraordinary variety of modes of formulating commands, requests, and pleas. They suggest that the poet had a very keen sense of the subtleties of each social situation, reflected precisely in the choice of verb forms and verbal periphrases, as well as accompanying formulas, with attention to hierarchies and personalities and to the complexities of each new context. Most notable in all this is the avoidance of demands. The characters treat each other with a degree of consideration that surely impressed the presenter's audience as exemplary, as an admirable use of speech that also implied consideration for the audience itself, and appreciation of its presence. It too was being gently urged— to keep listening, to sympathize and believe, to admire the poet's mastery, to come back for more.

There is a broad middle ground between the two extremes of vaguely illocutionary speeches and specifically hortatory verb constructions, a middle ground occupied by a variety of desiderative expressions which account for a large proportion of the direct discourse of the poem. The poem's presence, its distinctive expressive personality, difficult to demonstrate analytically, does come into sharper focus in the light of its directive language. A thoroughgoing comparative study of hortatory devices in the various epic or quasi-epic texts, *Fernán González*, *Mocedades*, and *Roland*, might bring out more essential verbal habits in each. Here a more modest comparison is appropriate and will suffice to characterize this aspect of the clearly individualistic poetic manner of each work.

Fernán González, though closest to the *Cid* in time and space, is the farthest from it in the mentality it represents. As a bookish composition undoubtedly reflecting the author's background as a studious individual, it concentrates on principles of belief and behavior, sometimes presented in disputatious form, largely ignoring the social function of the text in performance. It is perhaps fair to say that, in contrast with the *Cid*, it has no dialogue—only pronouncements. Hortatory speeches often evoke no reported rejoinder, as in the following instance. The count explains to the monk Don Pelayo that he is a fugitive, all in indirect discourse, and receives the following response, to which the poem reports no answer:

> Recudio l' monje e dixo: "Ruego t' por Dios, amigo,
> si fuesse tu mesura, ospedasses conmigo
> dar te e yo pan de ordio ca non tengo de trigo,
> sabras com as de fer contra 'l tu enemigo."
> El cond Ferran Gonçalez, de todo bien conplido,
> del monje don Pelayo resçibio su convido . . .
> (str. 235f)[3]

The self-deprecatory, apologetic phrasing of this invitation is typical of the poem's attempts at social interchange. It properly reflects the humility central to Christian teaching, but as used in this work isolates the individual and discourages the meeting of minds and wills that is so well evoked in the *Cid*. So the count Don Yllán assures a Muslim potentate of his intention to betray his king: "digote yo verdat, amigo Vusarban, / si non te do España non coma yo mas pan, / de mi non fies mas que si fues yo un can" (44b–d).[4] Speeches begin with ceremonious formulas: "oit me, cavalleros, si Cristo vos perdon" [Hear me, knights, may Christ pardon you] (58c,

---

3. "The monk answered and said: 'I beg you for the sake of God, friend, / if it is in your good judgment, take lodging with me. / I will give you barley bread, for wheat bread I have not. / You will learn how to act against your enemy.' / The count Fernán González, perfect in all virtue, / accepted the invitation of the monk Don Pelayo."

4. "I tell you truly, friend Vusarbán, / if I do not deliver Spain to you, / may I not again eat bread; / trust me no more than if I were a dog."

202c), but then move into summaries of reasoned arguments that are about to follow. The discourse is introverted. Where people answer each other, it is in the form of systematic argument. The hero even takes God to task regarding failures of communication: "non nos quieres oir maguer que te llamamos, / non sabemos con queja que consejo prendamos" [you will not hear us, though we call upon you; in our extremity we know not what counsel to take] (189bc).

The *Mocedades de Rodrigo* exhibits stylistic affinity with the *Cid* in introducing some of its hortatory speeches with "merçed" (176, 374) and "Oit me" (71, 391, 410), and by verbal periphrases: "mandat gelos dar" (351, also 278), "querria" (427), "pensemos de andar" (405), and other first-plural, "lleguemos" (1008), and third-plural forms, "Caualguen vuestros reynos, et non sean en tardar lo" (1006). As in the *Cid*, most direct discourse in the poem is hortatory, but with differences: requests and orders are often abrupt—"datme" is particularly common—and formulaic refusals form a more fully developed complementary category: "sola mente non sea pensado" (495). A curse also broadens the inventory: "La mj maldezion haya, et non le ayude omne nado" (200). Requests directed to the king may be formalized by lengthy amplification, "Rey don Sancho Auarca, por amor de caridat, / fijo del conde don Sancho, mj sennor natural: / vayamos..." (96–98). As in the *Cid*, an ecclesiastic uses a passive construction with *otorgar* and related verbs. The pope speaks: "de mj sea otorgado / a ti, Mjro, episcopus palentino mucho onrrado" (191–92), and the king: "ssea te otorgado" (523). A disclaimer or preemptive apology is also reminiscent of the *Cid*: " 'Merçed,' dixo, 'sennor, non lo tengades a mal. ... Dat me ...' " (374–76). In short, as seen in its hortatory modes, *Mocedades* clearly continues a stylistic tradition already highly developed in the *Cid*, though managing it with less of the authentic tact and subtlety of the skilled live performance. The formulas have become more automatic, and their meaning attenuated.

Finally, the *Chanson de Roland* is of interest, in part because Spanish dependence on French epic formulism has been accorded great significance by some critics. In the sententious style of this poem, polite introductory formulas occupying a line or more, characteristic of the *Cid*, are absent. Commands and desideratives are straightforward, often introduced by *car*. The command form of the verb, with *vos* as subject, predominates strongly, although variations are not rare: the future: "Nu ferez, certes" (255); with *voleir*: "De Carlemagne vos voeill oïr parler" (522); *poeir* in "jo i puis aler ben" (258); periphrases, "Ben seit vostre comant!" (616), "salvez seiez"

(428); a third-person optative, "Fust i li reis, n'i oüssum damage" (1102). More characteristic of the peculiar language of this poem are two directive types that stand in high contrast with each other. One is seen in the abrupt commands of Charlemagne when he vents his exasperation during the dispute about who should be named envoy to the Saracens: "Alez sedeir, quant nuls ne vos sumunt!" (251; in Bédier's version, "Retournez vous asseoir, car nul ne vous a requis!"), and "Alez sedeir desur cel palie blanc! / N'en parlez mais, se jo nel vos cumant!" (272, "Allez vous rasseoir su ce tapis blanc! N'en parlez plus, si je ne vous l'ordonne!"). The other type is seen in Ganelon's lengthy colloquies with the Moors, in which he repeatedly represents Roland as the only Frank who is a serious threat to them and so persuades them to embrace his plan to bring about the hero's death (370–616). For 199 lines he uses no imperative forms and only one desiderative formula, "salvez seiez de Deu" (427), before relating Charlemagne's alleged demands to the Moorish ruler Marsile. Finally, when the plotting is nearly complete, but only in response to the Moor's questioning, he recommends a course of action: "Lessez la folie, tenez vos al saveir" (569), with two more command forms, "enveiez" (588) and "livrez" (592). Ganelon is an expert speaker, the most skilled in all the poem: "Par grant saver cumencet a parler / Cume celui ki ben faire le set" (426–27, "Par grand art il commence, en homme qui sait parler bien"). His use of eloquence for evil intent has no parallel in the *Cid*, in which excellence in speaking is a virtue shared by the performer with the heroic characters, who practice persuasiveness competitively as a reflection of the highest values held by the poet.

The esteem attached to good speaking, which assimilates the performer and his characters to each other, goes far to explain why the Beni-Gómez are poor speakers, both in choice of topic and in execution—with the exception of the sharp-tongued Asur González, whose speech is pungent but inappropriate—later ages would say in bad taste. The clearest instance of verbal ineptitude is in the single developed speech of Count Garçi Ordóñez, uncle and adviser of the Infantes, presented earlier as the Cid's arch-enemy, "que mal siémprel' buscó" (2998). The threat so announced evaporates when the count chooses the worst possible topic, the Cid's beard, to bring up at the court of judgment, along with the implied argument that rank confers rights to commit outrageous abuses (3271–79). A comparable instance of poor speaking occurs in the *Iliad*, where Thersites' speech is deficient in heroic style, which is conceived as a "proportion of words and deeds" (Martin 1989, 111). Agamemnon is also rhetorically ineffectual (Martin 1989, 62–64). Asur's character is out of proportion, "es largo de lengua, mas en lo ál no es tan pro" (2173). If, in the *Cid* as in the *Iliad*, a speech may serve to evaluate the speaker, and not to advance the plot (Martin 1989, 67), the inappropriateness of the discourse of the Beni-Gómez takes on an artistic justification that merits the attention of the modern reader, who habitually separates words from deeds and values the latter more highly. In his answering challenge, Muño Gustioz points to his adversary's deficiency, associating his falseness with his offensive behavior: "¡Calla! . . . Non dizes verdad—a amigo ni a señor, / falso a todos—e más al Criador . . . ¡Fazértelo he dezir,—que tal eres qual digo yo!" (3383–89). In this last line, the discrepancy between saying and doing has become the basis of the formulaic words of the challenge. The same defect is cited by Pero Vermúdez against the Infante Fernando: "Lengua sin manos, —¿cuémo osas fablar?" (3328), and permeates all three challenges.

Whereas those of the heroic group address the accused directly, the Beni-Gómez speak only to the court or to the king to defend themselves, except in one instance where Fernando addresses the Cid, only to see his words redirected to Pero Vermúdez (3293–95): "a mí lo dizen, a ti dan las oreiadas" (3304). Choice and identification of the intended hearer, elaborately formulaic as seen earlier in this analysis, was conditioned by the relative rank of speaker and addressee and, in the court, by whether one was making or refuting an accusation. The Cid is obviously conscious of the implications of choosing his addressee, and the medieval audience would also take note of the failure to speak directly to an adversary, given the competitive nature of speech normal in oral culture (see Ong 1967, 193, 197–98, and Edwards and Sienkewicz 1991, 29).

The suggestion of a parallel between the *Iliad* and the *Cid* presupposes each to be a product of an oral culture, agonistically toned, empathetic and participatory rather than objectively distant, more situational than abstract (Ong 1982, 43–49)—regardless of the degree to which the act of composition was done orally. By contrast, the composer of *Roland* has taken a significant step into the world of writing, giving the most powerful voice to a character with evil intentions. The audience may find the traitor's verbal dexterity at once admirable and unacceptable as the familiar plot unfolds. The role of the presenter now changes in *Roland*, as he is distanced more clearly from the poet and from the villainous characters, and the audience becomes more aware of each distinct role, including its own, as it judges Ganelon's speeches as good argument on his part and good artistic creation on the part of the poet, but evil in their aims. These distinctions might be neither totally absent from a presentation of the *Cid* nor clearly developed in *Roland*, but the latter gives evidence that the genre is developing a greater degree of literary self-consciousness and control.

In the *Cid*, the exhortations and commands are phrased to be most acceptable to the hearer of the poem as well as to the fictional addressee. One system of social intercourse, one code of courtesy, and one set of hierarchies are recognized as valid and as applicable both to those imagined and to those present. The characters vie with one another in speaking well, as the minstrel vies with other minstrels. Most of their speeches are bent toward influencing others' behavior. In the *Iliad* a special category of such directive acts is recognized and given the name *épea pteróenta*, "winged words" (Martin 1989, 31–32). A sense of an analogous category may well have been conveyed by the paralinguistic communicative devices—the expressive use of the voice—of the live performer of the *Cid*. While that suggestion must remain a matter for speculation, it is clear that the sensitivity of each speaking personage to the subtleties of each social situation that develops—the hierarchies, debts owed, sex of speaker and listener, and the nature of the response being required, urged, suggested, insinuated, or merely counseled—all these are reflected in the delicate choice of linguistic forms. The resulting sense of presence, reminiscent of a ritual presentation, points to a habit of oral composition latent in the poem's background. The verbal etiquette seems to seize upon all the resources provided by the language and fortifies the sense of a ritualized existence, one that is intimately identified with a social group—the audience—that remains closely knit through its conversance with the subtleties of the language and customs. That etiquette is a powerful instrument for building the sense of community needed both by the *juglar* and by his listeners. In this connection we have noted how the language easily turns ironic when used with outsiders, as in the dealings with the moneylenders. A fine line is drawn between forms of expression that straightforwardly bolster group solidarity and those that do so by setting up oppositions between the group and those outside it.

In one significant instance, this is done to place the "good Moor," the Cid's tributary Abengalbón, in a favorable light, even accentuating his benign image by tingeing it with exoticism. As is normal for the poem's characters, he is introduced by his own words, which are perfectly proper but unlike anyone else's: in greeting the Cid's knights upon their arrival at his city of Molina, he affirms his loyalty by denying any ill-will: "¡Venides, los vassallos—de mio amigo natural! / A mí non me pesa,—sabet, mucho me plaze" (1478–80). In his next appearance he speaks even more oddly. In particular, he again denies any ill-will toward the Cid, apparently adding a note of Oriental resignation to his protestations of loyalty:

Ondrar vos hemos todos, — ca tal es la su auze,[5]
maguer que mal le queramos, — non ge lo podremos fer,
en paz o en guerra, — de lo nuestro abrá,
múchol' tengo por torpe — qui non conosçe la verdad.

(1523–26)[6]

The several negative clauses, along with *querer mal*, "guerra," and "torpe," all seem slightly superfluous and out of place on the occasion of a cordial reception, adding curious notes to the kiss on the shoulder (1518–19) and the highly original greeting, "¡Tan buen día convusco!" (1520), which does not resemble any other in the poem. *Convusco*, in particular, might have been recognized by many in the audience as corresponding to the ʿalaykum of Arabic greetings, as in *salaam ʿalaykum*, "peace (be) with you." Since "peace" should be wished by Muslims only to other Muslims (Muslim, like Islam, is formed on the same root as *salaam*), the substitute "good day," combined with ʿalaykum, "convusco," is a plausible calque on an Arabic greeting.[7] These insinuations of a mentality at once alien and attractive are good indicators of the finely tuned sense of linguistic identity that unites the minstrel both with his epic characters and with his audience.

Ceremonial Tableaux

Methods of presenting the Cid's existence as removed from the ordinary, yet at the same time a real, believable human being, have been brought out by some of the best literary commentary that has been done on the poem

5. Raquel also makes a reference to the Cid's *ventura*, a synonym of *auze*, which is somewhat unexpected in the given context. He requests a favor: "assí es vuestra ventura,—grandes son vuestras gananças. / una piel vermeia,—morisca e ondrada, / Çid, beso vuestra mano—en don que la yo aya" (177–79).
6. "We all ought to honor him, for such is his good fortune; / even if we wish him ill, we cannot do it [ill] to him. / In peace or war he will get some of our property. / I regard anyone as stupid who does not recognize the truth."
7. I am indebted to S. G. Armistead for information on the greeting.

(see, for example, Castro 1956, Salinas 1958, and Alonso 1973b). The hero's actions, words, and gestures are those of a man perfectly adapted to his station in life, but they are formalized, elevated, stylized—in a word, ritualized. Castro's remark to that effect has been noted (p. 43). We have suggested that the myth existed before it was linked with the Cid, that it provided the original framework for the story, that the beast belonged to the initiation account. The hero's idealized behavior is inherited from other, perhaps half-forgotten heroes. In less mythic parts of the poem, group as well as individual action is aggrandized through formal poetical language, as pointed out by Alonso in discussing the battle of Alcocer ("enbraçan los escudos—delant los coraçones . . ." [715]). Such passages oblige the critic to qualify claims regarding the "verismo" of the poem.

The ritual nature of the textual fabric is another condition essential to its elevated tone. Several passages will serve as examples of formalized action and speech. Constants in the fabric of these scenes are simplification, balance, and rhythmic repetition of what is done and said, resulting in a sense of fine tuning, of a controlled movement from the beginning to the end of each segment, which harmonizes with the paratactic manner of the poem and is enhanced by phonetic effects. As a first example we may take the initial meeting and dialogue between the Cid and Doña Jimena.

The poem prepares the meeting carefully, with phonetic resonances evoking the action being related. A laisse begins as the Cid arrives at Cardeña at dawn, as marked by the crowing of the cock, "Apriessa cantan los gallos" (235). Contrasting sounds announce his arrival on horseback in the second hemistich, "e quieren quebrar albores" (235). Six more rhymes in -or(es) (236–41) make sonorous echoes of the initial line. In strong phonetic contrast with his abrupt arrival is the line telling of the prayer of the abbot in the company of Jimena and her ladies—her first appearance in the poem: "rrezava los matines—abuelta de los albores" (238), with voiced continuants (in Old Spanish) z, v, voiced s, and the harmonious similarity of "abuelta" and "albores." The Cid arrives as in a procession. Jimena is also in a gathering visualized geometrically; as befits her status, she kneels together with five noble ladies (239). The abbot then moves also in formal procession, in a powerfully alliterative line: "con lunbres e con candelas— al corral dieron salto" (244), with sounds *con-lun-con-can-co* and *del-al-al-al*. The sharp initial sonorities accompanying the dawn melt into quiet words and solemn movement. The meeting is further delayed by the joyful reception by the abbot and his attendants, and delayed again as practical matters are seen to. Through these, the poem introduces the approaching meeting by showing the wife and daughters as the Cid's primary objects of concern—a motif to be confirmed at the end of the scene (283–84).

Finally, after all these preliminaries, Doña Jimena's appearance with her retinue is announced by a solemn "afévos." She presents herself with extreme formality, which she will maintain throughout the scene. As happens nowhere else in the poem, the usual two-line introduction to a speech (see p. 93) is doubled, with two lines by the narrator and two occupied by the formulaic exordium. If the length of the introductory phrasing can be taken as a measure of the importance of the speech, as is usually true in the poem, then the dialogue, conveying mutual respect, affection, and a complete meeting of minds of the two, during which the Cid states the purpose of his existence, surely expresses one of the poem's primary messages: the essential role of woman in society, to whom all the man's efforts are ultimately dedicated.

The presentation:

> Ant el Campeador doña Ximena — fincó los inoios amos,
> llorava de los oios, — quísol' besar las manos:
> "¡Merçed, Canpeador, — en ora buena fuestes nado!"
>
> (264–66)

Doña Jimena switches to the women's assonance, *í-a* (see pp. 131–32), summarizes the situation faced by all the women present, and requests nothing more than "conseio," words of support:[8]

> "¡Merçed, ya Cid — barba tan conplida!
> Fém ante vós — yo e vuestras fijas,
> iffantes son — e de días chicas,
> con aquestas mis dueñas — de quien só yo servida.
> Yo lo veo — que estades vós en ida
> e nós de vós — partir nos hemos en vida.
> ¡Dadnos conseio — por amor de Sancta María!"
>
> (268–73)

---

8. *Conseio* had a range of meanings not easily sorted out (Menéndez Pidal 1954–56, 591). Here the most appropriate, in view of the Cid's response, is probably the one found in *Fernán González*, where, after the destruction of Spain by the Arabs, the Christians are starving and desperate: "Perdieron dellos con miedo los sentidos, / matavan a las madres, en braços a sus fijos, / nos' podien dar conseio mugeres nin maridos, / andavan en grand miedo muchos enloquecidos" (95).

He echoes her factual tone. More notably, he patterns his speech after hers and repeats a number of her words and phrases. These will be underlined here, making allowances for the change of speaker. The Cid moves solemnly, "enclinó las manos" (274), and joins Jimena in weeping. His speech, modeled on hers, is the completely satisfying response she has asked for. It defines their respective roles and confirms their common feelings.

> "Ya doña Ximena, — la mi mugier tan conplida,
> commo a la mi alma — yo tanto vos quería.
> Ya *lo vedes* — que *partir nos emos en vida,*
> *yo iré* — e vós — fincaredes remanida.
> ¡Plega a Dios — e a *Sancta María*
> que aún con mis manos — case estas *mis fijas,*
> o que *dé* ventura — e algunos días vida
> e vós, mugier ondrada, — *de mí seades servida!*"
> (278–84)

Several of the repeated words are in the rhyming position, stressing the shared feeling, an effect intensified by the distinctive *i-a* assonance.[9] The phrases "yo lo veo" and "Ya lo vedes" bring out the harmony of perception: "to see" is often "to understand" in the poem, and is so used at other critical moments as well (see pp. 120 and 153). The repetition is not mechanical or monotonous to the reader; on the contrary, it is what gives power to these plain, objectively worded statements, which build to a moment of great pathos.

The scene is helpful in defining the difference between ritual and drama. Repetition of known facts by the speakers—known by themselves and by the audience—becomes a kind of incantation. Her words are apt for his message. Individual voices are blended, reaching toward universality as single personalities are submerged and feelings are joined with their conditioning circumstances (see pp. 143–44 for a comparable example at lines 666–78). The effect of anonymity recalls effects achieved by other tech-

---

9. Of course, sharing does not imply equality. Jimena requests support, but offers it only in the form of prayer (as he does also), and she refers to "vuestras fijas," while in turn he calls them "mis fijas" (although he speaks to her of "vuestras fijas" in 1768, when the topic is his role as "servidor" to the ladies). Ultimate responsibility rests with him. Moreover, a false note is struck in his hope of marrying the daughters "con mis manos." The sinister power of the Infantes de Carrión will take the matter out of his hands, "él vos casa ca non yo" (2204), and it will not be restored. In response to the marriage proposal of the princes of Navarre and Aragon, he avoids taking any initiative, telling the king, "Vós las casastes antes,—ca yo non, / afé mis fijas—en vuestras manos son" (3406-7).

niques in Greek theater, the masks and the chorus. If this scene were mounted with actors, it would be difficult to avoid banality; individual figures impersonating the characters on the stage, trying to "interpret" their individual feelings through the stylized language, would find themselves mouthing formulas at once too plain and too wordy to bring to life. The unifying words "yo lo veo" and "ya lo vedes" might be the most refractory of all, as their apparent emptiness would invite pomposity. Those words are in fact metatextual, structuring a participatory experience, not describing a perception to onlookers.

The words of prayer spoken by both man and wife underline the ritual quality of their dialogue. After this exchange they do one more thing together before his departure. They go to the church, where Jimena's prayer ends with the same sentiment he has expressed to her: "quando oy nos partimos,—en vida nos faz iuntar" (365).

The repetition and counterbalanced wording, with periodic rhythms of sound, word, and sense, can be even more marked in narrative segments. The actions and movements of the personages are visualized more effectively than in most medieval literature, in a stylized geometry that is synchronized with the flow of the poem's language. The effect would be intensified if the poem were chanted. The battle of Alcocer shows the technique in a type scene that was probably already traditional when it appeared in the *Cid*; it is repeated later in the poem (3615–22), resurfaces in the *Mocedades* (930–34), and has French analogues. It turns the great battle into a linguistic artifact, a sequence of balanced phrases, grammatical and conceptual parallelisms, and rhetorical patterns. It was treated masterfully by Alonso (1973b, 116–18); here a few lines are chosen for their almost mathematical patterning:

> trezientas lanças son, — todas tienen pendones;
> seños moros mataron, — todos de seños colpes;
> a la tornada que fazen — otros tantos [muertos] son.
> Veriedes tantas lanças — premer e alçar,
> tanta adágara — foradar e passar,
> tanta loriga — falsar e desmanchar,
> tantos pendones blancos — salir vermeios en sangre,
> tantos buenos cavallos — sin sos dueños andar.
> (723–30)

The language suggests familiarity with the experience of war but seeks a level other than the verisimilar. Authenticating details of battle, such as equipment, topography, and tactics, are indeed present in the poem, but the actualities of battle, such as fear, pain, fatigue, discouragement, and loss of comrades (some of which loom large in *Fernán González*), are sublimated as in a ritual reenactment. Here the most vivid evocation of carnage, perhaps, is "tantos pendones blancos—salir vermeios en sangre" (729), which can be taken as a deft play of two color words by a listener with a weak stomach, and yet would not offend the seasoned warrior as mere talk inadequate to the topic. Elsewhere in the poem, the repeated line "e por el cobdo ayuso—la sangre destellando" (501, etc.) conjures up an image that could itself be called distilled, perhaps of dewlike drops glistening in the sunlight. The reality of a blood-soaked sword, arm, and hand would in fact be gruesome, and a slippery or sticky mess to contend with in trying to manage the weapon. But the figures are seen from a distance; they are on display, like the Cid and Minaya in the council of war (see pp. 143–44).

A segment in which the linguistic structure takes on an iconic or representational quality, mimicking the skilled disposition of troops in an encampment, encompasses laisse 27:

> Bien puebla el otero, — firme prende las posadas,
> los unos contra la sierra — e los otros contra la agua.
> El buen Canpeador, — que en buen ora nasco
> derredor del otero,— bien çerca del agua
> a todos sos varones — mandó fazer una cárcava
> que de día nin de noch — non les diessen arrebata,
> que sopiessen que Mio Çid — allí avié fincança.
>
> (557–63)

Of the many phonetic and syntactic echoes of this passage, a select few many be noted. As the second hemistich of each line completes or complements the meaning of the first, the second line of each pair takes on the same function within the couplet (with the third line, "el buen Canpeador . . . ," as an extra insertion). The synonyms "otero" and "sierra" of the three first hemistichs twice are balanced by their antitheses "agua" and "río" in the following half-line. Along with various consonantal patterns, the vowel echoes of "Bien puebla el" and "bien çerca del" help bring out the unity of the first four lines. The heavy repetition does not produce an effect of unpleasant insistence or crudeness. (That this is true of the poem as a whole may be due in large part to the irregularity of the meter, which, if viewed as an asset rather than a defect, can be seen to lend flexibility and delicacy to the poetic form.) The words "que de día nin de noch non les diessen" make up a kind of phonetic palindrome, with "noch" as its axis, surrounded by negative *n*'s and reverberating *d*'s followed by front vowels. To be sure, many of the alliterations are provided by the language, but it is obvious in the first two lines, and probably true throughout, that the poet made the most of that raw material. The rhythmic patterning, which is continued into the next laisse, brings out the symmetry and hence the fixity, the "fincança" in the final summarizing word, of the Cid's position (one which, paradoxically, he later pretends to abandon in disorder). The versatility of the formulaic language is demonstrated when the Moors in their turn move in to besiege Alcocer, and the text almost repeats itself: "Fincaron las tiendas—e prendend las posadas" (656). This time the constant movement, not the "fincança" of the troops, is the main theme, used to bring out the menacing presence of the Moorish horde: "Creçen estos virtos . . . ; de día e de noch—enbueltos andan en armas . . . muchos son . . . grande es" (1657–60), with resounding Arabic military words "arrobdas" and "almofalla" to heighten the effect.

The prose version of laisse 33 found in the *Crónica de veinte reyes* expresses in simple narrative form the information that the poem develops into a chanted tableau. "Otro dia mando el Cid posar los unos contra el rio e los otros contra la sierra, e fizo fazer una cárcava aderredor de ssi, por guardarse de rrebate de dia e de noche" (Powell 1983, 124). Here the Cid is presented as a capable tactician and commander. In the poetic text, he establishes himself as a presence—a trick aided by slipping from singular to plural verb forms and back again. This blurring of distinctions between subjects reminds the reader of the Cid's first exchange with Jimena, in which he adapts her words to a statement of noble purpose. The poet's skill in the use of language is such that the *Cid* almost escapes the limitations of the "yo," as the poet exploits the grammar to convey the experience of feelings and opinions held in common.

In a more overtly ritual scene, the power of nonverbal communication and the intimate interrelationship of persons, perceptions, and places reach their highest expression. When, after years of separation, the wife and daughters arrive at Valencia, the poem partially repeats the pattern of their previous meeting. Again their face-to-face confrontation is delayed by a celebration. Again Jimena, at her husband's feet, speaks formally of her afflictions and her presence before him and before God, in the company of her daughters. As in their earlier meeting, the two weep and embrace. But there is a great difference: now they have a place to which they belong and which belongs to them. The Cid invites the women to see the great city "que vos yo he ganada" (1607).

> Adeliñó Mio Çid — con ellas al alcáçar,
> allá las subié — en el más alto logar.
> Oios vellidos — catan a todas partes,
> miran Valençia — cómmo iaze la çibdad
> e del otra parte — a oio han el mar,
> miran la huerta — espessa es e grand;
> alçan las manos — por a Dios rrogar
> d'esta ganançia — cómmo es buena e grand.
>
> (1610–17)

A ritual act of possession has been prepared. The instrument of possession is the women's eyes, which have never seen any view comparable to this one. Suddenly, surprisingly, the poet shifts attention to the eyes. In the absence of any word of grammatical subordination in this paratactic passage, they become the controlling agent that structures it, that assumes the subordinating power. With their structural control the eyes combine great emotional force. The "oios vellidos," full of amazement, embrace the three parts of the scene, "çibdad," "mar," and "huerta." The audience imagines simultaneously the beauty of the eyes, the astonishment they express, and the beautiful view they behold. The very simple language, balanced in repetitive cadences, is highly effective: synonymous active verbs "catan," "a ojo an," and "miran" and the plain adjectives "espessa" and "grand" all magnify the marvelous effect of this view, which neither poet nor audience has probably ever seen.[10] The ritual raising of the hands provides a fitting closure to a scene in which no word is spoken, and which makes no pretense to realism.

For the Cid, this joyful reception has been a recapitulation in reverse, not only of his leave-taking from his family, but also of his departure from Vivar. There, as here, the text concentrates on the act of seeing in relation to possession. At Valencia the poet chooses three rough synonyms of *ven*: "catan," "miran," "a oio an," and again "miran." At the poem's beginning it was "estávalos catando" and "vio," with a select inventory of telling details and with adjectives representing abandonment ("abiertas," "vazías"):

---

10. After the Cid's death in 1099, Valencia reverted to Moorish hands and was not reconquered until 1238.

"Vio puertas abiertas—e uços sin cañados, / alcándaras vazías,—sin pielles e sin mantos, / e siñ halcones—e sin adtores mudados" (3–5). The technique of constructing an imagined scene is the same in the two passages, perfectly adapted to convey either deprivation or abundance. The poet's sense of ritual dictates the emphasis on the visible scene, the identification with a place and its symbolic content, the sense of sight as an instrument of power—as seen again in "Todo el bien que yo he,—todo lo tengo delant" (1634). Elsewhere, as in the leave-taking from Jimena, "Yo lo veo," "Ya lo vedes," and with the young girl as well: "ya lo vee el Cid—que del rrey non avié gracia" (50), eyesight is the instrument of understanding. Repeatedly in the poem, to see is to know: to be aware (114), to recognize (1096), to foresee (1249). Scenes and actions rarely lie. The poem is made up of them. It is true that most stories are so structured, but in the poem the technique of visually linking action, place, and the characters' experience is particularly well developed and undoubtedly reflects habits of perceiving and thinking.

The next ascent to the tower is again for the purpose of seeing, but this time the landscape is covered with Moorish tents. Now the Cid wants the ladies to watch him in battle. Uncharacteristically nonchalant about the risks to them, he reassures them repeatedly, promising riches as well as a close look at the Moorish battle-drums that are terrifying them. The key verb continues to be *ver*:

> "Mis fijas e mi mugier — ver me an lidiar,
> en estas tierras agenas — verán las moradas cómmo se fazen,
> afarto verán por los oios — cómmo se gana el pan."
> (1641–43)

The hero will perform, doing what he does best against an exotic background of "moradas." The ladies are the subject of *ver* four more times in this and the next laisse: "alçavan los ojos,—tiendas vieron fincadas" (1645, and 1653, 1662, 1666b), and again when the Cid returns after the second day's battle: "¿Vedes el espada sangrienta—e sudiento el cavallo?" (1752). The two metonyms for male force and violence must be seen at close range. It is the counterpart of an initiation for the women and their attendants, and as in the male initiation, sexual sequels are implied. Now wealth is plentiful, and weddings are discussed (1763–69, 1802). Being watched by his womenfolk has been important to the Cid, "créçem' el coraçón— porque estades delant" (1655); for his part the poet seems to be so concerned with the visual experience that here he loses sight of the horror and danger of the battle, and a force of 4100 Christians defeats 50,000 of the enemy almost casually. It is the poet's "veriedes" transferred from the minstrel's audience to the Cid's audience, the female characters. The hero's actions toward the ladies are more spontaneous, less formalized, than usual; the poem gives him a new human touch without compromising his aura of greatness. A presenter who presumed to occupy his place at this moment, and to imitate him, would destroy the scene along with his own credibility.

The chief focus is not visual as in the preceding instance, but verbal, in the feasting that accompanies the reconciliation of the hero with the king. This feast, one of the most formalized episodes in the poem, provides a model against which to evaluate the treatment accorded the count of Barcelona. Both episodes are carried out with acute awareness of the etiquette of feasting, which is understood as a feature of the gift economy. Both exemplify the competitive nature of the proceeding, and both show some stretching of the rules, intended to place the Cid in a favorable light when compared to his competitor.

The scenes with the king (2013–67) are designed to bring him closer to the inner circle represented by the *mesnada* of the hero, all the while giving the latter the upper hand. In contrast, the actions with the count are meant to distance him even further from the chosen group, by reversing the ceremony of ritual feasting, normally an affirmation of alliance and friendship achieved by an appearance of camaraderie. In his pioneering study of the gift economy, Mauss (1923–24, 150–51) points out that even among friends, the links forged by receiving sumptuous gifts might become uncomfortably strong and entail unwanted future obligations, raising awkward problems for someone who would really prefer to decline an offer. Convivial eating was strongly symbolic of alliance and obligation; so one should not join an enemy for a meal ("Aussi ne doit-on pas manger chez son ennemi").[11]

The analogy of the invitation to a meal with a gift (one "gives" a banquet; see Benveniste 1973, 486), as well as the expectation to reciprocate, is

11. With reference to Indo-European society in general and Greek and Roman in particular: "The feast with an abundance of food, the expense which is purely ostentatious and intended to maintain rank, the festive banquet—all this would have no sense if those who had the profit of this largesse were not committed to requite it by the same means" (Benveniste 1971, 279).

made explicit by Abengalbón when Alvar Fáñez offers him a feast: "Plazme d'esta presentaia, / antes d'este terçer día—vos la daré doblada" (1532–33). (The word *presentaia* clearly means "ceremonial gift" in six examples where it designates offerings conveyed by Minaya to the king, is "gift" also in line 516, and, with apparent irony, refers to the money offered by the Moors of Castejón for the Cid's portion of the property he has seized from them [522].)

The particular interest of the official repatriation and reconciliation with Alfonso (1985–2012) derives from the hero's management of the entire ceremony. Having dressed up and picked his companions, he painstakingly secures the women in Valencia and heads for the Tajo. The king has already reached the appointed place, which gives the Cid (and the poet) the opportunity to inaugurate the new scene and action by his arrival. He then proceeds as planned, "commo lo comidía" (2020), first making extreme demonstrations of submission, on hands and knees, taking grass in his teeth, weeping: "assí sabe dar omildança" (2024). Taken aback by such excess, the king commands him to rise, "besad las manos—ca los piedes non; / si esto non feches,—non avredes mi amor" (2028–29). But the king is obliged to acquiesce to the scenario of the Cid, who respectfully demurs and remains kneeling, "inoios fitos sedié," asking for pardon "assí estando" (2032), that is, still on his knees, and for all present to hear. When the king pronounces his pardon, the Cid retains the initiative, "Yo lo rreçibo" (2036b), giving thanks first to God "e después a vós" (2037), and finally to the select group of followers, "e a estas mesnadas" (2038), who are acting as witnesses. For the Cid to perform each step properly and say exactly the right thing is plainly of some importance to the poet, who by these actions defines the relationship between the two men. And he puts to good use his own professional instinct for the nuances of oral performance. His hero has finessed the scene, making the most of its ritual character.

The further details of the proceeding continue to show the Cid in control to a surprising degree, and acutely conscious of the significance of each action. He invites the king to the first of the celebratory banquets that are to be given. Instead, Alfonso, attentive to the established proprieties, declares himself to be the host for the first day. The poet can then put the Cid in the advantageous position, able to offer the second feast and outdo his ruler: as all agree, "passado avié tres años—no comieran meior" (2067).[12] This

---

12. In the ballad "El Cid en las cortes," which Menéndez Pidal considered to be of epic origin, and which recalls imprecisely the law court at Toledo, the Cid recalls the king's role in

offering is part of his program of ceremonial giving, designed to build up his roster of *pagados*, of people who owe him favors.[13] The giving continues; the king is embarrassed, "enbargado" (2147), by the lavish presents he receives, and as the Cid has promised—"cuedo quel' avrá pro" (2130)—each wedding guest is to be offered great wealth (2257). Such a show of generosity was in fact not reckless or disinterested. The poem shows that not all those who might receive gifts are willing to do so and accept the attendant obligations: "Qui aver quier prender—bien era abastado" (2260, as again at the close of the cortes: "tales í á que prenden,—tales í á que non" [3501]). The carefully managed act of pardon and the apparently free but in fact tightly controlled giving provide two examples of the emphasis on memorable public acts characteristic of a culture still largely preliterate and too orally based to place much credence in written agreements made in private. These examples stand out too because the poet uses them to foreground the Cid at the king's expense—although I would not claim, like Edmund De Chasca (1972, 74–79), that moral rivalry between them is a chief theme of the poem.[14] Here the Cid exercises power—which only exists in its exercising—as part of the social ritual.

As for other ceremony, except for lines 2182–2204, where the progress and mood of the ritual proceedings are clouded by doubts about the Infantes, the more than two hundred lines that complete the second cantar after the Cid's pardon are completely given over to it: the king's highly public request and urging of the marriage, the delivery of the daughters and the Infantes, the gifts, the appointment of a sponsor, more gifts, the departure of hero and guests, the preparations and conferences before the wedding,

---

the marriages of Elvira and Sol, emphasizing in particular the feast he gave for the king at the meeting by the Tajo, and the wedding feasts: "cien cabezas matara—de mi ganado mayor / de gallinas y capones,—no os lo cuento, no" (Díaz Mas 1994, 112).

13. The custom and institution of gift-giving is treated more explicitly in the account recorded in the *PCG* of the second wedding of the daughters: "et quando al partir, non ouo y cauallero de quantos con los infantes vinieron a quien non diesse el Cid algo, a qual cauallo, a qual mula, a qual panno, a qual dineros, de guysa que todos fueron sus pagados" (2:631b31–48). The giving was supposed to have the appearance of disinterested spontaneity, which created an atmosphere of pretense that was reflected in the somewhat hypocritical use of the term *pagado*, literally "pleased," "gratified" (Duby 1974, 48, also Duggan 1989, 31, and Montgomery 1994).

14. The competition here was more like what prevailed in twelfth-century France: "The court was . . . a place of rivalry where everyone competed in extravagance" (Duby 1974, 234). This was true in Irish and Germanic as well as Roman and Romance cultures (Benveniste 1973, 228–79).

the palace and church wedding ceremonies, the celebration, and the conclusion. The educational or indoctrinating "encyclopedic" function of epic
(Havelock 1963, 43–49 et passim) is the primary motivator of this section.

The ritual behavior portrayed in this reconciliation, and to a slightly
lesser extent in all dealings with the king, has affinities with the poem's formalized introductions to direct discourse (pp. 93–95). A bridge between the
two communicative systems is the ceremonial kiss, required in many greetings and leave-takings (particularly those including the king), used often in
petitions, and frequently having contractual force. The part of the body at
which to plant the kiss is stipulated according to occasion and hierarchy; it
may be the feet, the hands, the mouth, the eyes; with Moors it is different:
the shoulder, neck, and exceptionally the arm or knee, according to copi-
ous data gathered by Menéndez Pidal on *besar* and its partial synonym
saludar (1954–56, 506–9, 837). *Besar*, with fifty-seven occurrences in the
poem, is among the verbs that most frequently replace the verb of saying in
introductions to direct speech. Solemn movements of the hands are also frequent reminders of the formalized action characteristic of the poem (Smith
1977, 231–42).

Nonparticipants

"Cozina" plainly means "feast" in the line introducing the Cid's offering to
the king beside the Tajo: "El Campeador—a los sos lo mandó / que
adobassen cozina—pora quantos que í son" (2063–64). This sense of the
word is corroborated in other texts (Menéndez Pidal 1954–56, 604–5). The
phrase *adobar cozina* also appears when the Cid holds the defeated count
of Barcelona under guard in his tent:

> de todas partes — los sos se ayuntavan;
> plogo a Mio Çid — ca grandes son las gananças.
> A Mio Çid don Rodrigo — grant cozínal' adobavan,
> el conde don Remont — non ge lo preçia nada,
> adúzenle los comeres, — delant ge los paravan.
> (1015–19)

The Cid's men have gathered and the feast is prepared. As always, it will be
communal; neither the Cid nor his men will abstain. Lines 1015–17, parat-

actically interrelated, make clear that the meal is part of the sharing of the spoils of battle. This is the occasion for the invitation to the count: "Comed, conde, d'este pan—e beved d'este vino" (1025). In speaking of "este pan," the Cid is not serving the count; he is partaking of the same food that has been placed before the prisoner.[15] The first line of the count's answer (1028b) again tells the listener that the hero is in the act of feasting. For three days, as the division of spoils, including goods and victuals, continues (1031), he will take no part:

> "Comede, don Rodrigo, — e pensedes de folgar,
> que yo dexar me é morir, — que non quiero comer."
> Fasta terçer día — nol' pueden acordar;
> ellos partiendo — estas ganançias grandes,
> nol' pueden fazer comer — un muesso de pan.
>
> (1028b–32)

Routinely, after a battle, the victor was expected to provide sustenance to any prisoner (Corfis 1983–84). It is not simply the sustenance offered, but the company proposed, that the count cannot accept. The Cid's solution to the standoff, which by now has gone far enough, is to allow the count to eat in the company of two of his own captured knights rather than that of his captor, and for all three to go free. The offer is not clear in the text when it is made: "e si vós comiéredes—don yo sea pagado, / a vós—e a dos fijos dálgo / quitar vos he los cuerpos . . ." (1034–34b); but the count evidently understands that he will have his own company, since he now happily accepts, and the meal is in fact shared with two knights: "con dos cavalleros — que el Çid le avié dados / comiendo va el conde . . ." (1051–52). The Cid makes no other concession; the meal still stands as a trial and a spectacle, a travesty of the good will that properly attends a banquet: "sobr'él sedié—el que en buen ora nasco: / 'Si bien non comedes, conde,—don yo sea pagado, / aquí feremos la morada . . .' " (1054–55). This could be a parody of the custom of reaching agreements while at table

15. The chronicles, in adapting this episode, do not show the Cid personally making the offer of food and drink (Powell 1983, 131–32; PCG 2:533b25–534b9). As often happens, the chroniclers remove all traces of malice on the hero's part and make the dialogue between the Cid and the count into a model of genteel civility, e.g., "El conde ovo grand plazer de aquello que el Cid dizia que le non daria nada de lo que le tomara" (Powell 1983, 132). The chronicles' common source also must have contained a sanitized version. The extant text of the *Poema*, too, obscured some of the interaction. The manuscript is corrupt at several points in the episode.

(though the poem provides no explicit evidence of that custom). The partial identification of banquet-giving with gift-giving may also account for the Cid's seemingly superfluous assurances that he has no intention of returning "un dinero malo" (1042, also 1069–75) of what he has taken from the count and his army. He knows the rules well, but on this occasion (as with the moneylenders) is making his own variation on them.[16]

I insist on the communal nature of the offered meal and the ritualistic form of the celebration, because the sense of community and ritualized activity are basic to the poem as a whole, as seen throughout this study, and to the image of the hero as head of a clan or tribe, opposed in varying degrees to all other such groups. The inversion or reversal of proper ritual has been seen in detail in the story of the Infantes de Carrión (pp. 42–51). The building of solidarity within the group has been observed in several instances. Its corollary, scorn for outsiders, is an extremely powerful reinforcement of that cohesion. The objects of humor and derision, namely the usurers, the count, the Beni-Gómez, are all outsiders whose values are inappropriate and who fail to adjust to the rules and customs of the privileged inner circle. Within this framework the Cid is an impeccable hero. Any abuse he metes out to outsiders is deserved and suitable. To expect him, in the literate twentieth century, to have a wider vision, to extend equal good will or fairness to every human being he encounters, is to place oneself among the deluded outsiders.[17] An effort to understand him as he is and, like it or not, to see ourselves in him, will teach us much more than attempts to justify his actions by standards other than his own. Achilles and Roland are hugely destructive in their fragile pride, Odysseus sometimes lies simply for the sake of lying, and the Cid, as a cultural icon, upholds his own values and gives affront to those of others. They are epic heroes because of these traits, not in spite of them.

The poet himself gives especially harsh treatment to the count as an outsider: "es muy follón" (1060). The only other personage to receive an explicitly negative evaluation from the author is the poorly balanced Asur González (see pp. 109–10). *Follón* has long been taken to mean "vanidoso," based on an imagined affinity with *fuelle*. But in fact the poet's

16. Critics, most recently Montaner (1993, 491–93), have been somewhat reluctant to see the Cid's conduct with the count as tribal rather than moralistic in a broad sense. But, unlike the *PCG* (2:533b28–29, 534a5) and its source, the chronicle of Lucas de Tuy (Tudense), the poem gives no hint that the Cid acted in a spirit of generosity toward his wealthy enemy.

17. On the outsider who does not "possess" the vernacular, known as a "lame," see Labov 1972, 258.

choice of this word is more damaging. He takes a Catalan vocabulary item meaning "iracundo," of Germanic origin, and cognate with French *felun*, "cruel, malvado," "vil," "traidor," also frequently identified with French *fol*, "necio, loco," and earlier Spanish *follía* "locura, imprudencia, maldad" (Corominas-Pascual 1980–91, 2:926–27). As in his use of *franco* (1068, in this episode), it is probable that the author took the occasion to mock not only the count and Catalans, but also French epic heroes and jongleurs. In *Roland, fel / felun* (nom. / acc.) and its derivatives occur a total of thirty-six times; *fol* and its derivatives fifteen times (Duggan 1969, s.vv.). Such a heavy incidence of abusive language is incompatible with the tone of the *Cid* and must have jarred on the ears of Spanish *juglares* as they came into contact with their northern colleagues. As for tribalism on the part of the *juglar*, it is of course pardonable even by modern standards.

"Over the course of the last two decades, it has gradually become clear that ritual, etiquette and other strongly habituated forms of practical discourse and discursive practice do not just encode and transmit messages, but they play an active and important role in the construction, maintenance, and modification of the borders, structures, and hierarchic relations that characterize and constitute society itself" (Lincoln 1989, 75). The structures as seen in the poem are specific to each society and automatically erect their own borders. Structures outside those borders are perceived simplistically, as poorly developed and crude; they are perceived in terms of convenient stereotypes and, of course, may be regarded as comical.

So, though the Moors are not usually objects of laughter in the poem, their loss of Alcocer to the Cid, taken as a literary creation, depends on a stereotype that had a basis in fact. When the Cid, after besieging the fortress for fifteen weeks, feigns a hasty retreat, the Moors rush out to seize his goods, leaving the stronghold unprotected, and are quickly defeated. No doubt they can be blamed for their greed and their imprudence, but a culture-specific factor gives a more satisfying sense to the event. The text provides a guide to it. On seeing the Christians retreating in apparent desperation, the Moors are moved to action: "Demos salto a él—e feremos grant ganançia, / antes quel' prendan los de Terrer—si non, non nos darán dent nada" (584–85). The poem continues to make fun of their extreme haste, to which the mention of "los de Terrer" offers the key. Terrer is the next Moorish settlement down the river, toward which the Christians are supposedly escaping. The Moors do not envision a collaborative Moorish action against the fugitives, which would stand a much better chance of success than a confused unilateral attack. The Cid plays on the well-known and fatal disunity of the Muslim population. Misled by him, the inhabitants of Alcocer go for double ("doblada," 586) or nothing ("nada," 585), trying to exclude their compatriots from any gain. Having erected unsuitable borders (to borrow Lincoln's term), they end with nothing.

Ritual as Opposed to Drama; Abstraction

The scene of the pardoning of the Cid provides an occasion for further consideration of the contrast between ritual and drama. It is dramatic in the sense that it is striking, forcefully effective, and appears to be taking place as it is narrated; but as a ceremony marking a change of status it is an exemplary ritual act, not drama in the sense of acting or pretense. It must be recounted and imagined, not reproduced. A minstrel might imply by gesture some of the physical movements of the epic personages, but no gesture is exact (Zumthor 1990, 155), and the poem's ceremonial framework would strictly limit any move to personify or impersonate the hero or other epic characters. Imitation or personalized interpretation of recounted acts would amount to interference, the interposition of an artificial resemblance of present experience to experience related. "Performance is experience and does not call for interpretation" (Zumthor 1990, 187–88). Resemblance is the stuff of metaphor. It can deceive as well as edify. The poem's mode of connecting the time and place of performance with those of the epic action is not through the intermediary of resemblance.

Saussure's doctrine of the "arbitrary" character of the linguistic sign, as refined by Benveniste,[18] helps to clarify the poem's communicative mode. Like the front and back of a sheet of paper, the signifier and signified are inseparable and have no intermediary agent connecting them, no relatively superficial resemblance to make an association. More intimate than metaphor is the relationship of contiguity—a metonymic relationship in the broad sense of that term as adopted by Jakobson, who made it seem— though apparently without ever coming out and saying so—that all mental associations are made either by metonym or metaphor—or of course both

18. "La langue est encore comparable à une feuille de papier: la pensée est le recto et le son le verso; on ne peut découper le recto sans en même temps découper le verso . . ." (Saussure 1949, 163); "Entre le signifiant et le signifié, le lien n'est pas arbitraire; au contraire, il est *nécessaire*" (Benveniste 1966, 49–53).

combined.[19] The dual nature of the sign, its condition as both signans and signatum, what Saussure misleadingly called its "arbitrary" character, does not involve or admit symbolism of resemblances. The *Poema* operates as an extended "arbitrary" linguistic sign, avoiding, for instance, the metaphor that is the linguistic mode of Gonzalo de Berceo, which is designed to portray two different worlds, the everyday and the marvelous, in terms of each other (see also p. 142). The *Cid* derives power from its reference to a single world, by minimizing its role as intermediary between the audience and the imagined action. To the extent that it achieves its goal, its meaning is not ulterior; the two sides of the sign create a single unity.

The poem's vision, like its language, is metonymic; in this resides the directness of its plain language, so powerful, for instance, in the first viewing of Valencia by the women (p. 119). As a plain, "arbitrary" word directly evokes an object, this plain narrative directly evokes events. Objects and events are rich in associations, but this does not mean that they have to represent something other than what they are. The content, even the wisdom, of the poem is in its events. We may as readers be obliged to interpret those events in symbolic, abstract terms such as honor and faith, but we can profit by peering into the world known through this poem, whose happenings are its substance, avoiding superimposition of the critic's abstractions, vague and not quite appropriate to the poem's idiom (see also p. 92). Still today, contemporary popular culture resists adequate characterization by intellectuals who are bent on appreciating it. Their abstract commentary remains at its fringes, making some larger sense of forms like television drama or advertising, which are not greatly concerned with making that kind of sense. The intellectualization of popular forms is a twentieth-century phenomenon. It is difficult to imagine a thirteenth-century Spanish scholar trying to interpret the *Poema del Cid* in terms of stated principles. The chroniclers approached the poem on its own terms. As history or lore it was, to be sure, subject to modification according to their desires or sense of propriety. If it did not make the sense they wanted, and sometimes when they did not understand it, they changed it; but they did so without departing from the narrative mode.[20]

19. "The dichotomy [between metonymy and metaphor] appears to be of primal significance and consequence for all verbal behavior and for human behavior in general" (Jakobson and Halle 1956, 79).

20. In comparing the two versions of *Siete infantes*, in the *PCG* and in the *Crónica de 1344* (see p. 15), Capdeboscq (1984, 204) shows in rigorous detail how modifications in the narra-

To appreciate the gap that existed between narrative and generalizing abstraction in the Middle Ages, one may recall the poor match made between the tales of *El conde Lucanor* and the final verses that purport to essentialize them. The *Cid* is even more alien to abstraction than are the *ejemplos*. Its apparently abstract vocabulary, when examined in context, turns out to refer to the dynamics of social interaction. *Amor* is a state of favor given by the lord, or lost, like *graçia*, or it is a favor done with *fazer*, or part of a pious formula, "por amor del Criador" (Montgomery 1991b, 128–29). *Bien* and *mal* likewise occur usually with dynamic verbs like *fazer* and *dezir*, and *mal* also with *buscar* and *querer*, or in the formulaic phrase of prayer *curiar de mal*. *Ondra* and *onor* are social words, meaning "esteem," usually associated with the hero's daughters. They are used with dynamic verbs *creçer*, *dar*, and *aver*, "to receive," and *ondrar* is usually "to honor publicly." These words are accurately understood, in the poem's lexical structure, through contrast with antonyms *desondrar*, *escarmentar*, *biltança*, obviously rather concrete. They refer to feudal relations, rankings, and preoccupations: "que é aver e tierra—e oro e onor" (2495). Their most abstract uses are in ritualistic formulas: *creçer en onor* (1905, 2198), which refers to weddings, and *creçer la ondra* (1861, 1883, 3433, etc.). Loftier or more impersonal abstractions such as justice, rectitude, or cruelty, are surely in some sense deep concerns of the poet, but are known only through actions and are not given names. When we speak of the epic as a poem of honor, or allege a moral rivalry between the king and the hero, we are speaking in terms that the poem does not use. Not just our language, but the concepts we formulate may well be inaccurate. "The worlds in which different societies live are distinct worlds, not merely the same world with different labels attached" (Sapir 1949, 162). The poem's language may be the more misleading because some of the labels, the words just cited, are familiar in appearance to the speaker or student of modern Spanish.

Abstraction depends largely on metaphor—the five words of the preceding statement are all metaphoric either as used (largely, on) or etymologically (abstract, "drawn away," depends, "hangs from," metaphor, "carry across"). The poem plainly had no inclination to make abstract statements like the one just analyzed. Nor would its language have been suitable for such a purpose. The critic who derives abstractions from the poem, as

---

tive of the later text put the blame for the tragedy much more squarely on Llambra, oppose her more clearly to Sancha, and give Mudarra a more distinctly heroic role.

though the original text were not capable of saying what it really meant, risks falling into chronological provincialism.

That the ritual manner of the poem is linked to narrative, with little reference to metaphor or to abstraction, is shown by the scenes cited in the preceding pages: the dialogue between man and wife, the council of war, the account of troop disposition, the battles, the moments of deprivation and possession, the feast, the public ceremonies. All of these help to set the elevated tone of the poem, and to them could be added, as instances of stylized action, receptions of travelers, itineraries, the incident at Corpes, and the scene at the law court, leaving only some of the poem's most prosaic passages as exceptions.

It is true of both ritual and poetry that form denotes, implies, or enhances content. A formal ritual, like a story, must have a recognizable beginning and end, and it must have a point. Its sense is likely to be much less explicit than that of a well-told story (Bell 1992, 183–84; Pratt 1977, 81, 110), and more liable to varying interpretations by different observers, but in performance it lends power to a story, as in this poem.

Formalized Language: Assonance and Personal Names

The ceremonial, formalized performance has a counterpart and reinforcement in the solemn, stylized language of the work. Some aspects of that idiom will be taken up next, with considerations on how it distinguishes itself on the one hand from everyday speech, and on the other, from the literary manner, from the meditated language of the studious author.

As noted earlier, "the underlying nuances of myth are felt to be somehow consonant with the surface of sound" (Friedrich 1986, 39). In a striking use of conventionalized language, the poem uses a particular assonance to mark passages devoted to its feminine characters. Five of the eight laisses in *í-a* (16, 41, 51, 109, 129) are devoted to Jimena and her daughters, another to the Virgin (112), another to a skirmish that takes place as the ladies watch (92), leaving only one (89) without a feminine connection. For this brief laisse an alternative motive suggests itself: it follows another one in *í-o*, which rhymes participles in *-ido* in four of its eight lines. The three *í-a* rhymes that comprise laisse 89 are likewise all made by participles. The pattern is similar to that of laisse 42, which follows one (or two) participles in -*ado* by one in -*ada* (and a form in -*ava*).

Other laisses dominated by Jimena's presence are in *á* and *á-a*, but never in *ó*, the assonance at the opposite phonetic pole from *í-a*. From their first appearance (213), the *í-a* series show a basic rhyming vocabulary of their own, associated with faith, hope, and the feminine, the commonest words being "María," "días," "missas," "rricas," "bida," and of course "fijas." For example, laisse 10, the longest one in this assonance, with nineteen lines, uses "María, "pida," and "fijas" each twice, along with seven past participles and three instances of the imperfect tense of the verb, leaving just three miscellaneous forms. Again, in laisse 41 the listed words account for four of the five rhymes. The *í-a* as leitmotif for the feminine is at once a brilliant touch and a very natural one, since a number of the listed words come easily into use when women are the topic.

The change to or from the *í-a* assonance can mark a break in tone or content. Jimena's first speech in the poem shifts to *í-a* after two initial lines in *á-o* (268, quoted on p. 114), and the feminine presence continues to dominate as the Cid answers her in the same assonance, repeating some of her key rhyming words. When the Cid brings news of the proposed marriage, Jimena and the daughters express their pleasure in *í-a* (2192–95), but his gloomy answer reverberates with negatives in *ó*: "non lo levanté yo," "nol' sope dezir de no," "él vos casa, ca non yo" (2199–2204). The poem's last *í-a* laisse follows one in *ó* and ends with the same somber note. It occurs at the point where male domination reaches its perverse pinnacle: the "serie gemela" at Corpes, rhyming "armiñas," "camisas," "bestias de la fiera guisa," and "non por bivas" and ending "¡Quál ventura serié—si assomás essora el Cid Canpeador!" (2749–53). The *í-a* ending could in part be a reflex of the historical names of the daughters, María and Cristina (note also the variant form Ximina [1424]). The two discarded names, with *í-a* and *i-í-a*, were perhaps too insistently repetitious in their vowel patterning to be acceptable when used along with words of associated sense like *niña* and *chica*, and when associated in the poet's mind with diminutive feminine endings. The name Elvira is excluded from rhyme, whereas the formulaic phrase habitually used in naming the young women, "don Elvira e doña Sol," contains the maximal vowel contrast noted above, of *í-a* with *ó*. Of the twenty-four occurrences of this phrase, twenty-three are in rhyme. Elvira is the silent sister, never heard speaking alone. The naming formula "don Elvira e doña Sol" could perhaps be seen, in a tentative hypothesis that would apply to the two contexts just cited (2199–2204 and 2749–53), as locating the feminine within the realities of the male-dominated world, represented by much-used rhymes such as "Campeador," "Carrión," "Criador," "Alfonso," "Muñoz," "Gustioz," "Vermuez," "Aragón," "León," "cort," "varon(es)," "Señor," and "nós" and vós" as they are used by the poet (even in the rare instances where "vos" does refer to women, as in 2185–2204, the pronoun is always in the objective case).[21]

Other vowel echoes and contrasts also appear to be exploited for artistic purposes. In the hands of an author who was in the habit of manipulating words to produce vowel rhyme, the way sound and content reverberate together is surely not wholly accidental in the line "tañen las campanas—en San Pero a clamor" (286), with five sequences of *a* plus nasal, or in "Apriessa cantan los gallos—e quieren quebrar albores" (235), already noted (p. 113). Nor is it likely to be mere coincidence that makes rhymes with "atamores," the Moorish drums that terrify the women in laisse 91, along with other evocative words: "alvores" (when battles begin [Lot 1946, 37]), "tremor," "atamores" (repeated), "pavor," (also repeated) (1657–72). As the women's fear diminishes in response to the Cid's reassurances, the fearful sound is abruptly interrupted by a contrasting signal bell struck by a Christian, "Viólo el atalaya—e tanxo el esquila" (1673), which initiates a successful sally in *í-a*, the one witnessed by the ladies. "Atamores" and "esquila" yield the same contrast of assonances that was noted above as phonetically maximal: a hostile and a friendly sound in words with corresponding connotations.

Other manipulation of vocabulary for the sake of rhyme supports the claim that the correspondences just noted are deliberate. Thus, *christiandad* and its synonym *christianismo* are always found in line-final position, making their respective assonances. *Ondrança* and *dubdança* are only used where they replace their synonyms *ondra* and *dubda* for purposes of rhyme. *Onor* rhymes in twelve of its thirteen occurrences; the exceptional instance means "property," not "ondra," which for its part never as-

---

21. In the light of the possible conceptual grouping of *í-a*, the women's assonance, and *í-o*, and the rarity of the latter rhyme, with a total of forty-four lines but none in the second half of the poem (after 1629) except in the declaration of Diego González before the court (3353–59b), it could be that his rhymes were intended to sound silly or childish, and his remarks laughable: "De natura somos—de los condes más limpios ... mientra que bivan—pueden aver sospiros," etc. The latter phrase may have appeared ridiculous in the given context, as something to be said of a jilted lover but not of a wife one has beaten and left for dead. A *juglar* who wanted to bring out the unmanly quality of these lines in performance could easily do so, and the withering response of Martín Antolínez would be in stark contrast: "¡Calla, alevoso,—boca sin verdad! ..." (3361).

sonates. *Desonor* in its five instances bears the same relation to *desondra*, as do *pavor* to *miedo*, and *rrictad* to *rriqueza*.

Among several other names that seem to evoke phonetic echoes in the poem, Muño Gustioz stands out with its exceptional sequence of back vowels. It appears twelve times in assonance, and more notably still, sixteen of its seventeen occurrences are in laisses in *ó*. The proportion of occurrences of the vowel -o- in many lines containing this name is distinctly higher than the 25 percent that is normal for -o- in the language of the poem (Montgomery 1980, 312): "Oyó la poridat—aquel Muño Gustioz (2364), "¿Ó eres, Muño Gustioz,—mio vassallo de pro?" (2901), etc. While this personage is historical, though little is known of him beyond his name, an apparently fictitious name such as Martín Antolínez, with its repeated initial and stressed vowels set off by echoing consonants, may have been a phonetically motivated invention. Concocted names are found in other epics; the *Roland* cites two companions called Gerins and Geres (1261, 1269) among the twelve peers, and the name of the Saracen queen Bramimonde surely has deliberate phonetic resonances; compare Germanic *brammon*, "to roar," hence "demand," "desire," etc. (Meyer-Lübke 1972, 113) and *mund*, "protector," as in Edmund.[22] But if the French names tend to the grotesque, the Spanish ones, historical or not, have a noble sonority fitting to heroes and to the grave manner of the *Poema*: besides Muño Gustioz and Martín Antolínez, consider Minaya Alvar Fáñez and Félez Muñoz.

Formalized Language: Metonymy and Parataxis

An instance has been noted elsewhere (p. 119) in which the textual content functions to produce a kind of mental and perceptual subordination analo-

---

22. In later Spanish tradition, the queen's Germanic-sounding name is transformed into Abrayma Mora, with a decidedly Semitic ring. Comparably, in *Mainet* the Moor Bramant of the *PCG* is Abrahin in the alternate version of the *Gran conquista de Ultramar* (see pp. 55–56). The feminine form of 'Ibrahim, plausibly 'Ibrahima, is of questionable linguistic authenticity, since it could only be accepted after the original meaning of Hebrew *Ab-*, "father," had been forgotten (personal communication from S. G. Armistead). Cf., however, Alexandra (Gk. *andrós*, "man"). Some distinctively masculine names are of course made feminine in French and Spanish, as Jeanne, Daniela, Fernanda, Sigismunda. Note also the apparent gender change from masc. -*mund* in Bramimonde itself.

gous to the effects usually achieved by subordinating pronouns. In that scene the eyes of the hero's wife and daughters embrace and organize their first view of the lands around Valencia, as the text adheres to its paratactic manner. As happens typically, the extralinguistic experience of the event takes the form of an accumulation of perceptions. In the conventional style of most texts, these perceptions are organized as principal and subordinate in subsequent retellings, as the mind interprets and hierarchizes the remembered experience. The poem, by contrast, stops short of a complete interpretation, preferring to take the experience on its own terms, as in the following passage, which even includes several antitheses with no explicit indication that they are present. The three subordinating words, *pues*, *antes que*, and *quién*, do little to mitigate the overwhelming parataxis.

> "Pues adelant irán tras nós, — aquí sea la batalla;
> apretad los cavallos — e bistades las armas.
> Ellos vienen cuesta yuso — e todos trahen calças,
> e las siellas coçeras — e las çinchas amoiadas,
> nós cavalgaremos siellas gallegas — e huesas sobre calças,
> çiento cavalleros — devemos vençer aquellas mesnadas.
> Antes que ellos lleguen al llano — preséntemosles las lanças,
> por uno que firgades — tres siellas irán vazias;
> verá Remont Verenguel — tras quién vino en alcança."
>
> (990–98)[23]

The poem jumps abruptly from one topic to another, as the commander might have shifted his gaze from point to point: prediction, decision, orders for preparation, the enemy's direction and equipment, the equipment of the Cid's troops, prediction, plan, the prediction repeated, result. The words achieve force through a pattern of antitheses. Because they vividly catch each aspect of the scene in meaningful order, subordination is not necessary to achieve coherence. It would constitute an authorial intrusion and only slow the pace.

The Cid's decisiveness, forcefully presented in the initial lines of this se-

---

23. "Since further on they will go after us, let the battle be here. Tighten [the girths of] the horses. They will come downhill and all have breeches and light racing saddles and loose girths. We will use [firm] Galician saddles and boots over breeches; a hundred of our knights should defeat [all] those troops. Before they reach level ground let us present our lances: for each one that you strike, three saddles will go empty. Remond Verenguel will see who it is he has come to pursue."

lection, all but disappears in the corresponding chronicle versions (which, since they resemble each other, may reflect a poetic source less forcefully worded than that of the extant *Poema*): "et si daqui nos ymos, empos iran fasta que nos alcancen. Et pues que de su contienda non nos podemos partir, meior sera que lo ayamos con ellos aqui" (*PCG* 2:533a42–45); "E ssi nos de aqui fueremos, tras nos yran, fasta que nos alcançen. E pues que de su entençion non nos podemos partir, mejor sera que lo ayamos aqui con ellos que yr fuyendo" (*Crónica de veinte reyes*: Powell 1983, 131).[24] The chroniclers' subordination of action to explanation leads them to lose sight of the main point, that by choosing the location of the battle, the Cid gains a critical tactical advantage. The chroniclers miss the positive character of his words and then simply omit the preparation and tactics sketched in the following five lines (1000–1004). Instead, at this point, the *PCG* makes the Cid continue speaking, further demonstrating its unresponsiveness to the poem's form of expression by this prosy dilution: "Et desta guisa uera Remont Verenguel tras quien viene en alcanço al pinar de Touar pora tollerme lo que yo auia ganado de los enemigos de Dios e de nuestra ley" (2:533b3–7).[25]

In another example, laisse 117 (2383–2402), the attack of Don Jerónimo contains no subordination except in an adverbial phrase "por la su ventura—e Dios quel' amava" (2385) and in an epithet, "el cavallo que bien anda" (2394). To be sure, the strict parataxis is less remarkable in a battle episode than it would be in most contexts. A further instance is the first part of laisse 95 (1711–31), in which the only subordinate expressions are brief authorial comments, "que non fueron contados" (1723), "ca muchol' andido el cavallo" (1726)—until the poet moves to results of the battle and subsequent occurrences (1731–40, etc.). Then, in dialogue, as is usual, subordination becomes common, though paratactic interfaces continue to mark the discourse, as at the beginning of 1766, 68, and 69, introduced by asterisks:

"Estas dueñas que aduxiestes, — que vos sirven tanto,
quiero las casar — con de aquestos mios vassallos;
*a cada una d'ellas — doles dozientos marcos de plata,

24. "And if we leave this place, they will come after until they catch up with us. And since we cannot avoid a battle, it will better to engage them here (than to flee)."

25. "And in this way Remont Verenguel will see who it is that he has come pursuing to the pine forest of Touar to take away what I have won from the enemies of God and our faith."

que lo sepan en Castiella - a quién sirvieron tanto.
*Lo de vuestras fijas — venir se á más por espaçio."
*Levantáronse todas — e besáronle las manos . . .
                                                    (1764–69)²⁶

The narrative passages of the poem, which have their own tense system
(see pp. 139–40), are also marked by heavy parataxis and notable syntactic
simplicity in comparison with the direct discourse. The contrast between
the two styles surely heightened the impression that the performer possessed and used a formalized, solemn language, unlike everyday speech,
and that the performance itself was accordingly a privileged occasion.
Ritual adopts "restricted codes of communication to heighten the formality
of movement and speech" (Bell 1992, 204). Even direct discourse can
at times be wholly paratactic, as in the speech of the young girl (quoted on
pp. 98–99), though it should not be forgotten that this is a special case in
which she acts as the voice of the poet and the group, in part repeating the
narrator's own words (42–43 reproducing 23–24, and 45–46 echoing
37–38).

As the paratactic mode conveys the effect of direct, unprocessed experience, a use of the relative adverb *quando* reflects a perception contrasting
with the often impersonal cause-and-effect relationship that is associated
with a large proportion of hypotactic constructions in medieval prose and in
the ordinary language of today, as typified by phrasing with *porque, como,
ya que,* medieval *pues que, por tal que,* as well as adverbials such as *por
ende, por esso.* Though of course *quando* is most often used in its temporal
sense in narrative, perhaps a fifth of its roughly 130 occurrences, with some
15 very distinct examples, represent a use that Menéndez Pidal termed
causal (1954–56, 395–96), but which is not equivalent to *porque.* Rather
than cause and effect, these examples express circumstance and response.
The response is a human one; the conditions have to do with changing for-
tunes or social situations. The response is often one of gratitude to God:
"E vós a Él lo gradid—quando bivas somos nós" (2861); "¡Grado a
Dios . . . quando tal batalla / avemos arrancada!" (792–93); and "Esto
gradesco yo—al Criador, / quando piden mis primas—don Elvira e doña

26. " 'These ladies-in-waiting that you have brought with you, who serve you so well: I
want to marry them to some of these vassals of mine. To each of them I give two hundred
marks of silver; let it be known in Castile what sort of person they have served so well. The
matter of your daughters [i.e., their marriages] will be seen to as time goes on.' They all arose
and kissed his hands."

Sol" (3446–47, also 3405, and similarly 2478). Three more refer to the family relationship with the Infantes: "Evad aquí vuestros fijos—quando vuestros yernos son" (2123) and "¡denme mis averes—quando mios yernos non son!" (3206, also 3222). Others reflect moments of agreement: "dad manero a qui las dé—quando vós las tomades" (2133) and "Quando a vós plaze—otórgolo yo, señor" (3415). Other variations are found at 365, 1220, 1298.[27]

The use of *quando* in these lines has the effect of locating the individual and his or her actions within a larger scheme, either social or divine—which in the poem are not very different from each other, since God is conceived as patron of the tribe or clan. The adverb seems to connote the personage's acceptance of his circumstances. The *Cid*'s focus on appropriate decisions and reactions to external forces represents an evolutionary step toward the self-conscious author, hearer-reader, and poetic personage, as compared with *Siete infantes*, whose direct, unreflective responses to events are in sharp contrast with its cognate work *Roland*. The French poem carries the process a step further than the last two lines just cited from the *Cid*. It gives *quand* a circumstantial application in just a few instances, but the condition determining the response is a human will—that of the ruler—whereas in the Spanish poem the will submits to the conditions expressed in the clause with *quando*. The same sense motivates Ganelon's last words before departing on his mission to the Saracens, which are: "Quant aler dei, n'i ai plus que targer" (338; Bédier: "Puisqu'il me faut aller, je n'ai que faire de plus m'attarder"). But Charlemagne's use of the word is markedly personal: "Alez sedeir, quant nuls ne vos sumunt!" (251, "Retournez vous asseoir, car nul ne vous a requis!"). And again, "Or irez vous certes, quant jol cumant" (328, "Vous irez certes, puisque je le commande"). The self-conscious making of decisions is clearly reflected in this linguistic use and reinforces the contrast with the unspoken external motivations of *Siete infantes* and the conforming to circumstance that characterizes the *Cid*.

Other subordinating items in the *Cid* also show a sense of language significantly different from what might be assumed upon looking at the

27. *Quando*, here translated by its normal equivalent "when," has the sense "given the circumstances that," "inasmuch as." Gratitude to God: "And give thanks to God when we are alive (2861); "Thanks be to God when we have won such a battle" (792–93); and "For this I give thanks to the Creator, when they ask for my cousins Doña Elvira and Doña Sol in marriage" (3446–47). Family relationships: "Behold here your sons, when they are your sons-in-law" (2123) and "Let them give me my possessions when they are not my sons-in-law" (3206). Other moments of agreement: "Appoint a sponsor for me to entrust them to, when you are taking them away" (2133) and "When it pleases you, I grant it, sir" (3415).

familiar words. In the *Cid*, *porque*, the cause-effect word par excellence in modern usage, does not usually refer to external circumstances as *quando* does, but rather links two clauses that have the same subject to introduce statements regarding one's self-esteem or emotional state. A typical example is, "que porque las dexamos—ondrados somos nós" (3360). The other item most commonly thought of as causal, *ca*, has a distinctive metalinguistic use. It identifies, not the cause of the action narrated, but the motive for relating that action. So in "Non viene a la puent,—ca por el agua á passado" (150), "ca" is roughly equivalent to "quiero decir que" or "lo digo porque," as also in "non se abre la puerta—ca bien era çerrada" (39) and "Cavalgad, Çid—el buen Campeador, / ca nunqua en tan buen punto—cavalgó varón" (407–8; Montgomery 1975).

The appropriation of these connecting words in social or personal situations and their use in facilitating interpersonal communication give evidence of an interactive sense of language derived from its function in the oral sphere, unlike the more mechanical, explanatory applications underlying *quando*, *porque*, and others, that characterize prose—essentially a written medium. Along with the notable scarcity of cause-effect language in the poem, the lack of transitional words in general, such as *mas* and *por esso*, merits attention. The speech of the young girl is a good example. Without the guidance of the situational and emotional context, her disjointed phrasing would be incomprehensible.

Formalized Language: Use of Tenses

The poem's choice of tenses, shared to a degree by *Mocedades*, presents a parallel to the use of *quando* just observed. While the tenses of direct discourse in the *Cid* are generally similar to those of other texts and of modern Spanish, the narrative voice employs a system more sensitive to verbal aspect than to tense. In direct discourse the distinction between past and present is a primary basis for tense selection—a fairly objective dimension. Aspect is more subjective, bringing out the manner of viewing an action or state, whether as an experience in progress (as usually with the Spanish imperfect tense) or as a distinctly delineated event (the preterite).[28] In the narrative sections of the *Poema*, the present, not the imperfect, is the most

---

28. The "heroic preterite" identified by Gilman (1961) is a subcategory of this broader type.

markedly imperfective of the tenses, and aspect overrides time-reference in its choice. So it is overwhelmingly preferred over past-tense forms for verbs whose lexical sense is imperfective, such as *ser*, *haber*, *tener*, *poder*, and *querer*, which report states, not events; it is also favored with verbs of motion *ir* and *venir*. A sentence like "Salieron de la eglesia,—ya quieren cavalgar" (1507) does not contain an example of the "historical present"; rather, it re-creates an experience as ongoing, evoking a sort of sensory environment within which the action takes place (see Montgomery 1991a, 364). Occasionally the effect of presence is reinforced by a demonstrative, as in "¡Dios, qué bueno es el gozo—por aquesta mañana!" (600), noted by Lapesa (1961, 39). The affinity with the circumstantial use of *quando* is clear in this instance. The presenter evokes the experience, rather than recounting it objectively, and draws the audience into it to bring himself, as first person, together with the audience as second person and the poem's actors as third. The effect is like that of a ritual; in fact the special use of tenses, as an accepted convention peculiar to the time and place of the performance, is a ritualistic adaptation of the rules of the language—not a revision of those rules, but a modification of viewpoint appropriate to a privileged occasion: "In all societies there exist speech events that are marked off from everyday verbal behavior by special rules of speaking" (Gumperz 1975, vi). The privileged linguistic form is used to address the second person, the audience, and invites its participation. On the other hand, the third person, the actor within the poem, applies the tenses in the manner of everyday speech. In this case, participation is invited in a way more familiar from other literature: the Cid speaks like everybody else, though better and more poetically, upholding a model of linguistic usage.

The linguistic habits just summarized show the language of the poem's non-narrative passages to be discourse-oriented and centered on human relations, rather than on essential ideas or principles (see also pp. 129–31). In its dynamism the poem does not seem to recognize the capacity of language for creating fixed concepts through verbal abstraction or definition. Modern critical efforts to essentialize, to say the *Cid* is a poem of honor or that it is an elaboration of a single nuclear line, "¡Dios, qué buen vassallo—si oviesse buen señor!" (20), are written from a perspective the poem does not adopt. These attempts to intellectualize have aims that the poem's participants, the *juglar* and his public, would not have shared and might even have scorned as alien to the tribal sense, which the poem brings into such sharp focus by emphasizing the contrasts between insiders and outsiders.

The *juglar*'s audience would have understood poorly if at all the desire—an outsider's desire (cf. Labov 1972, 256–57)—to identify eternal verities. Even the poet's near-contemporary, the author of *Fernán González*, lived in a world different from his, one in which the hero's faith was supposed to answer the larger questions of existence (Bailey 1993, 95–99). If "verbal interaction is the basic reality of language" (Vološinov 1973, 94), the poem is closer to that reality than is the great mass of literature, with its stronger anchoring in written models.

Metonymy, the Linguistic Artifact, Consensus, Sense of Place

In the foregoing pages, some specific observations have helped to account for the sense of directness and presence that marks the *Poema* and sets it apart from most other literature. These have included the association of given assonances with certain personages, making the women's presence virtually audible; the parataxis, which mirrors raw, unprocessed experience; the experiential, not objectivizing, use of subordinating words; and the participatory reference of verb tenses. It has been noted too that the circumstances that in other works would provide a background to a passage are instead made a part of it, as in the words of the young girl. Each of these characteristics is non-analytical, in other words arbitrary as the linguistic sign is arbitrary. That is, the signifier and the signified comprise a single entity, as symbolized by Saussure's sheet of paper (see p. 128). That *í-a* is the feminine assonance is arbitrary in the sense that there is no resemblance, only linguistic conventions (*-a* is feminine, *-í-* is found in most diminutives) that the poem elaborates and exploits. There is no identifiable intermediary point of association that connects *í-a* with the feminine.[29] As in each case noted above, the association is direct or, as Benveniste wrote, "necessary" (see note 18). A child not yet literate assumes this directness. Wanting to know the name of an object, she or he will ordinarily ask "What is it?" and not "What is it called?"

To explain the concept of the sign, Saussure took recourse to a

---

29. It may be that certain words are semiconsciously taken as models, such as *niña*, or the numerous feminine names like María and Elvira, in which case the metonymic association is combined with effects of resemblance. Neither the language nor the poem's form of expression can be strictly metonymic.

metaphor, that of the sheet of paper. New concepts and abstractions in general require the use of metaphors based on words of concrete meaning. The metonym, the association not by resemblance but by contiguity (proximity, contact, part of the whole, etc.) is exemplified by the "necessary" two sides of the sheet of paper. Since the relation between the two sides does not bear analysis, the relation between word and object—except in imitative words—admits no analytic dissection. This most basic and utilitarian semiotic mode, metonymy, is hard to describe or approach as an object of observation. As an instrument or a means of observation, it must yield to metaphor and imagination when the goal is to theorize or to cogitate creatively.

Gonzalo de Berceo, writing perhaps a generation after the *Poema del Cid* attained its extant form, enunciated a structure of metaphorical resemblances between this world and the next and presented himself as an interpreter of those resemblances. When he refers to the Virgin as "Madre del pan de trigo" (Berceo 1971, 659a), or to a Jewish child among Christian companions at Mass as "el cordero sin lana" (256d), the figurative speech attracts attention for its aptness and prompts reflection on its connotations; it does not allow the reader to forget that it is an artifact. Berceo constructs his world in the same way, inviting the reader to see life as a pilgrimage, or faith as an intermediary—brokered by himself—between the known world and the world beyond. The twentieth-century reader is well aware of the fragility of that link: the metaphor is too obviously a human creation, supremely admirable though it may be. As an intellectual construction, it is allowed to develop patterns of thinking that can disengage themselves from observed reality. But it invites reflection regarding its structure and implications, as the metonymic language of the *Poema del Cid* usually does not.

The *Poema*, as is well known, contains very little metaphoric language. Undoubtedly it has symbolic levels of meaning, some of them profound. I suggest, however, that it can be read most profitably by beginning at its own level of signification. This is not always easy to do. As readers, we like symbolism and are inclined to dismiss passages or lines in the poem that seem to be routine or automatic or insubstantial, even though the attentive reader will surely agree that the poem rarely wastes words. We also like to pick out the important events or statements, with an eye to summarizing, applying our own mental hypotaxis, which we may call perspective, to the experience of reading the text, and in the process intermingling previously held ideas and knowledge to draw our own inferences. Surely the medieval listener did some of this also, but the poem discourages the individual interpretation, appealing to the tribal sense and consensus that made survival possible in its time.

If the metonymic language of the poem leaves little room for interpretation, it also conceals the author's role as an individual developing his ideas through the narrative medium. A case in point is the council at Alcocer, where the sense of group solidarity is made into a screen hiding the deadly danger facing the Cid and his men. The Cid's creation of a false sense of safety could be dangerous in a real situation, but here it is the poet who speaks and the audience's reaction that counts. The poet's art of illusion, like that of his hero, develops an atmosphere of consensus that beguiles the audience.

At Alcocer, the Cid and his knights are under siege by a huge Moorish army. Their situation is becoming desperate. The leader calls a council of war. He outlines the situation: provisions are low, escape is not possible, and his troops are seriously outnumbered. He requests a group decision as to what is to be done:

> Mio Cid con los sos — tornós' a acordar:
> "El agua nos an vedada — exir nos ha el pan.
> Que nos queramos ir de noch — no nos lo consintrán;
> Grandes son los poderes — por con ellos lidiar,
> dezidme, cavalleros, — cómmo vos plaze de far."
> (666–70)[30]

To the Cid's request for a group opinion from his "cavalleros," Minaya gives the "first" answer—in fact, the only answer. His response echoes the leader's remarks as he speaks again of the provisions, the inevitability of battle, and their own inferior numbers. The appeal to the "cavalleros" is at the surface level of the discourse; Minaya's response is on the content level as he voices the only possible decision. The Cid praises him for making the correct recommendation, saying he could not have done otherwise, really admitting that he has staged the scene; but the two voices are those of authority figures, not actors, and not one authority supported by a yes-man. Through the poet's art of illusion, the hero's praise is extended also to the audience:

---

30. "The Cid consulted with his men: / 'They have cut off our water, we will run out of bread [i.e., food]. / If we try to get away by night, they will not allow it. / Their numbers are great for us to fight against. / Tell me, knights, what is your pleasure.' "

Primero fabló Minaya, — un cavallero de prestar:
"De Castiella la gentil — exidos somos acá,
si con moros non lidiáremos, — no nos darán del pan.
Bien somos nós seisçientos, — algunos ay de más,
en el nombre del Criador, — que non passe por ál,
vayámoslos ferir — en aquel día de cras."
Dixo el Campeador: — "A mi guisa fablastes;
ondrástesvos, Minaya, — ca aver vos lo iedes de far."
(671–78)[31]

The poem, through Minaya, recognizes only three pertinent considerations and countenances only one response. The question was not really a question at all; it left no room for deviation, as the Cid confirms in his final comment. What is most noteworthy in this exercise in mind-control is how it would have worked also on the performer's audience. It is true that they have the advantage of knowing the favorable outcome of the battle beforehand. Still, they would be drawn into the decision-making process and would feel the safety of tribal consensus, reinforced by the verbal symmetry. Minaya's words may almost be passed over as redundant by the modern reader who takes the poem as a source of information, but for the medieval listener they would effectively fortify the sense of participation and unanimity. The repetition of words and concepts by two respected figures creates an effect of ritual, as in the first meeting of the Cid and Jimena, where worthy, proper intentions are also intoned. In the present instance, the combined unity and correctness, synonymous with strong morale, gain force by implicit contrast with the fragmentation and greed of the Moors of Alcocer, portrayed just four laisses earlier (see pp. 127–28). But the artificial sense of safety in consensus is abandoned on the next morning when the battle is about to be joined, and the Cid expresses the brutal fact that it will end either in victory or death, and that in the second case the castle's defense will be irrelevant: "Si nós muriéremos en campo—en castiello nos entrarán, / si vençiéremos la batalla,—creçremos en rrictad" (687–88)—a rare admission on his part of the hazards of war.

In the scene of the council the repetition of words by a second voice

---

31. "First spoke Minaya, an excellent knight. / 'From noble Castile we have come to this place, / if we do not do combat with the Moors, they will not let us eat (bread). / We are a good six hundred, and a few more; / in the name of the Creator, let it not fail to be: / let us go to the attack tomorrow, on that very day.' / Said the Campeador: 'You have spoken my way. / You do yourself honor, Minaya, as you were bound to do.' "

serves much the same function of highlighting concepts—an editorial function—that would in other texts be achieved by hypotaxis. This manner of
organizing verbal expression, identified with the tribal mentality, corresponds to Roman Jakobson's metonymic or syntagmatic axis of discourse,
the axis of combination, as opposed to the paradigmatic axis of replacement, which is the realm of metaphor (Jakobson and Halle 1956, 69–77;
Jakobson 1981, 27–28). The Cid's discourse is incomplete in that it is
phrased as a question, although the answer is explicitly present in his mind.
Minaya's response functions to reinforce the foregone conclusion by
putting it into words that both echo and complement those of the Cid.
Since he chooses different words, an element of replacement is present. "A
competition between both devices, metonymic and metaphoric, is manifest
in any symbolic process, either intrapersonal or social" (Jakobson and
Halle 1956, 80, where "symbolic" subsumes "linguistic"). The competition, particularly in this instance, lends power to the message.

The opposition between these two modes of association is profound.
The metonymic or contiguous mode here operates as a tool of cohesive
tribal thinking—which is far from dead in today's world. When seen in an
unfavorable light it may be called prejudice. It is instructive to view it posi-
tively as the poem does, as a tool for survival, whether directed against a
group in some way regarded as inferior, such as the moneylenders or the
too-eager Moors of Alcocer, or against a person resented as privileged, like
the count of Barcelona. The outsiders need to be manipulated and defeated;
the insiders must remain a close-knit group, and this also requires manipulation, as in the scene just considered and in the hero's many dealings with
his men. The primacy of group thinking comes into focus in the third cantar, as the Infantes become a threat to the Cid's dominance of the *mesnada*
when he is forced to prohibit his vassals from mocking them: the failure of
consensus, if the cause were not removed, could have destroyed the group
(see p. 50).

The forces at work are not abstract; they affect the social organization.
They are made to operate also on the audience. A good audience will respond well, will react to the broad range of the poem's verbal content and
will know that the feelings communicated are as essential as the information. As good narrative, the poem does not invite or need an ulterior interpretation. It is a presence, not a mediator between the listener and remote
happenings. Its metonymic mode extends beyond the grammar of sentences
and laisses or paragraphs to condition its larger portrayal of reality, as its
overall conception also determines its details—although the modern stu-

dent may be obliged to approach the matter analytically, beginning with small linguistic units.

It is clear that the *Poema* differs radically from near-contemporary narrative works such as *Fernán González* or the writings of Berceo in its distinctively metonymic idiom. *Mocedades*, on the other hand, though it clearly inherits the epic language known to us through the *Cid*, fails to integrate events, concepts, and feelings as does the earlier poem. *Mocedades*, as a rule, is simply disjointed, requiring the audience or reader to remember or imagine the interrelationships that would provide continuity between lines of poetry and between sections. The sense of a strong guiding force, the mind of a poet always conceiving the poem as the sum of its parts, so strong in the *Cid*, is lacking in *Mocedades*.

Another phenomenon of combination, or uninterpreted association, is seen in the identification of each action with its location. The *Poema* makes this link regularly. Particularly in its early part, each scene, with its action, is situated in a new location or begins with a departure: "Allí piensan de aguiiar" (10), "por Burgos entrava" (15), "adeliñó a su posada" (31), "a la puerta se llegava" (37), "a oio se parava" (40), "tornós' pora su casa" (49), "partiós' de la puerta" (51), "llegó a Sancta María" (52), "salió por la puerta" (55), and "en la glera posava" (56). The connection of action with place is no doubt predictable in a text relating travels (though nothing like it occurs, for instance, in *Fernán González*). Thirty-nine arrivals and departures can be counted before the battle of Castejón (436).

To take another example, in relating the wedding celebration, the poem details arrivals to and departures from four locales. The palace is prepared (2205–7), and to bring out the sense of place, the poet invites the audience to imagine being there and taking part (2208). Within the hall, he visualizes the proceedings in terms of movements and symbolic changes of position. The participants file in, "son iuntados" (2209); "cavalgan los iffantes,—adelant adeliñavan al palaçio" (2211); "entraron . . . Reçibiolos" (2214); "delant se les omillaron / e ivan posar" (2211–15); and "es levantado . . . 'Venit acá' . . . 'métolas' . . . 'dadlas' . . . Levántanse . . . metiógelas en mano . . . 'dovos' . . . los rreçiben . . . van besar la mano" (2219–35). The departure for the cathedral (2237) follows, and the scene shifts to the bishop's preparations and reception of the party (2239). Again a departure (2241), then to the river's edge (2242) for a tourney, then a return to and arrival in Valencia and the alcázar (2248), with a summary characterization to close the episode: "rricas fueron las bodas—en el alcáçar ondrado" (2248). Each scene, however brief, receives a frame including both entry or arrival and exit or departing movement. This rather ponderous structure exemplifies the habit of clearly localizing each action, of organizing scenes hierarchically, here in a series, each with its opening and closure, with the long member of the series similarly subdivided. The sketchy outline of action leaves much to the audience's imagination, but the places are explicit, giving a foundation for the imagination to build on, a locale where given actions are necessarily carried out, with comings and goings serving to mark out each place together with its activity.

The use of verbs of motion can provide a kind of punctuation and organization that in other texts would be achieved at least partly through hypotaxis. The technique may be demonstrated by reexamining the passage just considered, though only a complete analysis of the poem would establish to what extent it is uniformly applied. The preparations for the weddings and their celebration, with ninety-six lines (2175–2269), contain twenty-four verbs of motion: "assomaron," "fueron," "entrava," "Venides," "vengo," "son iuntados," "cavalgan," "adeliñavan," "entraron," "ivan posar," "venit," "salieron," "adelinnando," "Al salir," "dieron salto," "Tórnanse," "an entrado," "entrassen," "yas' van," "rricos' tornan," "yas' ivan," "partiendo," "se parten," and "Venidos," along with fourteen other verbs that denote location or change of location: "Afélos," "sed," "rreçibiólo," "adugo," "Metívos," "enbiaron," "Reçibiólos," "es levantado," "métolos," "Levántanse," "metiógelas," "afévos," "rreçiben," and "espidiéndos," in addition to a few borderline cases like "dóvos" and "tornássedes." In this same selection, for comparison, there are just twenty-three subordinating words—plus six more in epithets.

By telling of many movements and by restricting the presentation to externals, without any indication of motive, reason for the action, or emotions attending it (except in 2213), this formalized scene develops a ritualistic tone. The seemingly mechanistic activity is reminiscent of *Siete infantes*, although in the *Cid* a sense of personal motivation and initiative clearly underlies it. In this scene from the *Cid*, the rituals are those of courtesy and propriety, whereas in *Siete infantes* all action seems to take the form of predetermined responses to a similarly preordained and limited set of stimuli. As a sequential form of communication, ritual is analogous to parataxis in speech. Ritual may on occasion be accompanied by a spoken commentary or punctuated by the sound of drums or bells, for instance, in which case these interpretative supplements function in a manner comparable to grammatical linking made by *quando, pues que,* etc. The scene just recalled seems to proceed in silence, although it contains verbs of communication, such as "enbiaron" and "Reçibiólos." The parataxis, with the many verbs of motion, heightens the visual aspect of the scene at the expense of all other impressions. Then the silence of what should have been a joyous wedding ritual is broken by the Cid's unhappy words, with the deep feeling they express: "Pues que a fazer lo avemos,—¿por qué lo imos tardando?" (2220). Subsequently, during and after the speeches, the many movements continue until the end of the wedding celebration (2270).

The pattern seen here, with action largely manifested as movement followed by interpretative commentary by one of the characters, is habitual in the *Poema del Cid*. The first four laisses of the poem follow this model strictly (compare p. 96), except that the fourth has two summaries, the second being supplied by the authorial voice instead of by a direct quotation. Though the model is later varied greatly, especially in laisses beginning with direct discourse, identification of locales continues to be a basic structural device of the poem, reflecting the metonymic mode of association. The strong sense of place—much stronger than in *Fernán González* or *Mocedades*—gives power to the *Poema* and is emblematic of its understanding that reality and emotional satisfaction are based on "in" and "with," which (in actual experience) are visible or in some other way sensory relations, and not "like," which involves the imagination. The difficulty of approaching the metonym (which "easily defies interpretation," Jakobson and Halle 1956, 81) and of understanding the identity or unity of the signans and the signatum—Saussure's sheet of paper, Jakobson's "codified contiguity" (1981, 44)—stem from the need to take recourse to metaphor in order to manage abstractions. Eric Havelock recognizes the analogous problem as applied to texts representing "primary orality"—which would be based on purely acoustic laws of composition—but reaches an analogous impasse: the term "oral text," referring to a recorded oral composition, is an oxymoron; the parallel term "written word" is partly a metaphor; e.g., Homer in written form is no longer an instance of primary orality. Havelock's comments, which would approach an understanding of the metonym, necessarily end on a negative note: "Literate habits and assumptions *and language* are the warp and woof of modern existence [emphasis mine]. . . . [I]n primary orality, relationships between human beings are governed exclusively by acoustics. . . . The psychology of such relationships is also acoustic." The literate mind deals with linguistic creations as "some kind of material existing in some kind of space." This and other metaphors are "a necessary means of communication, but their constant use . . . illustrates the peculiar difficulty of thinking about primary orality and describing it. We lack a model for it in our consciousness" (Havelock 1986, 65–66). Little wonder that the critic falls back on phraseological resemblances between the *Cid* and Berceo or *Roland* and sees them as signs of a common intellectual background.

The Language of Tradition

What kind of oral language can preserve tradition? "The answer would seem to lie in ritualized utterance, a traditional language which somehow becomes formally repeatable like a ritual, in which the words remain in a fixed order" (Havelock 1986, 70). But the words and their order will not remain fixed in popular memory; within the patterns of repetition, variations will set in as on a template or in a matrix, utilizing for example synonymy, e.g., "Allí piensan de aguiiar,—allí sueltan las rriendas" (10), with virtually synonymous hemistichs, or verbal patternings as in "a la exida de Bivar—ovieron la corneia diestra / e entrando a Burgos—oviéronla siniestra" (11–12), with rhythmic antitheses. The repetition with variation may occur at any level, from the phone ("comed, conde" [1025, etc.] and "tañen las campanas—a San Pero a clamor" [286]) to the word, to incidents, and even larger structures: the "series gemelas" (laisses 51, 73, 129); the two encounters with Raquel and Vidas; the two with Jimena at Cardeña; the two battles that comprise the taking and the defense of Alcocer; the two fortresses occupied on the way to Valencia, Castejón and Alcocer; the two great battles in defense of Valencia; the two encounters between the Cid and the king, on the Tajo and at Toledo; the two demonstrations of cowardice by the Infantes, with the lion and in battle; the two outrages planned or committed by them, against Abengalbón and against their wives; and so on,[32] as well as groups of three such as the missions to the king and the various triads at the law court.

The amount of repetition to be found at all levels in the *Poema* is extra-

---

32. Repetitions and replications of this kind are basic to the structure of Spanish epic and medieval epic in general. They are an essential cultural element: "We are discovering the existence of close ties between parallelism in poetry and in mythology, including ritual. The role played by parallelism in the tradition and creation of myth reveals ever new and unexpected possibilities in the structural properties of parallelism. This role brings out in particular the significance of binary structures at different levels of cultural anthropology, thus still opening new vistas for an interdisciplinary study of parallelism" (Jakobson and Pomorska 1983, 104).

ordinary. Perhaps even more remarkable is the fact that it is not usually very noticeable to the reader, and hardly ever bothersome. This is a sign that the text is successful as poetry; repetition is likely to be deadly in prose. Prose is nearly everywhere the child of writing; preliterate prose, such as saga, is exceptional in world literary history. Tradition-based epics such as the *Poema del Cid* stand at the juncture of orality—language heard—and literacy—language seen and accordingly preserved. With writing comes authorial self-consciousness and an increased ability to manage the mechanics of a text—to limit excessive repetition, perhaps, or to organize its parts to increase its coherence. Whether the *Cid* has undergone such revisions with the aid of the tool of writing is a question to which no answer will be attempted here. It does seem clear that the poet (perhaps more than one) has some of the self-conscious independence of spirit that comes with the skills of reading and writing, and that he has taken some bold measures to bend his story to convey messages that are of his time rather than inherited with the tradition—making his hero a skilled and eloquent politician, for instance, and weaving together the Cid's rehabilitation before the king and the growing threat posed by the Infantes. At the same time, the author knows and respects the archaic formal language that is preserved as part of the tradition, "since it is built on the instinct to conserve rather than to create, and must exclude the casual idiom and unpredictability of current talk" (Havelock 1986, 74). This is seen, for instance, in the parataxis and the related phenomenon of metonymy, in the special narrative tense system, which was surely not the author's invention, in epic epithets, in quaint expressions such as "fincaredes remanida" (281), and undoubtedly in old-fashioned vocabulary such as *tiesta* (used only once, and in rhyme), *huebos*, *virtos* for "troops," and a special use of *qui*, which alternates with *quien* in some grammatical environments but is particularly found in expressions having a proverbial ring: "qui en un logar mora siempre,—lo so puede menguar" (948, also 126, 424, etc.). So the stately language of the past, preserving the wisdom of bygone generations for the contemporary ingroup, lends authority to the text, even as the poet's sense of self, in Greece a post-Homeric (i.e., Socratic) discovery according to Havelock (1986, 114), makes itself felt as a creative force.

Old Spanish Epic as a Corpus

When the various Old Spanish epic texts are examined together, two aspects come to the fore. One is a common tradition ultimately reflecting a mythic background, clearly recognizable although treated very differently in each of the texts. The other is the uniqueness of each text at the linguistic and stylistic levels. The differences at these levels reflect contrasting world-views, which also determine how each story is constructed in its larger narrative dimensions and how it selects and brings out its themes.

Some sense of the contrasts can be observed in the various ways of identifying truth or reality. In an orally based culture, these are not ideas developed in the form of definitions but represent perceptions and beliefs that come into play in each new situation that arises. They are not fixed concepts but operational modes that produce given types of reactions to given stimuli. Thus, when faced with disagreement or potential disagreement, characters display patterns of behavior conditioned by their society. In *Siete infantes*, as the brothers travel to meet Ruy Velázquez in Moorish territory, their tutor warns them at a certain point that there will be no returning if they press on. This information goes against the course of action perceived by the infantes as proper according to their military code. Gonzalo's response, tacitly that of all seven, is an angry demand that the tutor be silent, and an implied threat to strike him dead if he speaks further (see pp. 76–77). The response to disagreement is simple and direct: destroy it and if necessary destroy its source—still today an all-too-effective way of obtaining unanimity. The tribal unit preserves its integrity by purging dissent. Truth or reality is the same thing as group opinion. This mentality pervades *Siete infantes*. It determines its action when Gonzalo hears Doña Llambra's immodest praise of her nephew, and his direct response is to challenge and kill the nephew. The wheels of the story are thus set into motion and continue to turn as each provocation produces an immediate result until the final retribution is accomplished. Only an outsider, Almanzor, is not caught up in the machine and is able to modify the course of events. Questions of truth, cohesion, honor, and freedom are bound up together, but questions are scarcely asked; even the narrative voice seems to have little independence of the code and its inexorable workings. Only by the fact that it is tragic does the story possibly imply a critical perspective on the code. But it is not clear whether as tragedy it represents a detached authorial stance or a passive acceptance of the tragic nature of existence.

The *Poema del Cid* deals also with truth and freedom as dynamics rather than as principles, but in remarkably complex and subtle ways. Consensus within the group is built in and receives eloquent expression in some of the poem's best passages, such as the first meeting of the hero with Jimena and the council of war at Alcocer. The poet and presenter exercise(s) great control in extending the sense of unanimity to include the audience. He achieves this by demonstrating that knowledge, which is derived from the group as a circle of opinion, is the equivalent of power. Agreement, clearly a matter of life or death in *Siete infantes*, is hardly less important to survival in the *Cid*. The narrative device of reinforcing group consensus by encouraging scorn for outsiders is in almost constant use. The threat to unity posed by the Infantes de Carrión in Valencia, as members of the Cid's family who have failed as warriors, reaches to the foundation and fabric of the warrior band. The leader is forced to prohibit his men from making jokes at the brothers' expense, giving evidence of a diversity of opinion in which he must present himself before the *mesnada* as hypocritical or self-deluded. The divergence of belief strikes at the roots of his authority and is all the more threatening because it must go largely unexpressed. It does come to the surface when he asks Pero Vermúdez to look after the two Infantes in the battle against the Moors under Búcar, and Pero, who already has supported the Infante Fernando's false claim of a successful exploit, declines in blunt terms: "que oy los ifantes—a mí por amo non abrán; / cúrielos qui quier,—ca d'ellos poco m'incal" (2356–57). The falsehood is only cleared up, as far as the audience is informed, in the court of law, when Pero relates the true story of Fernando's cowardice (3313–28). The challenge there begins with the word "Mientes." The declaration of surrender that ends the duel, "Vençudo só" (3344), has carried with it in tradition the formula, "Mentí por esta boca," focusing on the central issue of truth and falsehood. The loser, repudiated by the group, is excluded from the number of those who speak truly.

The identification of truth with the insider must have an intimate link with the metonymic mode of thought and expression that characterizes the poem. The unity of opinion reaches into the group's patterns of perception, and perception mirrors reality, including inner reality, a fact often expressed by the poem, as in "Alegrós'le tod el cuerpo,—sonrrisós' de coraçón" (3184). The signifier and the signified are one. It may be revealing, in this connection, that among the poem's few expressions of similarity that are not formulaic (like "blancas commo el sol," said of women and of swords), a majority are deftly linked to falsehoods. Garçi Ordóñez, represented as the Cid's arch-enemy, twice uses comparative expressions to convey his envy and displeasure at the Cid's military successes: "semeia que en tierra de moros—non á bivo omne" (1346) and "por tan biltadamientre—vençer rreyes del campo, / commo si los fallasse muertos—aduzirse los cavallos" (1863–64).[33] As though to show the error of these remarks, both are contradicted by the king. Through Garçi Ordóñez, the spokesman for the Beni-Gómez, who elsewhere seems to show himself as a poor speaker (see p. 109), the poet may be condemning comparisons as idle and illusory, presenting the personage as a manipulator of the truth and creator of vacuous ironies—irony being understood as a play on the divergent perceptions of reality held by different people. The Cid's deceits, in contrast, are effective, because they play on the misperceptions of adversaries—he uses *semeiar* only once, when hoodwinking Raquel and Vidas (157). Knowledge shared within the group brings power and success. Except where his sons-in-law are concerned, the Cid is always in full possession of the realities of each situation, along with their attendant ironies, and expresses them straightforwardly. He sees clearly, and what you see is what you know; *ver* is often "to understand" in the poem (50, 82, 1096, 1249, etc.). And his "cavalleros" see things his way. As in Homer (Block 1986, 182), communal experience does not lie.

The importance of unanimity is reflected in the poem's massive use of *todos*, with 120 instances, and the repeated scenes of group rejoicing, as in 1083–84, 1601, 1799–1800, or agreement as in 1692, etc., or, more elaborately, in the three parallel sets of lines recognizing God and Minaya as bestowers of collective joy and wishing the latter a long life (924–34). The central theme, shared knowledge, receives direct attention when Minaya returns from his first diplomatic mission "Todo ge lo dize—que nol' encubre nada" (922); but usually the references are more oblique. For instance,

33. "It seems that in the land of the Moors there is not a living man" (1346); "by so vilely conquering kings in the field, / as though he found them dead, leading away the horses" (1863–64). *Semeiar*, "to seem," is used when the Cid lies to Raquel and Vidas—"a lo quem' semeia,—de lo mío avredes algo" (157)—and again when the king makes a disastrous decision (2977—also in 1875, 2414). *Commo si* is found three more times, where the narrator speaks: "assí posó Mío Çid—commo si fuesse en montaña" (61), where the Moors of Alcocer are hoodwinked: "De guisa va Mío Çid—commo si escapasse de arrancada" (583), and when Elvira and Sol first meet Alvar Fáñez, who is to take them home after Corpes: "Atanto vos lo gradimos—commo si viéssemos al Criador" (2860). One additional comparative expression, "assi commo . . . commo si" (2137), is used in a legal transfer of power to a proxy.

False appearances also come in for comment in the *Odyssey*, but in contrast with the Cid, Odysseus receives praise for elaborately lying to Penelope: "He knew how to say many false things that were like true sayings" (Lattimore translation, 19.203).

group members express confidence or certainty regarding the king's future actions, to be based on their own success: "aun çerca o tarde—el rrey querer me ha por amigo" (76), "esto feches agora,—ál feredes adelant" (896), with God's word to the hero, voiced by the archangel Gabriel, as the guarantee that royal favor will some day be forthcoming (409). Insider knowledge, often the key to victories, is contrasted explicitly with the ignorance of an outsider in the prelude to the battle with the count of Barcelona, who mistakenly says "¡sabrá el salido—a quién vino desondrar!" (981), while the Cid has the true word: "¡Verá Remont Verenguel—tras quién vino en alcança...!" (998). And the performer includes the audience among those who know (see also Rico 1993, xi–xiii).

The Infantes, on the other hand, are much given to secrets, though—for purposes of the author—they are usually not successful at keeping them. Not only are their confidences sometimes overheard (2320–24, 2660–65), they seem unable to distinguish between private and public matters, as when they carry out the crime of Corpes in an atmosphere of stealth, intending to dishonor the Cid's family but not cognizant of the king's involvement in the marriage and the shame they will bring to themselves— even though Sol reminds them of it (2733; see p. 51). Among the good men and true, facts are enunciated in narrative form, as common experience cannot be falsified.[34] Examples are the Cid's inspirational speech to his troops before battle, "Después que nos partiemos—de la linpia christiandad..." (1116–21), which merges into a directive, and Minaya's encomium of the hero: "Echástesle de tierra, — non ha la vuestra amor..." (1325–33), as well as the many other recapitulations of previous events that provide orientation for the listener, who also must share the knowledge.

Fernán González, as a poem derived from a presumed epic source, plainly reacts against any assumption that the group is the repository of truth, or that perceptions are dependable sources for it. The monkish author's devotion to doctrine and to humility are incompatible with the kind of tribal familiarity with God and the confident optimism that mark the *Cid*. The unfamiliar, however inappropriate, appeals to him more than perceived reality, as in a simile he adopts to relate the incident of the lecherous archpriest who discovers the fugitive count in a wood with the princess Sancha. When the priest sees the moment as a chance to take advantage of

---

34. "The 'true' is identical with the 'real' only insofar as it can be shown to possess the character of narrativity" (Zumthor 1987, 6).

the lady, as the poet declares, "plógo l' qual si ganasse a Acre e Damiata" (652d; Catalán 1980, 135). This reference was arcane enough to be unknown to the scribe of the Escorial manuscript of the poem, who wrote "Amiaça." For the author, true experience, if it is even relevant, may come from an obscure book. The count denies the validity of perception in another passage, where his troops see a great fiery serpent in the sky on the eve of the decisive battle of Hacinas (str. 471–73). Though they all have seen it and he has not, he explains that it is a creation of the Moors intended to demoralize them, and that as Christians they need fear nothing but God. So the authoritarian voice, far from deriving from the group's realities, calls them insubstantial. As for the word *verdat*, it refers twice to the Divine and five times is a reinforcing filler in speech, "por verdat vos lo digo" (645c)—as also in the *Cid*, but in the latter poem it usually applies to the realities of a situation as recognized through experience and observation, or to the integrity of a person: "¡Calla, alevoso,—boca sin verdad!" (3362).

Mocedades uses the word *verdat* in two instances, one similar to that just cited from the *Cid* (345) and one in a formula of refusal. To instructions given him by his father, Rodrigo responds, "Et esso non seria la verdat" (400), and proceeds to issue instructions of his own. This form of refusal or denial is also found in the *Cid* (979, 2417), where it may correspond to the poem's situational, dynamic sense of reality, but in *Mocedades* it appears rather as an inherited formula, whether epic or vernacular. In general, this poem takes little interest in observed reality. It recalls traditions as verbal forms rather than as living culture, and its admixture of bookish and diversely traditional elements does not allow for the development of a genuine worldview. The poem is interesting, rather, as an example of how the vital sense can be drained from oral traditions as they turn to mere forms, though still preserving vivid memories of tales that were once essential to the culture. The collective thinking that *Fernán González* had been at pains to obliterate has in *Mocedades* become redundant, as the hero has ceased to be its guide and spokesman.

Whereas the *Cid* poet brings God, hero, *mesnada*, and audience together, the author of *Fernán González* isolates his hero from the deity and from his men by making him engage in disputation with both. The count's righteousness dehumanizes him. Like his author, he is a lonely figure. The Rodrigo of *Mocedades*, though his adventures may be gripping, is also isolated by being unreal, unbelievable, and asocial.

The Cid, in contrast with these isolated figures, is a consummately social being, as evidenced by his skill in manipulating friends and outsiders, and in his adroit command of the conventions of courtesy (as seen on pp. 122–23)—an indispensable quality from the point of view of the linguist: "politeness . . . is basic to the production of social order, and a precondition of human cooperation" (Gumperz 1991, xii). A deeper verbal structure is outlined by Benveniste, who points to parallel relations between the rules of courtesy and the acts they prescribe, on the one hand, and myth and ritual on the other: "[Le rite et les formules de politesse] ne se tiennent dans une relation semiologique que par l'intermédiaire d'un discours: le 'mythe' qui accompagne le 'rite'; le 'protocole' qui règle les formes de politesse" (1974, 50).[35] Implicit in this statement is an appreciation of how a society as a collectivity creates a mode of determining what it knows to be true and right.

In its social awareness as well as in other senses, the *Cid* stands at the pinnacle of the Spanish epic production that has come down to us. A pinnacle presupposes a trajectory, and the four texts chosen here for consideration, whose deep differences have been emphasized, present themselves as fairly representative points along such a path. Albert Lord traces a long-term evolution: "The poet was sorcerer and seer before he became 'artist' " (1965, 67). *Siete infantes*, with its inexorable reactions to stimuli, its parallels and cycles, has the rhythm of a ceremonial dance. It alone contains a seer, a sage whose wisdom is based on the reading of omens, who cannot extract himself from the heroic tragedy he sees unfolding around him. The poetic tradition, functioning as author, seems similarly impotent, unable to control the course of events except by providing a final retribution that saves a generation, perhaps understood as the race itself—though it sacrifices most of its principal actors.

Lord pursues the evolutionary process in these terms: "It is from the dynamic life principle in myth, the wonder-working tale, that art derived its force. Yet it turned its back on the traditional significance" (1965, 221). The *Cid* has not gone quite so far; it has turned the traditional tale of initiation on its head, but with a vivid appreciation of its meaning. The hero is victorious over the dire threat posed by the failure of his sons-in-law, a failure presented in terms whose primitive character lends them authenticity.

---

35. "Rites and politeness formulas are held in a semiological relationship only by the mediation of a discourse: the myth that accompanies the rite, the stated principles that govern the conventions of politeness."

The hero, unlike the Infantes, is moved by a sense of purpose; he is a man emerging from the facelessness and the collective imperatives of the myth to appear as an individual with his own initiative and a clearly idealized role in society. So, besides bravery and prowess, he has tact, a finely tuned sense of humor, and conscious, articulate devotion to family and ruler.

Again the linguist takes a generalizing view: "Narratives must participate in the langue of previous narratives in order to seem plausible to an audience, especially if that langue is part of the audience's knowledge" (Chafe 1990, 234). The poet or poets of the *Cid*, working from the ancient tale, have deliberately changed its meaning in the process observed by Lord (1965, 221). James Burke advances a different hypothesis that gives abstract form priority over the narrative, according to which the poet inserted epic material into prefabricated rhetorical categories (1991, 51). The lion, for instance, is "the symbol that links the three poetic syllogisms that function in the poem" (89). In Burke's view the composer would have picked up at least some amount of "loose logical thinking" (21–22, 37) as he learned to read and used it to transform the tradition. Burke offers some acute insights, but he may have the basic process backward: "The general observations that one may abstract from the particulars of a story—observations about nature or about life—are not to be taken as the equivalent of a story" (Brooks and Warren 1959, 681). Burke's implication that literate habits of thinking penetrated easily into the medieval mentality is contrary to the findings of oralist scholarship. As for the accessibility of formal logic to ordinary people, it has been declared "impossible to find any significant public participation in the belief systems found among elites" (Bell 1992, 185). The syllogisms identified by Burke, challenging to the acuity of the modern reader, would have been inaccessible to the great majority in a medieval world in which written culture was confined to isolated islands in a "sea of orality" (Zumthor 1987, 127–28) and where literacy may have been "completely irrelevant to other roles in a traditional society" (Olson and Torrance 1991, 2). The materials gathered in the present book show the poem as essentially popular, by whatever paths its extant shape may have been reached. Without a comprehending and responsive oral audience, the poem as we know it would have had no reason for existing.

Lord continues to trace the evolution of poetic folk narrative as follows: "The nontraditional [i.e., literate] literary artist, sensing the force of the traditional material whence his art was derived, but no longer comprehending it, no longer finding acceptable the methods of the tradition, sought to compensate for their lack by intricacies of construction created for their own sake" (1965, 221). That *Fernán González* only partly conforms to this analysis is largely due to the limitations of its author's talent. He does take up a heroic theme, and he does repudiate the traditional langue or idiom along with the group mentality. His attempts at decorative complication are sporadic, for instance "Acre e Damiata," but his ingenuity is insufficient to allow for development of an elaborate style.

Lord's preference, needless to say, was for the oral forms. He perhaps never knew a medieval epic text quite as decadent as *Mocedades*, which has excellent passages recalling an earlier poem or poems, as well as traces of long-standing tradition such as the initiation—but in a version that is often incoherent stylistically, structurally, and conceptually. Instead of replacing the group mentality by another ideology, it simply lost sight of that mentality, along with the heroic ideal, as social conditions changed. The poem will nevertheless continue to merit study by readers concerned to know how it declined and what it preserved. It constitutes a true laboratory case in the decadence of an oral tradition no longer respected, no longer strong enough to anchor a firm standard of literary quality.

Frontiers

The various Old Spanish texts are not usually studied together in quite the way that has been undertaken here: to see what light they throw on one another when examined thematically and stylistically. The topic has also brought in, almost by its own agency, some transnational and transgeneric considerations. The tales and traditions seem to be poor respecters of frontiers. As they wander, however, they do adapt themselves with remarkable agility to the new cultures and historical situations they encounter. The interpenetration of the experience of life and of literature can intensify both those experiences in an atmosphere of foreign contacts—though, on the other hand, if the Old Spanish material is a good indicator, the interplay among fictions representing unequal cultural levels can easily be counterproductive (*Fernán González, Mocedades*). Since many instances of crossfertilization have come into view in the course of this study, most have been dealt with only summarily. If some of the probes offered suggest lines of further inquiry to a few readers, their presence here will be justified.

The productivity of cross-cultural contacts may indeed find a reflection in the story lines of these tales. The border crossing is one of only two elements shared by all nine of the principal tales examined. Only the killing[36]—certainly an essential element of the initiation—is as common. In part, to be sure, the many incursions are due to the warlike theme of the tales, since warriors necessarily invade each others' territories. But the contact with foreigners or outsiders is more than a simple mechanical circumstance. It opens up the narrative plots and the characters' perspectives, giving them an awakening and revivifying impulse which they communicate to the group in diverse and unpredictable ways. The effect is the more noteworthy because it plays against the unifying tribal instinct which is a primal force in the Spanish epic—brilliantly espoused in the *Cid* and less overtly potent but still fundamental in the other epic tales.[37] All these compositions were made with clear consciousness that an ingrained drive to group unity was a necessity for survival, spiritual and physical, and that it presupposed conflict with other groups. But paradoxically, this necessity carries with it the inverse proposition: the group and the identity of its individuals are only conceivable in terms of outside contacts, without which stagnation and presumably eventual extinction would result.

Full demonstration of these points would involve much repetition of material already presented. A few examples will recall the variety and creative ingenuity with which cross-cultural motifs are developed. Some time after his initiation, Cúchulainn is required to go to Alba (Scotland) to continue his training as a warrior. There he fathers a son. On his departure for home, he leaves instructions for his son's eventual journey to Ulster. The instructions are couched in such a way that when the son arrives, the hero must enter into combat with him. One of them must die, and since the son shows the potential to outperform the father, Cúchulainn makes unfair use of a magical weapon to destroy his contender. His normal straightforward habit of killing innumerable enemies is in this case turned into a very different impulse, contradictory and tragic. The usually indomitable, single-minded hero acquires a painfully human dimensionality. The reader senses that the border crossing and the mystique of the stranger have the effect of opening up the tale and giving it a degree of maturity that would not have been available to it if confined to its home ground.[38]

---

36. The killing is reduced to defeat in the case of the count of Savoy.

37. For the *Poema del Cid* as a frontier work, see Montaner 1993, 22–23.

38. This episode was cited earlier (p. 86) as an instance of the critical view taken by the tradition of the purportedly exemplary career of the hero.

Like Mudarra, Cúchulainn's son Connla (or Connlaoch) is born of a princess in a foreign land after his father's departure, is trained as a great hero, receives a ring, sets out to find his

In *Siete infantes*—where the primary conflict is between clans or sub-clans—the other world, that of the Moors, is a place of sacrificial death and regeneration. Only there can treachery take its full effect, and there lives the ruler who determines the ultimate course of events in Castile. Without the decisions of the outsider, Castile would languish for a generation and more—under continued clan warfare if Almanzor had not approved the Moorish ambush of the seven brothers, or under the blighting domination of Ruy Velázquez if Almanzor's orders had not led to the birth of Mudarra. The dependence, moral as well as political, of Castile upon the neighboring land is more explicit in this tale than in the others. The seer Nuño Salido declares the crossing of the frontier between the two regions to be prohibited, the entry into the land of no return. The line itself seems to generate narrative invention, to introduce a world of the imaginary where life and death hang in precarious balance. In the world beyond, supernatural forces hold sway and strange things occur. The *Cid*, too, gives special treatment to the lands of the Moors. Not only are they realistically viewed as a source of material wealth—a stimulus too, however removed from myth—but the border is crossed at night, the land beyond is barren and hostile, and the Cid and his men must keep wandering and struggling, making night raids like outlaws, until they subdue Valencia. The "tierras estrañas" of Valencia are also the scene of the Infantes' unnatural failures. Corpes is in a no-man's land across the Duero, which is a traditional barrier between Christians and Moors and the scene also of the visits of other-worldly characters, Gabriel in the *Cid*, Lazarus in *Mocedades*, the Virgin in a popular miracle story (*PCG* 2:426–27). In *Mocedades* the young Rodrigo crosses (by implication) the Pyrenees as well as the "Rhone" to take the noble Savoyarde as a prize of war; then, the prompt birth of her son is strangely efficacious in bringing peace to the warring nations.

Since all the tales contain significant border crossings, perhaps enough has been said to identify the frontier or the water barrier as a kind of lever or spring that propels plots in unexpected directions and yields novel narrative elements. The Pyrenees have a comparable function in *Roland* and other French epics (e.g., *Galien*; see Monteverdi 1945, 354, and Menéndez Pidal 1969, 493), in the *Condesa traidora*, and less directly in *Mainet*. The cross-cultural fertilization may well reflect the experience of minstrels, both

---

father and has a hostile encounter with him on his arrival (Cross and Slover 1936, 172–75). The resemblances are worth noting, but unless related correspondences can be found, they are rather too isolated to suggest a meaningful interpretation.

French and Spanish, along the Way of St. James, who would have found a great impulse to artistic innovation in their mutual contacts, and so would be alert to stimulating elements in the traditional narratives they and others brought to that linguistic and artistic frontier. A similar kind of excitement is undoubtedly felt by scholars, explorers of the imagination who today look across national borders to discover perspectives on other mentalities and on their own.

The view across frontiers taken in this study has made it possible to propose motivations and sense for a number of narrative details that have usually been disregarded as insignificant or as outlandish products of errant imaginations. Among these, for example, are Gonzalo's use of a hawk as a weapon and his later act of bathing his hawk, Rodrigo's passive acquiescence to a betrothal he claims to regret accepting, the similarity and even identity of the complaints voiced by the vicious Llambra and the idealized Jimena, Ganelon's act of throwing off his cloak, the Infante Diego's choice of a wine press as a place of refuge. The transnational perspective is also useful in that it provides a backdrop of essential similarities against which the differences among the various manifestations of the initiation tale stand out, offering glimpses into their significance and making visible the mechanisms of textual evolution. Additionally, the tools provided by today's disciplines of linguistics, philology, and stylistics help to account for the peculiar immediacy of the stories under study, particularly the *Poema del Cid*, by bringing out their ritualistic nature and a unity of form and content that represents a metonymic mode of thought and perception.

None of the matters just noted have been treated exhaustively in these pages. Rather, as a preliminary step, the intention, or the hope, has been to draw up a context for them.

Seen in the light of Irish and French counterparts, the Spanish lore stands out for its way of integrating the feminine element into its fabric. The woman is the center about which the hero's life revolves, as seen in the case of the Cid at two stages of his existence. Her role in his initiation, in his transformation into a hero and model of proper action, is fundamental and indispensable, as her power overcomes his poorly directed animal aggressiveness to make him a potentially worthy husband and a vassal committed to supporting the king. In time, all his effort will be devoted to her well-being and that of their daughters. In the poem (as not in historical fact) the Cid's family consists only of women. The continuity and prestige of the family group will be the standard by which he measures his success (282–84, cited p. 54). All this is seen coherently and cumulatively in the young Rodrigo and the mature Cid, and by negative example in the Infantes de Carrión.

The images of womanhood developed in the epic transcend clichés to portray impressively complex feminine personalities. At the same time the epic demonstrates the origins of the simplistic, polarized stereotypes that recur in medieval literature: the submissive, supportive wife and mother as opposed to the scheming, treacherous, mysteriously powerful witch. In the world known through the epic, the overweening concern was the survival, by no means assured, of individual, family, and clan. Roles were not chosen; the man had to be a fighter and the woman had to support him. He also had to provide her protection, and she needed to accept it. Both had strictly limited spheres of activity, though as a rule her limitations were greater. Alternatives were not available to them, because in principle, as the epics, especially in their initiation segments, repeatedly demonstrate, defeat meant death for him and violation for her. Given the strictures and the brutality of existence, the system was not immune to malfunction. To the brutal man, the treacherous woman appears as counterpart, and in such cases the simple basic scheme quickly becomes complicated. The resentful woman might manipulate other men to achieve the destruction of a hated man (Llambra), or might implant a fear and distrust of women in her male child during his first, formative years. This last process does not appear in the epic, which is rarely concerned with childhood, but it is implicit in the fact that the epic expresses that kind of fear and distrust—a deep-seated realization by the man that the woman can withhold the affection and support that makes his life worth living (as when Gonzalo murders Alvar Sánchez over a question of female approval). On such a basis the warring society, through its myth and tradition, produced predictable stereotypes: the aggressive woman, Llambra or the *Condesa traidora*, and the weak or corruptible man who does her bidding—Ruy Velázquez or Garci Fernández. A good woman was not weak. Jimena overcomes Rodrigo at his initiation and must be as strong as he in later adversity. The mutual support is superbly communicated in the scene where they first meet in the poem. Their minds also meet. She imparts strength by requesting support: "¡Dadnos conseio!" (373). He gives expression to deep understanding of her words by echoing them, and in turn imparts strength by pledging his life to their mutual cause: "¡e vós, mugier ondrada—de mí seades servida!" (284). Each member of the pair is essential and speaks with appropriate dignity. Critical comment regarding feminine submission and abnegation in the epic will be wide of the mark if it always takes the man as "other." In contrast with the Cid and Jimena is the unbalanced pair formed by Doña Llambra and Ruy Velázquez. Mysterious, uncontrollable evil emanates from the woman, and the man is as helpless as a child before it. Though he moves among men, he surrenders his will to her. In the *Poema del Cid*, the Infantes de Carrión do not make good marriages; they are unfinished products of the heroic pattern. They are weak and vicious, but they do not originate and diffuse evil in the manner of Doña Llambra.

None of these characters has been created out of a manipulative agenda. They incarnate genuine hopes and fears that will remain alive as long as the warring society continues to exist. When it becomes obsolete (as already adumbrated in the *Poema del Cid* when the hero becomes a statesman), the archetypes will lose their relevancy, but the still male-dominated society will cling to them, degrading them to stereotypes no longer suitable as tribal warfare is absorbed into more inclusive political organisms. Still, when war again arises, the instinctive territorial urges may reassert themselves; bringing death to men and violence to women.

Out of the harshness of living at war, the epic erects a structure in which tribal cohesion, reinforced by ritual repetition of traditional lore, gives comfort and strength, endows life with a sense of purpose, masks its rigors, and bestows upon it dignity and even beauty. As the voice of a highly developed though largely illiterate culture, it speaks with all the depth and authenticity of an entire people. And that voice exerts its peculiar power over others far removed in time and space. A comment once written on the *Poema del Cid* can apply to all the epic texts, especially when they are taken together: "cada nueva lectura descubre en el *Mío Cid* renovados atractivos, no sospechadas complejidades" (Castro 1956, 8). Growing out of their culture and adapted to ceremonial performance, the poems were able to integrate the verbal medium with a group experience of which we are privileged to obtain glimpses. André Malraux, immersed in his study of ancient sculpture, was moved to declare: "Nous avons passionément remonté le temps—vers l'instinct" (1949, 1:123). In the presence of the epics, our experience is like his: the age-old artifacts touch the fibers of our being, drawing us into their world.

WORKS CITED

Acutis, Cesare. 1978. *La leggenda degli Infanti di Lara: Due forme epiche nel medioevo occidentale.* Turin: Giulio Einaudi.

Alonso, Dámaso. 1973a. *Obras completas.* Vol. 2. Madrid: Gredos.

———. 1973b. "Estilo y creación en el *Poema del Cid.*" 1973a:107–47. A 1940 lecture first published in *Ensayos sobre poesía española* (Madrid: Revista de Occidente, 1944), 69–112.

———. 1973c. "El anuncio del estilo directo en el *Poema del Cid* y en la épica francesa." In 1973a:195–214.

Armistead, S. G. 1955. "The *Gesta de las Mocedades de Rodrigo*: Reflections of a Lost Epic Poem in the *Crónica de los reyes de Castilla* and the *Crónica general de 1344.*" Ph.D. diss., Princeton University.

———. 1963–64. "The Structure of the *Refundición de las Mocedades de Rodrigo.*" *Romance Philology* 17:338–45.

———. 1974. "The Earliest Historiographic References to the *Mocedades de Rodrigo.*" In *Estudios literarios de hispanistas norteamericanos dedicados a Helmut Hatzfeld con motivo de su 80 aniversario,* 25–34. Madrid: Ediciones Hispam.

———. 1987. "La 'furia guerrera' en dos textos épicos castellanos." In *Studia in honorem prof. M. de Riquer,* 2:255–69. Barcelona: Quaderns Crema.

———. 1990–91. "Gaiferos' Game of Chance: A Formulaic Theme in the Romancero." *La Corónica* 19:132–44.

Bailey, Matthew. 1993. *The "Poema del Cid" and the "Poema de Fernán González": The Transformation of an Epic Tradition.* Madison, Wis.: Hispanic Seminary of Medieval Studies.

Bandera Gómez, Cesáreo. 1969. *El "Poema de Mio Cid": Poesía, historia, mito.* Madrid: Gredos.

Barnard, Mary. 1966. *The Mythmakers.* Athens: Ohio University Press.

Bédier, Joseph. 1926–29. *Les Légendes épiques.* 3d ed. 4 vols. Paris: Payot.

———, ed. 1905. *Le Roman de Tristan par Thomas.* 2 vols. Paris: Firmin Didot. Reprint, New York: Johnson Reprint, 1968.

———, ed. 1960. *La Chanson de Roland.* Paris: L'Édition d'Art H. Piazza.

Bell, Catherine. 1992. *Ritual Theory, Ritual Practice.* New York: Oxford University Press.

Benveniste, Émile. 1966. *Problèmes de linguistique générale.* Vol. 1. Paris: Gallimard.

———. 1971. *Problems in General Linguistics.* Vol. 2. Trans. Mary Elizabeth Meek. Coral Gables, Fla.: University of Miami Press. Originally published in French as volume 2 of Benveniste 1966.

———. 1973. *Indo-European Language and Society*. Trans. Elizabeth Palmer. London: Faber & Faber.

Berceo, Gonzalo de. 1971. *Obras completas*, ed. Brian Dutton. Vol. 2, *Los milagros de Nuestra Señora*. London: Tamesis.

Bloch, Maurice. 1977. "The Past and the Present in the Present." *Man* 12:278–92.

Block, Elizabeth. 1986. "Narrative Judgment and Audience Response in Homer and Virgil." *Arethusa* 19:155–67.

Bowra, C. M. 1952. *Heroic Poetry*. London: Macmillan.

Brault, Gerard J., ed. 1978. *The Song of Roland*. 2 vols. University Park: Pennsylvania State University Press.

Bremmer, Jan. 1988a. "What Is Myth?" In Bremmer 1988c, 1–9.

———. 1988b. "Oedipus and the Greek Oedipus Complex." In Bremmer 1988c, 41–59.

———, ed. 1988c. *Interpretations of Greek Mythology*. London: Croom Helm.

Brooks, Cleanth, and Robert Penn Warren. 1959. *Understanding Fiction*. 2d ed. New York: Appleton-Century-Crofts.

Burke, James F. 1991. *Structures from the Trivium in the "Cantar de Mio Cid."* Toronto: University of Toronto Press.

Burkert, Walter. 1979. *Structure and History in Greek Mythology and Ritual*. Berkeley and Los Angeles: University of California Press.

———. 1983. *Homo Necans: The Anthropology of Ancient Greek Sacrificial Ritual and Myth*. Trans. Peter Bing. Berkeley and Los Angeles: University of California Press.

———. 1988. "Oriental and Greek Mythology: The Meeting of Parallels." In Bremmer 1988c, 10–40.

Butler, Isabel, trans. 1932. *The Song of Roland*. Boston: Houghton Mifflin.

Campbell, Joseph. 1959. *The Masks of God: Primitive Mythology*. New York: Viking.

Capdeboscq, Anne-Marie. 1984. "La Trame juridique de la légende des Infants de Lara: Incidents des noces et de Barbadillo." *Cahiers de Linguistique Hispanique Médiévale* 9:189–205.

Caro Baroja, Julio. 1974. *Algunos mitos españoles*. 3d ed. Madrid: Ediciones del Centro.

Castro, Américo. 1956. "Poesía y realidad en el *Poema del Cid*." In *Semblanzas y estudios españoles*, 3–15. Madrid: Ínsula. Also published in *Hacia Cervantes* (Madrid: Taurus, 1957), 3–17.

Catalán, Diego, ed. 1980. *Reliquias de la poesía épica española* [ed. por] Ramón Menéndez Pidal. 2d ed. Madrid: Gredos. (Page references are to the second of two series of pages contained in the volume, except where the first series is specified.)

Chafe, Wallace. 1990. "Some Things That Narratives Tell Us about the Mind." In Bruce K. Britton and A. D. Pellegrini, eds., *Narrative Thought and Narrative Language*, 79–98. Hillsdale, N.J.: Laurence Erlbaum.

Chotzen, Th. M. 1933. "Le Lion d'Ovein (Yvain) et ses prototypes celtiques." *Neophilologus* 18:51–58, 131–36.

Colum, Padraic, ed. 1967. *A Treasury of Irish Folklore*. 2d ed. New York: Crown.
Cook, Robert Francis. 1987. *The Sense of the "Song of Roland."* Ithaca: Cornell University Press.
Cooper, Louis, ed. 1979. *La gran conquista de Ultramar*. 4 vols. Bogotá: Instituto Caro y Cuervo.
Corfis, Ivy A. 1983–84. "The Count of Barcelona Episode and French Customary Law in the *Poema de mío Cid*." *La Corónica* 12:169–77.
Corominas, Joan, and José A. Pascual. 1980–91. *Diccionario crítico etimológico castellano e hispánico*. 6 vols. Madrid: Gredos.
Cross, Tom Peete, and Clark Harris Slover, eds. 1936. *Ancient Irish Tales*. New York: Henry Holt.
De Chasca, Edmund V. 1972. *El arte juglaresco en el "Cantar de Mio Cid."* 2d ed. Madrid: Gredos.
Débax, Michelle. 1982. *Romancero*. Madrid: Alhambra.
Deyermond, Alan D. 1969. *Epic Poetry and the Clergy: Studies on the "Mocedades de Rodrigo."* London: Tamesis. A paleographic edition of the poem is included on pp. 222–77.
———. 1976. "Medieval Spanish Epic Cycles: Observations on Their Formation and Development." *Kentucky Romance Quarterly* 23:281–303.
———. 1988. "La sexualidad en la épica española." *Nueva Revista de Filología Hispánica* 39:767–86.
———, ed. 1977. *"Mio Cid" Studies*. London: Tamesis.
Díaz Mas, Paloma, ed. 1994. *Romancero*. Barcelona: Crítica.
Dillon, Myles, ed. 1968. *Irish Sagas*. Dublin: Mercier.
Duby, Georges. 1974. *The Early Growth of the European Economy: Warriors and Peasants from the Seventh to the Twelfth Centuries*. Trans. Howard B. Clarke. Ithaca: Cornell University Press.
Duggan, Joseph J. 1969. *A Concordance of the "Chanson de Roland."* Columbus: Ohio State University Press.
———. 1989. *The "Cantar de mio Cid": Poetic Creation in Its Economic and Social Contexts*. Cambridge: Cambridge University Press.
Dumézil, Georges. 1942. *Horace et les Curiaces*. Paris: Gallimard. Reprint. New York: Arno Press, 1978.
———. 1969. *Heur et malheur du guerrier: Aspects mythiques de la fonction guerrière chez les Indo-Européens*. Paris: Presses Universitaires de France.
Dunn, Joseph, ed. 1914. *Táin Bó Cúailgne*. London: D. Nutt.
Dunn, Peter N. 1962. "Theme and Myth in the *Poema de Mio Cid*." *Romania* 83:348–69.
Edmunds, Lowell, ed. 1990. *Approaches to Greek Myth*. Baltimore: Johns Hopkins University Press.
Edwards, Viv, and Thomas J. Sienkewicz. 1991. *Oral Cultures Past and Present. Rappin' and Homer*. Oxford: Basil Blackwell.
Eliade, Mircea. 1958. *Birth and Rebirth*. New York: Harper and Row.
———. 1963. *Aspects du mythe*. Paris: Gallimard.
———. 1974. *The Myth of the Eternal Return*. Trans. Willard R. Trask. New York: Pantheon.

Friedrich, Paul. 1986. *The Language Parallax. Linguistic Relativism and Poetic Indeterminacy*. Austin: University of Texas Press.

García Montoro, Adrián. 1972. *El león y el azor: Simbolismo y estructura trifuncional en la épica medieval española*. Madrid: Ediciones "R."

———. 1974. "La épica medieval española y la 'estructura trifuncional' de los indoeuropeos." *Cuadernos hispanoamericanos* 285:554–71.

Gerli, E. Michael. 1992. "Poet and Pilgrim: Discourse, Language, Imagery, and Audience in Berceo's *Milagros de Nuestra Señora*." In Gerli and Sharrer 1992, 39–51.

Gerli, E. Michael, and Harvey L. Sharrer, eds. 1992. *Hispanic Studies in Honor of Samuel G. Armistead*. Madison: Hispanic Seminary of Medieval Studies.

Gifford, Douglas. 1977. "European Folk-Tradition and the 'Afrenta de Corpes.' " In Deyermond 1977, 49–62.

Gilman, Stephen. 1961. *Tiempo y formas temporales en el "Poema del Cid."* Madrid: Gredos.

Gumperz, John J. 1975. "Foreword." In Mary Sanches and Ben G. Blount, eds., *Sociocultural Dimensions of Language Use*. New York: Academic Press.

———. 1991. "Foreword." In David R. Olson and Nancy Torrance, eds., *Literacy and Orality*. Cambridge: Cambridge University Press.

Hanaway, William L., Jr. 1978. "The Iranian Epics." In Oinas 1978, 76–98.

Harney, Michael. 1994. Review of Burke 1991. In *Hispanic Review* 62:407–8.

Havelock, Eric A. 1963. *Preface to Plato*. Cambridge: Belknap Press of Harvard University Press.

———. 1986. *The Muse Learns to Write: Reflections on Orality and Literacy from Antiquity to the Present*. New Haven: Yale University Press.

Herslund, Michael. 1974. "Le *Cantar de Mio Cid* et la chanson de geste." *Revue Romane* 9:69–121.

Horrent, Jacques. 1987. "L'Épopée dans la Péninsule ibérique." In Rita Lejeune et al., eds., *Les Épopées romanes*, pt. 1/2, sec. 9. Vol. 3 of *Grundriss der romanischen Literaturen des Mittelalters*. Heidelberg: Carl Winter.

Hymes, Dell. 1981. *"In Vain I Tried to Tell You": Essays in Native American Ethnopoetics*. Philadelphia: University of Pennsylvania Press.

Jakobson, Roman. 1981. "Poetry of Grammar and Grammar of Poetry." In *Selected Writings*, vol. 3, *Linguistics and Poetics*, 18–51. The Hague: Mouton.

Jakobson, Roman, and Morris Halle. 1956. *Fundamentals of Language*. The Hague: Mouton.

Jakobson, Roman, and K. Pomorska. 1983. *Dialogues*. Cambridge: MIT Press.

Keen, Maurice. 1984. *Chivalry*. New Haven: Yale University Press.

Knudson, Charles A. 1968–69. "Le Thème de la princesse sarrasine dans *La Prise d'Orange*." *Romance Philology* 22:449–62.

Krappe, Alexander H. 1924. "The *Cantar de los Infantes de Lara* and the *Chanson de Roland*." *Neuphilologische Mitteilungen* 25:15–24.

Labov, William. 1972. *Language in the Inner City: Studies in the Black Vernacular*. Philadelphia: University of Pennsylvania Press.

Lacarra, María Eugenia. 1980. *El "Poema de Mio Cid": Realidad e historia*. Madrid: Porrúa Turanzas.

————. 1993. "Representaciones de la feminidad en el *Cantar de los siete infantes de Salas.*" In Philip E. Bennett et al., eds., *Charlemagne in the North: Proceedings of the Tenth International Conference of the Société Rencesvals*, 335–44. Edinburgh: Société Rencesvals, British Branch.

Lapesa, Rafael. 1961. "Del demostrativo al artículo." *Nueva Revista de Filología Hispánica* 15:23–44. (*Homenaje a Alfonso Reyes.*)

Lejeune, Rita. 1961. "Le Péché de Charlemagne et la 'Chanson de Roland.' " In *Studia Philologica. Homenaje ofrecido a Dámaso Alonso*, 2:339–71. 3 vols. 1960–63. Madrid: Gredos.

Lévi-Stauss, Claude. 1958. *Anthropologie structurale.* Paris: Plon.

————. 1962. *La Pensée sauvage.* Paris: Plon.

Lincoln, Bruce. 1989. *Discourse and the Construction of Society.* Oxford: Oxford University Press.

Littleton, C. Scott. 1966. *The New Comparative Mythology: An Anthropological Assessment of the Theories of Georges Dumézil.* Berkeley and Los Angeles: University of California Press.

Livy. *The History of Rome.* Loeb Classical Library. 1919.

Loomis, Roger Sherman. 1959a. "The Oral Diffusion of the Arthurian Legend." In Loomis 1959b, 53–63.

————, ed. 1959b. *Arthurian Literature in the Middle Ages.* Oxford: Clarendon Press.

Lord, Albert B. 1965. *The Singer of Tales.* New York: Atheneum.

Lot, Ferdinand. 1946. *L'Art militaire et les armées du Moyen Age.* Paris: Payot.

MacCana, Proinsias. 1983. *Celtic Mythology.* Rev. ed. New York: Peter Bedrik.

Malraux, André. 1949. *Psychologie de l'art: Le Musée imaginaire.* 3 vols. Genève: Albert Skira.

Martin, Richard P. 1989. *The Language of Heroes: Speech and Performance in the "Iliad."* Ithaca: Cornell University Press.

Mauss, Marcel. 1923–24. "Essai sur le don: Forme et raison de l'échange dans les sociétés archaïques." *L'Année Sociologique* 1:30–186.

Menéndez Pidal, Ramón. 1924. *Poesía juglaresca y juglares.* Madrid: Centro de Estudios Historicos.

————. 1934. *La leyenda de los infantes de Lara.* Madrid: Hernando.

————, ed. 1954–56. *Cantar de Mio Cid.* 3 vols. Continuous pagination. 3d ed. Madrid: Espasa-Calpe.

————. 1957. *Poesía juglaresca y orígenes de las literaturas románicas.* 6th ed. Madrid: Instituto de Estudios Históricos.

————, ed. 1965. *Crestomatía del español medieval.* Vol. 1 of 2. Madrid: Gredos.

————. 1969. "Los Infantes de Salas y la epopeya francesa—influencias recíprocas dentro de la tradición épica románica." In *Mélanges offerts à Rita Lejeune*, 1:485–99. Gembloux: J. Duculot.

————. 1986. *Flor nueva de romances viejos.* 28th ed. Madrid: Espasa-Calpe.

————. 1992. *La épica medieval española desde sus orígenes hasta su disolución en el Romancero.* Ed. Diego Catalán y María del Mar de Bustos. Madrid: Espasa-Calpe.

Meyer-Lübke, Wilhelm. 1972. *Romanisches etymologisches Wörterbuch.* Heidelberg: Carl Winter.

Michael, Ian, ed. 1980. *Poema de Mio Cid*. 2d ed. Madrid: Castalia.

Montaner, Alberto, ed. 1993. *Cantar de Mio Cid*. Barcelona: Crítica.

Montaner Frutos, Alberto. 1987. "El Cid mito y símbolo." *Boletín del Museo e Instituto "Camón Aznar"* 27:121–340.

———. 1992. "Las quejas de doña Jimena: Formación y desarrollo de un tema en la épica y el romancero." José Manuel Lucía Mejías et al., eds. *Actas*. II Congreso Internacional de la Asociación Hispánica de Literatura Medieval. Alcalá: Universidad de Alcalá de Henares.

Monteverdi, A. 1934. "Il cantare degli infanti di Salas." *Studi medievali* 13:113–50. Reprinted in Angelo Monteverdi, *Saggi neolatini* (Roma: Edizioni di "Storia e Letteratura," 1945).

Montgomery, Thomas. 1975. "Grammatical Causality and Formulism in the *Poema de Mio Cid*." In *Studies in Honor of Lloyd A. Kasten*, 185–98. Madison, Wis.: Hispanic Seminary of Medieval Studies.

———. 1980. "Vocales cerradas y acciones perfectivas." *Boletín de la Real Academia Española* 40:299–314.

———. 1988. "Cycles, Parallels, and Inversions in the *Leyenda de los Siete Infantes*." *Olifant* 13:41–54.

———. 1990–91. "Marking Voices and Places in the *Poema del Cid*." *La Corónica* 19:49–66.

———. 1991a. "Interaction of Factors in Tense Choice in the *Poema del Cid*." *Bulletin of Hispanic Studies* 68:355–69.

———. 1991b. "Las palabras abstractas del *Poema del Cid*." *Cahiers de Linguistique Hispanique Médiévale* 16:123–40.

———. 1994a. "Traces of an Ancient Economic System in the *Poema del Cid*." *Romance Philology* 47:308–18.

———. 1994b. "A Ballad and Two Epics." *La Corónica* 23:23–34.

Nagy, Gregory. 1990. *Greek Mythology and Poetics*. Ithaca: Cornell University Press.

Newstead, Helaine. 1959. "The Origin and Growth of the *Tristan* Legend." In Loomis 1959b, 122–33.

Northup, George Taylor, ed. 1928. *El cuento de Tristan de Leonis*. Chicago: University of Chicago Press.

The Odyssey of Homer. Trans. Richmond Lattimore. 1975. New York: Harper & Row.

Oinas, Felix J., ed. 1978. *Heroic Epic and Saga. An Introduction to the World's Great Folk Epics*. Bloomington: Indiana University Press.

Olson, David R. 1994. *The World on Paper*. Toronto: University of Toronto Press.

Olson, David R., and Nancy Torrance, eds. 1991. *Literacy and Orality*. Cambridge: Cambridge University Press.

Oman, C. W. C. 1953. *The Art of War in the Middle Ages, 378–1515*. Revised and edited by John H. Beeler. Ithaca: Cornell University Press.

Ong, Walter J., S.J. 1967. *The Presence of the Word*. New Haven: Yale University Press.

———. 1982. *Orality and Literacy: The Technologizing of the Word*. London: Methuen.

O'Rahilly, Cecile. 1976. *Táin Bó Cúailgne*. Dublin: Dublin Institute for Advanced Study.

Paris, Gaston. 1900. "Les Sept infants de Lara." In *Poèmes et légendes du Moyen Âge*, 215–51. Paris: Société d'Éditions Artistiques.

Parker, Robert. 1987. "Myths of Early Athens." In Bremmer 1987c, 187–214.

Pastré, Jean-Marc. 1994. "Tristan musagète." In *Wodan: Griefswalder Beiträge zum Mittelalter*, vol. 30, *Europäischen Literaturen im Mittelalter*, 321–31. Greifswald: Reineke Verlag.

Pokorny, Julius. 1959–69. *Indogermanisches etymologisches Wörterbuch*. 2 vols. Bern: Francke.

Powell, Brian. 1983. *Epic and Chronicle: "El Poema de mio Cid" and the "Crónica de veinte reyes."* London: Modern Humanities Research Association.

Pratt, Mary Louise. 1977. *Toward a Speech Act Theory of Literary Discourse*. Bloomington: Indiana University Press.

Primera crónica general de España. 1955. Ed. Ramón Menéndez Pidal et al. 2 vols. Madrid: Gredos.

Quin, E. G. 1968. "Longas Macc N-Uisnig." In Myles Dillon, ed., *Irish Sagas*, 55–66. Dublin: Mercier.

Richthofen, Erich von. 1954. *Estudios épicos medievales*. Madrid: Gredos.

———. 1989. *La metamorfosis de la épica medieval*. Madrid: Fundación de Investigación Española.

Rico, Francisco. 1990. *Breve biblioteca de autores españoles*. Barcelona: Seix Barral.

———. 1993. "Estudio preliminar." In Montaner 1993, xi–lxiii.

Riquer, Martín de. 1959. "El fragmento de *Roncesvalles* y el planto de Gonzalo Gustioz." In *Studi in onore di Angelo Monteverdi*, 2:623–28. Modena: Società Tipografica Editrice Modenese.

———. 1968. *La leyenda del Graal y temas épicos medievales*. Madrid: Editorial Prensa Española.

Ross, Anne. 1960. "The Human Head in Early Pagan Religion." *Proceedings of the Society of Antiquaries of Scotland* 91:10–43.

———. 1986. *The Pagan Celts*. Totowa, N.J.: Barnes & Noble.

Salinas, Pedro. 1958. "La vuelta al esposo: Ensayo sobre estructura y sensibilidad en el *Cantar de Mio Cid*." In *Ensayos de literatura hispánica*, 45–57. Madrid: Aguilar.

Sanches, Mary, and Ben G. Blount, eds. 1975. *Sociocultural Dimensions of Language Use*. New York: Academic Press.

Sánchez Romeralo, Antonio. 1992. "Lengua, habla, oralidad y poesía en 50 aforismos de *Ideolojía*, libro inédito de Juan Ramón Jiménez." In Gerli and Sharrer 1992, 257–72.

Sapir, Edward. 1949. *Selected Writings of Edward Sapir in Language, Culture, and Personality*. Ed. David G. Mandelbaum. Berkeley and Los Angeles: University of California Press.

Saussure, Ferdinand de. 1949. *Cours de linguistique générale*. Paris: Payot.

Segre, Cesare, ed. 1989. *La Chanson de Roland*. Translated from the Italian by Madeleine Tyssens. 2 vols. Geneva: Librairie Droz.

Sharrer, Harvey L. 1992. "The Spanish Prosifications of the *Mocedades de Carlomagno*." In Gerli and Sharrer 1992, 273–82.

Slings, S. R. 1992. "Written and Spoken Language: An Exercise in the Pragmatics of the Greek Language." *Classical Philology* 87:95–109.

Smith, Colin. 1977. *Estudios cidianos*. Madrid: Cupsa.

Spitzer, Leo. 1938. "Le lion arbitre moral de l'homme." *Romania* 64:525–30.

Such, Peter, and John Hodgkinson, trans. 1987. *The Poem of My Cid*. Warminster: Aris & Phillips.

Vaquero, Mercedes. 1990. *Tradiciones orales en la historiografía de fines de la Edad Media*. Madison, Wis.: Hispanic Seminary of Medieval Studies.

Vicens Vives, Jaime. 1969. *An Economic History of Spain*. With the collaboration of Jorge Nadal Oller. Trans. Frances M. López-Morillas. Princeton: Princeton University Press.

de Vitry, Jacques. 1971. *The exempla*. . . . Ed. Thomas Frederick Crane. New York: Burt Franklin. Reprint of 1890 edition.

Vološinov, V. N. 1973. *Marxism and the Philosophy of Language*. Trans. Ladislav Matejka and J. R. Titunik. New York: Seminar Press.

Wailes, Stephen L. 1978. "The *Nibelungenlied* as Heroic Epic." In Oinas 1978, 120–43.

Wartburg, Walther von, et al. 1948–. *Französisches etymologisches Wörterbuch*. Tübingen: Mohr.

Zumthor, Paul. 1987. *La Lettre et la voix*. Paris: Seuil.

———. 1990. *Oral Poetry: An Introduction*. Trans. Kathryn Murphy-Judy. Minneapolis: University of Minnesota Press.

INDEX